WHY *I Had to*
Murder *My* MOTHER

WHY
I Had To
Murder *My*
MOTHER
A Memoir

KATHARINE LEPPARD

T

The manufacturer's authorised representative in the EU for product safety is
Authorised Rep Compliance Ltd, 71 Lower Baggot Street, Dublin D02 P593 Ireland
(www.arccompliance.com)

Troubador Publishing Ltd
Unit E2 Airfield Business Park
Harrison Road, Market Harborough
Leicestershire LE16 7UL
Tel: 0116 279 2299
Email: books@troubador.co.uk
Web: www.troubador.co.uk

ISBN 978 1836281 801

British Library Cataloguing in Publication Data.
A catalogue record for this book is available from the British Library.

Printed and bound in Great Britain by 4edge Limited
Typeset in 12pt Minion Pro by Troubador Publishing Ltd, Leicester, UK

Front cover painting by Katharine Leppard

For

Cherie
Michele
Chris

Such fun and happy memories

Contents

All happy families are alike; each unhappy family is unhappy in its own way.

Leo Tolstoy, *Anna Karenina*

Foreword

I started writing this "memoir" while my mother was alive—very, very much alive. Only now that I've murdered her can I put it into your hands and ask you to read it. Perhaps doing so will make you complicit, will fold you into the crime, much as I have been folded into my mother's terrible behaviour throughout our lives together. Please try to forgive me—as *I* am trying to forgive *her*.

I wonder what telling this story really means, what the purpose of all this remembering might be. Redress? Revenge? Repair?

Perhaps, when it comes down to it, the purpose of remembering is ... to forget.

Prologue

Little Holt

Friday 3rd April, 1964

Darling Keithie,

I received your long letter today—the one you wrote on Easter Monday. I am mystified, and indeed I really thought you must have been drinking until I came to the end and saw your PS which said you hadn't had a drink all night.

Firstly, darling, I love you dearly and love you for what you are. I wouldn't want to change you one bit, and I am very proud of you. I want you and need you, and I feel lost without you.

I do wish you could understand that I am not different from other women. Interested in the home and always seeking to improve. I know this is right because it always comes out in conversation—even yesterday and today when I've had people to tea, it has come up and we all come to the same conclusion, that no sooner is one goal reached, than we start off on another tack.

You have given a whole list of things about me that you say I must change—material outlook, strain, rush, tension and hate. How am I to do it?

I think the material side is natural but perhaps I could stop "wanting" a bit. Strain—I do find life a strain—simply because I have landed myself in an environment to which I don't belong. I don't go around asking for sympathy because of my bad home life as a child, but I don't suppose there is another person in our present walk of life that has had such a bad start and a continual struggle. I'm now on the same level. Naturally it's more of a strain for me.

The "rush" part is all the same thing. I loathe any day to go by when I haven't achieved something, otherwise I'm not satisfied. I told you I had to force myself to clean the car the other day but it made me feel better because I felt it wasn't a day wasted. Yesterday and today I had people to tea and I felt the same way about this. It is the same with the garden. I like to think at the end of the day I've done the job I intended doing. This is part of my makeup and I'm sure I won't change. Whenever I sit back and don't care it is usually the time when I am miserable and have no incentive. Dorothy R. is worse at this than I am, so I'm not the only one. I do believe too that it gets David down a bit.

Tension: this is something I could do something about but if only I knew how. If only I could calm down and feel at peace with the world, I too would think it marvellous. When things go right, I occasionally have this release of tension, I feel an entirely different person—almost the same way as when I've had a gin. (I mean a gin—the effect one has on me if I have one about 6pm.)

But how can I do it? I do get ratty and disturbed over the least thing. I realise now more than ever what I must be like when I see Katharine behaving exactly the same way.

Hate: This hate is really resentment. The only person I feel hate towards at the moment is your mother. This may sound very cruel, and I don't suppose it really is hate, purely resentment. I won't go into any more details there, because it won't do any good.

You ask me to accept you as you are darling, with all your inadequacies. I won't ask the same of you darling, because one thing I must conquer is losing my self-control. This I will strive to do. But please accept some of my faults.

You mention numerable times our rows in February. Although I make them develop into something simply dreadful, I truly think that on both occasions you were the one who sparked them off... (1) was the boiler and the bowler hat. The boiler I'd done for 6 months and resented you saying I didn't understand it—the bowler hat you knew I was right about, and we found out at cost to us all. (2) Was your mother's birthday present—all the secrecy. I know you're only trying to be kind to her but when you ask me repeatedly to put things in their true perspective about money, and you at the same time reckon your mother's present warrants stepping up the overdraft, I just don't see it. It isn't as if she ever puts anything out in your direction (you or your children). If she was generous herself it would be different. I shall never forget her meanness at Christmas, and her failing to offer to help out but failing to even provide for her own liabilities, e.g. petrol on Boxing Day.

Well lovie, I've gone down the list now. I feel a pain when you say you've had an inferiority complex out there, and I feel deeply for you my sweet. Being short of money and having to behave like a peasant is the basic trouble. People don't understand, and then perhaps think you're odd and aloof. It's always nice to feel wanted. I was feeling rather much the same over Easter and felt the need for the security of you.

My whole life is meaningless without you. We must learn to live peacefully together because we are just what each other needs. One thing we must do and that is make a vow that we'll never have scenes in front of the children for it will affect them for the rest of their lives. We must make a firm rule.

It's late, darling, and I must change the subject to tell you that much to my surprise a man from Lombard Bank came this evening. This must be more thorough than Mutual Finance as I believe he intended asking a whole heap of questions regarding salary and mortgage per month. I mildly suggested that I thought this was over-doing things a bit and so he settled by satisfying himself that this was in fact your home and that he's seen enough to convince him we are reasonable sort of people.

I was rather embarrassed because he wasn't the

usual type of chap on this sort of caper—rather old school tie—I hardly had the courage to tell him that we thought the "10 year scheme" better after all—eventually I did but he really did advise against it. Apparently, most of the interest is paid in the beginning, so if ever we settle up, we should still have paid the high percentage of interest; which in fact I had previously thought we'd escape. So, darling, if it's not too upsetting for you, we're still on 5 years.

I am so tired, I really must go up to bed. I've been dead tired recently.

I was pleased when Jill Emery said how smart the white trellis was. She noticed without any prompting and also noticed the improvement in the drive—the odd change I've made in the bed.

The lawn that I put lawn-sand on has turned black almost showing all the moss. I'm dying to rake it all out but can't for 2 weeks. The other parts you seeded last year are looking very nice and green. Yes, sweetie, I'll save the levelling for you!

Goodnight love, God bless and keep you safe.

All my love as always,

Your own Rachel

O nce I knew for sure that my mother was dead, I dug this letter out from amongst a heap of paperwork. I'd glanced at it guiltily two or three years earlier but, feeling it was private, I hadn't read it properly, let alone digested anything in it.

It had been written by my mother to my father two months prior to his return from a year at sea (I haven't come across his original letter to her because she destroyed most of them after his return). When she replied to my father, she clearly had no idea what he'd been doing with his off-duty time in Singapore; none of us knew at that time. Nor did we know how her finding out—and, more crucially, how she *reacted* to finding out—was about to change our lives … forever.

1

The Whore in Singapore

L et me begin at the beginning. Or at least at the beginning of things starting to go horribly wrong: when a family life that had seemed so perfect started to dissolve into a nightmare that would last for almost six decades, leaving us all struggling to stay afloat.

It's 1964. I'm eight. I can see myself as clearly as if it were yesterday, running out of the last mid-afternoon prep-school class, certain that my father will be waiting to greet me after a year away at sea. As I rush out of the school gate, I see him at the end of the gravelled track, standing there in his naval uniform, waving, gold braid glinting on his sleeves, a sharp navy-and-black-rimmed hat topped with pristine white. "Daddy, Daddy!" I run into his open arms, and he picks me up and throws me into the air before embracing me and holding me to his chest. All my friends are watching. I am so happy and so proud. I treasure that memory.

My five-year-old brother and I have been ticking off the weeks and counting down to the big day. Our mother is equally excited, and for a whole week has been dusting, vacuuming, and proudly polishing our still part-furnished and half-decorated house to make it look its best. After school, just two days away from "Daddy's return", my brother and I sit on the sofa with our Marmite sandwiches and glasses of milk, watching *Blue Peter*, listening to the rattle of pots and pans and catching the aroma of special home-cooked food wafting in from the kitchen.

And if that isn't enough, my mother has somehow found the extra time and physical energy to tend an acre of garden: mowing the grass and keeping the drive and pathways pruned back and the roses blooming. She has stayed up late most nights doing housework. My mother is a perfectionist, and so very proud of it. "If something's worth doing, it's worth doing well, darling." It is as simple as that.

All my school chums and, it seems, most of my mother's friends, know about the forthcoming *big* day ... but it is to be made even *bigger* by the near-death experience of myself, my mother and brother, and two other school children.

It's my mother's turn to do the "school run", driving us in our Austin Cambridge A40. The car is probably eight or ten years old, and certainly looks it—black, bulbous, and bouncy—but it goes like a bomb and, unfortunately on this occasion, even faster than that! Its brakes are going to fail at the top of the steep hill leading down to the school entrance.

Quick thinking on my mother's part will make her scream for us to get on the floor as we hurtle down the hill.

If she allows the car to torpedo out onto the busy high street junction below there are going to be serious casualties; so instead of negotiating the slight bend on the hill she will bravely drive straight on, ploughing into a dense eight-foot-high leylandii hedge. The bonnet of the car will go up in the air and mount the top of the hedge, the wheels still spinning, the boot buckling under the weight of the tilting car, now angled back precariously. But stopped we will be … and we will have only just missed hitting a dozen or so young children arriving for school on the other side of the hedge.

Although shaken, we're all okay. The whole school comes out to look at the car on top of the hedge, with much excited chatter. My best friend Genny, however, is more interested in my mother's outfit and can't help but stand and marvel: leopard-skin leggings with feet through loops and into flat pumps, a fitted, pink, three-quarter-length-sleeved shirt with an orange silk scarf wrapped sumptuously round her head, worn like a giant Alice band, revealing curls of blond hair. At thirty-five, she is an extremely good-looking woman. Genny is so impressed and wants to know why *her* mother can't dress like that!

I don't think any of the onlookers really understand how close to being fatal our crash has been … except, perhaps, for the schoolteachers and the headmistress who, during assembly, say prayers for my mother.

My parents were married in 1954 having met two years before, when they were stationed at a naval air base in Cornwall. My father, Keith, was a fast-climbing-the-ranks twenty-seven-year-old lieutenant pilot in the Fleet Air Arm and my mother Rachel, at twenty-two, "the youngest Chief Petty Officer" in the WRNS (the Wrens), a fact she boasted about all her life.

Not only was she in charge of the rum and cigarette rations for officers and ratings, but on night duty she would patrol the dusky area between the men's and women's sleeping barracks to ensure there was no "hanky-panky". Any couples caught in the beam of her torch would be ordered "to break it up" and then named and shamed, regardless of rank. As part of their punishment, she could—and did—withhold an individual's rum and cigarette ration, knowing that my father would come and sweet-talk her into reinstating the ration, especially when the offending "chap" was a member of his own squadron.

My mother liked to brag that she could have married at least three other men; one of them in fact became her fiancé, "a millionaire" no less, but, charming as he was, she ditched him a week before their planned wedding day.

My father worked hard at wooing her and pulled out all the stops. Going a notch up and considerably higher than any other suitor, he "borrowed" (courtesy of the Ministry of Defence) a twin-seater Vampire jet to pick up my mother on a Friday afternoon from Cornwall and take her to his new air base in Scotland for the weekend, returning her to her Cornish base later on the Sunday.

This was one of the "perks of the job" back then, sanctioned by the unofficial "turn of a blind eye". It impressed my mother no end—and it's not hard to see why it wouldn't. She wasn't so appreciative, however, of my father's aerobatics en route, unable as he was to stop himself showing off. *She* was unable to stop herself throwing up.

Both my mother and my father came from relatively ordinary beginnings. My paternal grandfather was in banking, so on leaving grammar school, my father took a temporary job at the bank, until he was old enough to join an Admiralty scheme which had identified him as a potential officer whilst he was still at school.

My mother, five years younger, came from Bradford, the daughter of a blacksmith who had died when she was eight, in circumstances that were never made very clear. (She was always vague about the details and seemed to forget that she had given two differing accounts over the years: he was killed in Leicester during the war; or he was killed in a road traffic accident after spending the evening in the pub with his mistress. I know the latter was closer to the truth.)

As a result, apparently, my grandmother went off the rails and took to drink, men, and the bingo hall. My mother had three brothers (the uncles I never met) and an older sister who became an important professor, teaching mainly in Canada. "She had the brains, but I had the looks," said the younger sister.

My mother's childhood was unhappy: left most of the time on her own at home, abandoned by her older siblings, and denied the love and attention of her own mother. She never wanted to talk about her previous family life or anything to do with Bradford, though always maintained she was proud of her Yorkshire roots—"but of course not since Bradford was taken over and ruined by the Pakis."

Joining the Wrens at a young age was her ticket out—a chance to distance herself from her working-class family and immediate surroundings. She was christened Betty Rachel Smith, but as well as gladly giving up her maiden name when she married my father, she chose to drop "Betty" and become "Rachel". Her real first name, the one that remains on her passport and National Health Insurance records, is all that remains of Betty.

Rachel and Keith were always fiercely competitive, in work and in play and in their social circles. From their marriage in 1954 until the moment at the school gates in 1964 on that infamous afternoon of my father's return, they had enjoyed ten years of harmonious, traditional, married life—although, to be pedantic, the year away at sea would make it strictly only nine.

My father had been appointed Commander (Air) to the fleet carrier HMS *Victorious* in the Far East. In 1964, the year he was away, my mother was a full-time housewife with a lot on her hands and very little money. It seemed the monthly allowance my father gave her was never enough; naval salaries didn't amount to very much. Running the house and car, buying school uniforms, and feeding us was a struggle and, though I never remember going hungry, I know my mother did.

Communication back then was by written correspondence and Mum and Dad kept in touch via (at least) thrice-weekly letters written on thin blue airmail paper with stripy red-and-blue-edged envelopes sent via the BFPO (British Forces Post Office).

Early in the morning of the day of my father's return, whilst my brother and I are at school, a telegram arrives, addressed to my father. My mother signs for it and, imagining it is urgent—a death in the family, maybe—opens it. The telegram is short and to the point: it is a declaration of love for my father—"I'm missing you madly darling"—from a woman called Ginnie, in Singapore.

"The Whore in Singapore" is born—the larger-than-life evil witch whom we never meet and who during the ensuing six decades is to be the focus of nearly every single row between my parents. I will lose count of the times that this rhyming title of shame is hurled at my father—abusively, violently—by my mother.

Memory behaves in strange ways. Perhaps as a response to shock—like suffering amnesia after a car accident—I have absolutely no recollection of my father's first night back at home. That day of his return, when he embraced me at the school gates, was the very last occasion I remember feeling love and affection towards my father. It was also the last day of normal, loving, family life.

Rage, Rage ...

They say that "shit happens", and it most certainly does. Guilty of poor judgement, or temptation based on opportunity, my father had seriously fucked up. And had got caught. But life moves on and, most of the time, we learn to forgive and forget; even if we don't entirely forget, we mentally move on. But not my mother. She *could not* and *would not* forgive ... or make *any* attempt to forget. And she certainly chose not to walk away.

Many years later (and not that long ago) whilst clearing out the now abandoned house at Little Holt, I discovered a letter from my father to my mother, written only a few months after the fateful telegram had arrived on our doorstep. In an old shoebox stuffed with letters from my mother to my father there was just one from my father to my mother, the envelope marked with a red cross—presumably made by my mother who had, no doubt, destroyed the rest of his lifelong letters to her.

Reading it, my breath was taken away to see evidence of how deeply in love they'd clearly been, and how utterly desperate my father was to save his marriage (and, of course, his career). It endorsed, also, just how deeply upset and traumatised my mother had been by his disloyalty.

J.S.S.C. (Joint Services Staff College)
Latimer, Bucks
3rd November, 1964, Tuesday pm

My beloved Rachel,

I am still in a state of shock and bewilderment after our telephone conversation at lunchtime. I can only repeat darling, that all your accusations are utterly untrue, and that I have been completely truthful to you about our visit to Japan. I am in despair of ever being able to prove my sincerity and to restore your faith in me which I must do and put an end to this torture for both of us.

I don't know which way to turn, but feel that a meeting with Peter C. might help, (despite the embarrassment and departure from normal etiquette). Despite your views, he is a very sincere and kind-hearted man who, incidentally, thought very highly of you.

I implore you not to cause damage to the Navy (& the Lucys, Lachlans, Baldwins etc) and utter ruin and destruction for ourselves and our children.

With God's help, we can overcome our problems and have untold pleasures and happiness to look forward to, despite the terrible pain I have caused you sweetie.

Please, please darling Rachel, try to put the past behind you, for if you don't, the alternatives are too horrible to contemplate. I know this is easy to say and I do understand how deeply your mind has been hurt, but Andrew, Katharine and I all need you with all our hearts and it would break all of us should you turn your back.

Even at these desperate times, I love and adore you my darling, if only I could "communicate" with you on the same frequency.

Please remember that my whole life revolves around you and that love of twelve years cannot be erased, despite my ghastly deviation.

I am deeply in love with you darling and will give you all my strength and support over these next critical months. Please, please accept it, we can and will triumph and achieve warmth and happiness together which we can never experience apart.

I am always,
Your devoted,

Keithie

It will be another three years before my brother and I are sent to our boarding schools; during that time, we will be subjected to parental arguments way off the Richter scale. There is no shortage of physical fights, too, resulting in hospital visits. Through the nights, my parents scream and shout; plates and pictures are smashed; my father's clothes are thrown out of the window; stiletto heels are hammered into his now bald head.

One evening my mother stabs my father through the arm with a carving knife. She's locked him out of the house; he's climbed onto the flat roof outside my bedroom window and is in the process of trying to break the window to undo the latch. Frightened to the core, with my father balanced on the roof outside, pleading with me to open the window whilst my mother rages and promises she'll kill me if I do, I just stand there sobbing.

The physical fighting is extreme. They go on and on and on … At night in bed I cower under my blankets, terrified, unable to sleep with the noise of shattering glass and china and the exchange of screamed verbal obscenities, many of which I don't understand, but I do know they're bad. At some stage in the night, it will go relatively quiet, but inevitably a deep sobbing sound will creep along the landing from my parents' bedroom and seep under my bedroom door.

My mother's rages are extreme, and she'll sometimes turn on me and my brother, completely out of the blue, hurling out the most dreadful verbal abuse along with occasional physical violence. One evening I'm in the bath, listening to them shouting at each other, when the bathroom door opens and Mum screams for me to get out of the bath. As I do so, she grabs me by the hair and drags me from the bathroom, across the landing carpet to my bedroom, throwing me against the brick fireplace. I can't remember what she was yelling; I'm traumatised, blubbering. Dad goes crazy and rushes in, shoving my mother out of the room. He kneels beside my wet, naked, shaking body, and, in shock and tears himself, holds me tight, assuring me that "she doesn't mean it, she really loves you so very much."

I *did* know my mother loved me, even though it was clear that she struggled to show it. She wasn't like other mums, didn't like being unnecessarily "touchy", and hated being kissed on arrival at parties by people she said she hardly knew. When I was unwell, she'd bring food and drink to my bedside, but there was never any special TLC. It was then that her no-nonsense, practical approach would come to the fore. "If you're going to be sick, make sure it's in the bowl." Dad explained to me once that she found it difficult to show love and affection because she didn't get enough of those emotions herself as a child.

My brother and I were not particularly close, but I'd say we had a reasonable brother–sister relationship. However, during those long nights of raging battles, he and I used to stay in our respective bedrooms, too scared to come out, because our parents were out of control. On at least two occasions, in the dead of night, my brother and I, wearing just our pyjamas, were bundled off in a car by my parents' best friends; we both stayed with them for a week or so, having been told "Mummy is not well and is spending some time having a rest in hospital." On another occasion, when Mum went into hospital for a few days, we were told it was to do with "women's problems". (For me, it was hugely significant and revealing to find out, fifty years later, that she had, in fact, had an abortion.)

In many ways, staying away from home, and not being at school, was extremely good news: it meant a break from the terrifying rows, and staying with my best friend Genny and her parents was fun; they had a swimming pool and a ping-pong table. Despite Genny's father also being in the Navy, they were a far more liberal family; discipline—around bedtime, for example—was far more relaxed.

Then there were the suicide attempts. On one occasion my mother took an overdose of sleeping pills. She was always taking herself off to bed for whole days at a time, suffering from depression, but one day, on coming home from work, my father found my mother semi-conscious in bed. In shock and panic, he called for me and asked me to keep talking to her, telling me to repeatedly shake her so as not to let her fall asleep, whilst he called for an ambulance. "If she falls asleep, she'll die," he said.

As a young child, I had no understanding of marital "ups and downs" and adult reactions to betrayal and deceit. What I *did* know, however, was that my father was at fault and had caused this catastrophic breakdown in our family life. "Do you know what your father was doing on your eighth birthday, Katharine?" my mother, with eyes bulging, spat at me. "He was fucking a whore in Singapore." I didn't know about "fucking", and I was certainly none the wiser about the meaning of "whore"!

Over the years I will learn more … lots more. It appeared that my father had also fucked the same Whore from Singapore at the Strand Palace Hotel, London, on a day he was supposed to be visiting the Admiralty. My mother, astonishingly, hired a private detective to have my father followed during his next Whitehall-based appointment, until he eventually got wind of it. She then resorted to doing her own research and contacted a few of my father's fellow officers on HMS *Victorious* to quiz them about what they knew of his affair in the Far East.

My mother was "a woman scorned"; nothing was going to stand in her way in uncovering exactly what had happened, and where, during the past year. This was highly embarrassing for my father and his colleagues, and no doubt, extremely worrying for them, should their wives want to start asking similar questions of them. One can imagine that defending extramarital affairs whilst they were away at sea for a year on the grounds that they'd been lonely might just not have cut it!

Times were different then; my parents were already married with children when the sixties arrived. Having been through the deprivations and traumas of the Second World War, they were considered—and considered themselves—to be too old to enjoy the sexual liberation that was taking place or for my mother to benefit from the feminist wave that came shortly afterwards, something my mother deeply resented (looking back, I can understand why).

Perhaps it was this resentment, as well as the hurt and anger caused by my father, that transformed my mother from what I thought at the time was an almost perfect, loving, stay-at-home wife into a radically different woman: a process that started on the day of my father's return and would continue to gather pace over decades.

For most women at this time, divorce was just not an option—marriage was for life until death, in sickness and in health. A married woman took on her husband's name, promised to "obey" him and, unless—in the most unlikely of circumstances—she had independent income or property in her own name, became financially and economically dependent on him. There was stigma attached to divorced women at that time—huge social demotion amongst friends, mainly other married couples, where women were fiercely protective and suspicious of their husbands when in the company of a divorcee, whose moves were closely scrutinised.

A wife's social standing came from the success of her

husband's career, but as my mother continually trotted out, "behind every successful man, there's a *cleverer* woman." My mother had already helped drive and support my father's advancing career and she most certainly didn't want to be a divorcee. Deeply distressed and depressed, there seemed no options open to her, other than—and I honestly don't think, at this stage, she planned it this way—to *punish* my father.

My father had always been the head of the family: what he said, went; my mother was entitled to her own opinion … but only just. My mother neither drank nor smoked nor shopped for herself. But all this was to change; slowly at first, but then with determined acceleration. She would take off to London for the day with my father's credit card, or, in the early days, just a cheque book, and run up hefty bills, buying herself outfits at Harrods and other leading fashion boutiques. My father had always been overdrawn and went crazy when his bank statements arrived, when he'd find the bottom line was much worse than expected.

My mother started drinking whisky and gin and buying cigarettes, deliberately blowing smoke into my father's face (he never smoked and disliked it intensely). She would bait him: "If it was okay for the Whore in Singapore to smoke, then it's certainly okay for your wife." Yes, she had discovered the Whore had been a smoker! Not only that, but she had found receipts for several items of jewellery my father had bought for this woman in the Far East. This was too much to bear, especially when my mother had been starved of an appropriate income for the entire period her husband had been away, and she'd had to fend for herself and her two young children.

So begins the power struggle in my parents' long, and long-suffering, dysfunctional marriage, in which my brother and I are used like pawns on a chessboard. At every opportunity my mother will put my father down and remind us of his deceit. "Never trust a man, Katharine" comes out repeatedly as I inch away from the man I've been sitting with on the sofa.

Over time I can't bear for my father to be anywhere near me, let alone show me affection. The more he tries to show his love, and his remorse, the more I pull away. With my brother, there is less of an issue; he's that much younger than me, and unable to fully understand what is going on. Perhaps the father–son bond is easier for my father to maintain. Over time, another level of combat appears in the family: that of the females versus the males.

My father remained the breadwinner, and my mother played at being his "wife", but on *her* terms. The Navy was a military institution, steeped in the traditions of etiquette and protocol, and a naval wife had a big part to play. She'd give him support when it suited her—and not, when it didn't; or better still, she'd throw in emotional blackmail, threatening, usually at the last minute, not to attend a dinner party or naval function with my father's high-ranking bosses.

And when she does attend, with her good looks and charm, she is able to hold the attention of the mighty medalled men round the table and can get away with lines such as "The trouble with Fleet Air Arm aviators is they never know when to shut the hangar door!" This works on one level, but leaves my father squirming in his chair, not knowing what she is going to say or do next.

In a letter my mother wrote to me at boarding school, some years later, she asks: "Did Daddy tell you his boss Admiral G. is now Sir Admiral G.? He has just been knighted. We are going to have him and his wife to dinner." My father knew only too well that to progress in his naval career he needed his wife's support, and boy, did his wife know it too.

I was to discover, many years later, that the Whore in Singapore had, in fact, been another naval officer's wife!

2

School for Officers' Daughters

Grenville
Stoatley Hall
Royal Naval School (for Officers' Daughters)
Haslemere, Surrey

14th Sept 1967

Dear Mummy and Daddy

I have such a lot to tell you. I am enjoying myself very much so far but I can not say yet wether I am going to like boarding here because I have not been here long enough.

There are lots of new girls but I am one of the youngest.

We have got a nice form-room called Hermes and a new teacher Miss B.

As you know I am in HMS Onslaught and sleeping next to C.M. The dorm is meant to be haunted, of course I don't belive it.

I went to see the headmistress Mac yesterday and she asked where I lived. I said Kingsley-Green

Haslemere and she asked me why I was a boarder when my parents were at home three miles away and it was awfull I did not know what to say.

How is Andrew and the animals, all of you in fact? How did the trip to Somerset go?

I am afraid I can not write to you very oftern because we have not a lot of spare time. I must go now. Please write to me.

Love Katharine xxx

PS. My skirt is not allowed. Matron said I was not allowed to wear the skirt so I am afraid you will have to get me one with in the next 8 or 9 days. Please will you try and get me one other wise I will be in trouble. PPS the supper bell has just gone so I must go.

Perched on a hill, over two hundred meters above sea level, at the end of a narrow lane two miles outside of Haslemere, sits the austere Royal Naval School for Officers' Daughters. Where the lane ends, it is a right turn, through big heavy wooden gates along a grand driveway to the imposing Stoatley Hall, the main school building.

Alternatively, a left turn takes you along a dirt track leading onto a huge expanse of National Trust heathland which stretches for miles, where you can find yourself lost in the Devil's Punchbowl, or "spook" yourself thinking about the hangings that took place on Gibbett Hill during the eighteenth century. For over six years, every single time I am driven up the long, winding, and dreaded school lane

Me, with my parents, on my first day at boarding school

to be deposited at the isolated and forbidding building at the top, I feel sick. Cold, sweaty, and sick.

My first journey up the hill is for the start of the autumn term. Aged eleven, little do I know that as a "new girl" I am going to experience some traditional initiation surprises! I feel sick with fear of the unfamiliar, so scared of being away from home for the very first time. I have no idea about what lies ahead; how could I possibly have had an inkling?

It is especially difficult to understand (and, to this day remains so—although, in retrospect, boarding school was perhaps the safest place for me to be) why I am being sent to a boarding school when my parents live only three miles away, particularly when I discover fairly quickly that I could have been one of the "day girls", or, as the boarders label them, "day bugs". Many of the boarders have fathers who are stationed overseas; *my* father's daily commute alternates between home and the Admiralty in Whitehall,

London, and home and the Royal Navy Base in Portsmouth. My mother is a stay-at-home mum and a proud housewife (or has been up until quite recently).

Stoatley Hall is the oldest part of the school, a rambling but quite grand mansion boasting heavy oak panelling in the main hall, hung with oil paintings of past headmistresses and patrons—Lord Mountbatten of Burma is the school's patron. Front-of-house first impressions are, indeed, impressive! To the rear, there is a huge modern extension, circa 1950, housing the dining room and the house rooms, Grenville, Rodney, and Drake. The locker rooms are in the basement along with the boot room, a room specifically dedicated to the cleaning of shoes … and other less well-publicised activities.

There are dormitories on the first floor of the old building and the top two floors of the newish building, along with the "ablution block" and numerous lavatory cubicles spread at regular intervals along the corridors, sporting unpleasantly stained oak seats (often wet and smelly) and equipped with Jeyes toilet paper (using this is like wiping your bottom with non-stick greaseproof paper). Dormitories for the Lower and Middle IV house between six and eight pupils, with half of the beds for new girls and the other half for the older and wiser second-year girls, the idea being that the latter will help the newbies settle in.

The duty of the "head of dorm" is to check off the contents of each new girl's trunk: the exact number of pants, socks, Airtex shirts, games clothes, and two sets of skirts and jumpers ("mufti") for after prep and weekend wear. Each item must be identified by a stitched-in name tag with your full name and house. We are allowed two pairs of flat shoes: a brown pair to be worn everyday with our grey jumpers and skirts, and a black pair of lace-ups to go with our formal school navy suits which look not dissimilar, funnily enough, to a Wren's uniform! Instead of a tie, we have to wear a "tippet"—a stiff piece of black ribbon in the shape of a "V" which is attached to a length of elastic worn under your shirt collar. Fortunately, there are no Wrens' hats. We are, however, permitted one bedtime toy: mine is "Yorkshire Ted", who emits a nursery-rhyme tune when you squeeze his tummy.

After the checklist has been completed, bath rota lists are handed out, giving you the time and the day of your bathroom slot: three baths a week, two of which are at night and one in the morning (showers were far too modern for RNS, not even as a facility one would have thought essential after games). On the same list are rules for how often you can change your clothes: for instance, one pair of grey girls (thick, brushed-jersey knickers) to last a whole week, three pairs of linings (big white knickers to go inside the grey girls) per week, two pairs of long grey socks with garters! Little wonder classrooms frequently had a rather unsavoury whiff and the teachers, on entering a classroom, frequently demanded the window monitors take their responsibility more seriously.

A major part of boarding school induction takes place on a pupil's first night; it is, as I am to learn, "based on tradition". Lights are turned off by Matron at 20:30 and we are told there is to be strictly no talking, although this is one of the easier rules to get away with breaking. Inevitably there are a few snivels from girls who are already homesick. To cheer things up, the Middle IV head of dorm, C., asks the Lower IV new girls, one by one—to create more drama—if they are "innocent or guilty". Each time C. asks the question, the other three Middle IV girls emit squeals of delight. Neither I nor the other new girls understand— guilty of what?—but C. insists we answer. One by one, we do. "Innocent." This produces more snickering and gales of laughter from the Middle IVs.

And so begins our introduction to the "Facts of Life", none of us having a clue on the subject, other than some previous mention of "periods", which from now on, we are told, will be referred to as "the Curse". (My prep school induction to "the Birds and the Bees" had only extended to being told to use a sanitary towel when the time came, and I was still grappling with how you could possibly walk round as normal with a towel tied round your waist instead of a skirt!)

"The Facts of Life" are quite shocking to the four of us Lower IV girls, even more so when practical lessons start. Over the course of several nights, we have to gather round a chosen girl and her bed. The head of dorm, armed with a torch held appropriately under a lifted sheet, pin-points, rather like a biology teacher, the vagina and clitoris, but with added explicit information about how they function and what delights lie in store there for the future. There is certainly no sexual excitement on my part; rather I am frozen rigid with fear. This is a very big step up from playing "Doctors and Nurses" at the ages of six and seven. (I now realise that for the sexually more aware Middle IV girls, it did, however, provide huge titillation.)

A dorm event equally exciting but not quite as educational, is my first "fire practice"—certainly something to write home about.

> I must tell you what happened on Saterday evening. I told every one that I thought the firebell was going to go that night and I was right, it did go. It was when we had the lights out and we just all lay in bed and the bell went. It was very loud and it went on ringing. Head of dorm yelled to us to get up and she switched on the light and shut all the windows. When we had put our dressing gown and hard shoes on we rushed down the stairs out of the front door and in to the dark dark drive. We could bareley see where we were going. We reached the gym and we had to yell our names out. Mac was there too. She said we were going to have another firebell very soon. We all went back to our dorms and talked about what had happened till we fell asleep.

The first long "wake up" bell of the morning sounds at 06:45 hours, followed by two shorter bells at five-minute intervals. Another long bell rings at 07:00 and if you're not out of bed when the matron enters to check she'll rip the sheets off your bed, tossing them onto the floor, and she'll "smack" your bottom. (Oh yes, smacking was allowed then, or perhaps it was the case that it went largely unnoticed, despite it still not being entirely appropriate.)

The breakfast bell sounds at 07:45. You can only leave your dormitory after matron's bed inspection (hospital corners looking perfect, of course) and her general dorm inspection: clean surfaces, all clothes and shoes stored in their rightful place in the limited and now bulging wardrobes and drawers.

The dining hall is huge—big enough to accommodate 230 boarders, plus seventy "day bugs" at lunchtime. There is a multitude of long tables, from ten-seaters up to sixteeners, each table headed by the obligatory one or two prefects, also known as "table monitors". The dining room is on the first floor of Stoatley, and you can smell it way down the approaching corridors—it isn't the food, though, but the revolting smell of industrial bleach.

Dual-aspect windows, one complete walled side and, situated at the other end, a large, hatched area with a heavy wooden roller blind, which, when up, reveals the sometimes-smiling Spanish catering staff, ready to dollop food onto our plates. When the hatch is slammed down this means there are no "seconds" (not that it ever bothers me, as I am having trouble eating anything at all). Each table has a number and there is a seating plan that changes each week. Tables are called up to the hatch in turn and, depending on where your table is situated, it can be a long, lonely, daunting walk up the main aisle between the tables—the fear of being stared at is overwhelming.

Breakfast is an informal affair; fortunately for me, what you eat isn't monitored, though you still have to use your name-tagged white-linen napkin accompanied by your individual napkin ring for easy identification. You can help yourself to cornflakes or toast, or both. In giant metal urns there is tea that looks, and smells, like dirty dishwater. Or you can help yourself to a glass of milk. (Perhaps that is why, to this day, I can't drink tea, or milk for that matter.)

Over the course of my first three years at RNS, my white napkin will become a vital aid in the disposal of revolting food at lunchtime. I gently slide my meal off the plate and into my lap when the prefect and table monitor are looking the other way and then roll it up and place it under my grey jumper, depositing the contents down the lavatory after filing out of the dining hall. Grey became the new white as I didn't have access to Persil when washing out my napkin afterwards.

Some daily routines have remained constant over the years. Listening to the BBC Radio Four Greenwich Time Signal, aka "the pips", is one of those. From 07:45 until the BBC News at 08:00 we are allowed to talk—in hushed tones—but, on the stroke of the first "pip", compulsory silence descends on the dining hall and the Radio Four news begins. We only have to listen to the "main points", which last between eight and ten minutes, depending on world events and how much attention the "radio monitor" has being paying before flicking up the switch on the skirting-board plug.

The "radiogram" is positioned on a purpose-built shelf, approximately seven to eight feet from the ground. The brown, twined, electric cord reaches down to the floor plug so it can only be switched on and off at floor level and this means, of course, that the radio remains permanently tuned to BBC Radio Four, making it impossible for miscreants to tune in to Radio One or Radio Luxembourg.

There is a radio monitor rota—everyone must have a turn—and believe it or not, the responsibility, and the risk of "bishing it up" in front of 230 girls, weighs on us heavily. (Over fifty years on, still at more or less the same time, but now with black coffee in hand, I smile as I switch the radio on, and, indeed, off, whenever I choose—my partner allowing.)

At 08:40 hours, booted and suited and wrapped in heavy wool navy cloaks with distinctive, red-lined hoods, we gather outside the back door of Stoatley, getting "crocked-up" in preparation for the crocodile march to our morning lessons. These take place in Kilmorey, an ugly brick and concrete building with several flat-roofed classroom extensions, the academic part of the school and a good ten-to-twelve-minute downhill walk via a narrow twisty path just within the school grounds, running parallel to the tarmacked road of Farnham Lane.

Kilmorey houses the Assembly Hall and the Chapel, both of which double up as venues for in-house drama and music productions as well as Saturday afternoon cinema. I can still remember the sound of the stacking and un-stacking of those brown-canvas metal-framed chairs, laying them out, row upon long row, according to, and depending on, the precise function. What I can't pinpoint is exactly at what point my fear of feeling trapped when seated in the middle of a long row began, but I do know that it coincided with the start of my food phobia.

After House Rooms at 08:55 we file, in silence, to the main hall for Assembly, which consists of a couple of hymns, a prayer and some school notices being read out— usually general information about special events involving lectures, games fixtures, and summons for individuals to report to their house mistress or their dorm matron.

Once a week on a Friday morning, assembly will include "Mac on the Mount", an address from the headmistress to broadcast the names of the girls to be awarded Merit Marks, and those of the girls who had received Conduct Marks, along with lengthy details of each disgraced girl's misdemeanours. Three Conduct Marks in one term automatically will lead to expulsion, so getting just the one is considered a big bad deal.

Mrs McC.—"Mac"—is formidable in every way, and even the staff are scared of her. "She gives me the shivers," I write in one of my first letters home to my parents. Late-sixties and near retirement, she is a short, dark-grey-haired Scot, with a pair of small brown tortoiseshell half-glasses perched midway down her nose. When she looks at you, it's always from over the top of her half-rims and, often— except for when speaking at Assembly—she has a glass of gin in one hand and a cigarette in the other. And when she stares at you, you can't help being transfixed by the long, curling ash on the end of her cigarette and by trying to guess whether it will fall on her generous bosom or on the floor.

Lessons are very standard-syllabus fare—forty minutes per class with a few "doubles" (double Maths being my favourite, *not*!). The teachers are split evenly between male and female and range in age from between thirty to sixty, although at the age of eleven they all look quite old to me.

It very quickly becomes apparent that there are three types of teacher: those to be feared (Maths and French); those who are dead boring and intense (Religious Instruction, Chemistry, Biology, Geography); and those who are really interesting and fun (sadly, there was only one—my English teacher—although now I come to think of it, the woman who taught Art was a bit "groovy").

I'm not sure how I passed my Eleven Plus Entrance Exam, other than perhaps the Naval School must have had a shortfall of new applications that September and, desperate for the not-insignificant fees, they probably lowered the pass mark to fill those spaces. Due to my father's various postings around the country, I had, since the age of five, attended four or five different infant and prep schools. The Navy housed us in married quarters, and I was sent to an array of local schools, as was my brother (who had been born in Scotland, whilst I had been born in Wales).

So, it was little wonder that I was somewhat behind when I started at the Naval School. Perhaps allowances were made but, at that stage, my dyslexia would not have been a factor (I only discovered it myself in my late teens when taking shorthand dictation and writing numbers completely back to front). It seems almost inconceivable now to look back to the sixties and seventies and find a world where dyslexia, anorexia, OCD, ADHD, Asperger Syndrome, bulimia, and anorexia were either not recognised or, if they were, were simply swept under the carpet by the post-war "stiff-upper-lip" generation.

It was fortuitous, then, that I was good at something: sport! How I loved "Games", and my teachers, and the thrill of being praised for something. Double games was my ultimate joy, whether lacrosse, netball or tennis, even if it was raining. Athletics wasn't really my forte, although I did enjoy throwing the discus and javelin. I must have looked amusing, with my matchstick-like physique and weighing only six stone (as, indeed, I did right up until the age of seventeen).

Writing Home

The bullying started only a couple of weeks into the first term.

Yesterday I had a horrid time in our singing lesson. I was leaning against a chair and C. pulled it away and I went flat on my face. I have got brurises all over my knees and I hurt my thumb. But I am in one piece. Also yesterday, I went upstairs to change into my skirt and jumper and I found my bed in a terrible mess and I expect you know who did it. C. of corse. And then they all teased me for not making my bed propaly. Also about a week ago I went upstairs at bed time and they told me they had swaped my matress and all my bed cloths over with J. C's matress and bed cloths. It was because J.s matress was very lumpy and horrid. I have had to stick up with J.s matress now all the time.

Bullying is not unusual at boarding school—any

school, in fact—but it certainly amplifies the trauma of being away from home and still trying to find your way: who your friends are ... and who definitely aren't. Some say this is a character-forming experience, an exercise in learning from a young age about survival, even if you're not one of the fittest.

> Darling Katharine, ... I wonder if you have used your lax stick yet. I do hope you will manage to get into the netball team ... I do so much hope darling that you are feeling happier. I have given it a lot of thought and I am sure it is only a question of time before you truly settle down to boarding, and then you'll simply love it. It can be so much fun. It is a great shame that C. is upsetting you and I think the only way to overcome it is by being so nice to her that she will be too ashamed to be anything but nice to you back. Do try never to join in an argument, it is always best to say nothing. Just try and be pleasant and as helpful as possible. Daddy and I do so want you to get on well and to have a good report at the end of term. ... God bless darling, we think of you all the time. Lots of love, Mummy.

The advice from my well-meaning mother certainly didn't work. "I've tried my hardest to be friends with C. and I have even had a talk with her to ask if she will be nice to me, but it does not work." Encouragingly (for my parents), my report said otherwise: "This is a pleasing first report. Katharine has looked much happier of late and is now, I think, a well-integrated member of her form."

For the first two years I was bullied mercilessly, but during that time I watched, waited, and clocked the skills required to become a bully myself, a prelude to becoming just plain bad!

In the meantime, a mixture of bullying and being homesick must have led to my fear of sitting mid-row during Assembly and feeling trapped which, in turn, was tied up with my fear of sitting on a prefect-headed table at lunch and supper. Being made to eat my food at home was one thing, as the food was good, but at school it was revolting and I just couldn't eat it, let alone finish it.

I can feel that gagging sensation now as I recall what it was like to have a piece of fatty meat parked in the side of my mouth whilst being watched by a prefect as I tried to summon up the courage to swallow. I developed a fear that I was going to be sick on the plate and be embarrassed and exposed in front of the whole school. The napkin trick often came in handy, but there were occasions when I simply missed a meal by locking myself in the basement lavvies.

Something similar happened in Assembly: I had a phobia of not being able to get out of the hall in time to be sick unless my chair was on the end of a row. This fear was very real—my hands would sweat and shake, my tummy gurgled, and I would have to keep swallowing an excess of saliva. It was some sort of panic attack. My problem was that there was no choice about where you sat: the chair you had to sit in was the one you'd ended up standing by after filing in.

So, often, as we filed from our house form rooms at

08:55, down the long corridors to the assembly hall, I would neatly swerve off to the right, through a heavy swing door, into the cloakroom housing multiple toilet cubicles. I'd hide myself in the one right at the end, just in case someone came in, pulling the loo seat down to sit on, lifting my feet up from the floor so as not to be seen under the three-quarter-length partitioned walls.

I didn't have anorexia, but I certainly had an eating disorder that went on for years and I stayed very thin, not eating properly. I survived on cereal at breakfast, a biscuit at break time (I couldn't cope with the tepid, or even warm, bottled milk), bread and jam at teatime, and the occasional apple. My main sustenance was "tuck"—sweets, sweets, and more sweets. (It seems "sweets" was the generic term for any type of sweet or biscuit or bars of chocolate—so say my diaries. Little wonder that my generation now have mouthfuls of amalgam!)

Sunday lunch was the one meal I could just about cope with (actually, if I'm honest, it was just the pudding). Usually a "roast", albeit with very grey fatty meat, but always followed by ice cream and chocolate sauce. When the bell for seconds sounded, there was a stampede, although not when one of the "feared" teachers was on duty who demanded a controlled queue so you could only get up and stand in line when your table number was called.

Weekends at school were not much to write home about; but write home we had to—on Sunday mornings if we had an Evensong service, and Sunday afternoons if we had the Service in the morning. We had to sit for an hour in the foul-smelling dining-room with the elbows of our jumpers sticking to the tabletops that hadn't been wiped down properly.

Basildon Bond writing paper (in the main), fountain pen and ink; our name and house name had to be written on the back of the envelope for the duty member of staff to check that each girl had written to their parents. There was always a strong suspicion that certain girls had their letters intercepted and read.

We all had our own supply of stamps, though repeatedly had to write home asking for more when the stamp stock was dwindling, rather like the supply of "sweets". Letter writing was *the* form of communication (even when not at boarding school, telephone calls were considered an unnecessary expensive luxury).

I would write to my parents at least twice a week and they would take it in turns to write back, though my mother, to be fair, did more than her share (the general rule of thumb within married couples of that era). There were two postal collections and deliveries each day. A letter could arrive at its destination the same day it was posted, especially when it was only three miles away with a stamp costing 4d, or 1.5 pence in new money!

Grenville, RNS
26th Oct, 1969

Dear Mummy and Daddy,
I am very very sorry about my last letter but I have just found it at the back of my locker, so I am sending it

34

with this weeks. Thank you very much for your letter, it cheered me up very much.

Last Sunday night I left my locker key down in the woods and so five of us with a senior went down with a torch (not only to get my key but to see a certain den which had been made several years ago). Anyway, we went down and got back okay. Then the next morning Mac had something to say in assembly. She said anyone that went outside last night to stand up and come to the front. So many people stood up, some seniors. But what made me cross that many others had gone out and had not stood up. Anyway, for our punishment we had to learn the school rules off by heart. Anyway, we did and then we had to write them out without looking and sign them.

I just hope you don't mind too much.

I am getting so sick of sleeping in Thursley dorm, its so far down the hill to walk to at night. I don't like it at all and I don't like Miss H. She is so nasty to me. I don't know why, I have just given up with her. I am looking forward very much to coming out and the time is getting closer. It is half term on Friday and I hope that comes quickly.

Today we are going to have to start to do a quiz (Mac's idea). Everyone is fed up because it takes all our free time up and now we have no free time on Sunday at all. In the morning we have the Service followed by letter writing, followed by organised walks, followed by lunch. After lunch we have siesta followed by tea, followed by the quiz followed by supper and bed and that is our Sunday. Also we are wearing suits all day today as Mac says so.

The only thing that has been nice was Pop in the gym on Saterday, apart from the fact that we have been stopped from going after supper.

Mac has been in an awful temper lately. In the alcove she put up a notice about Shelter or something and at the top she put "Read this if you have time poor little rich girls in this school" (or words to that effect).

I went for a walk with Jane yesterday and you can't walk anywhere without seeing chestnuts. We have been slightly beaten with our record of 300 by someone else with 1,450 chestnuts.

Well time is running out now. Longing for the end of term.

All my love, Katharine xxxxx

PS: Sorry about all the complaints.

Although letters from my father were less frequent than from my mother, he was always very loving and encouraging; he would always sign off "Your affectionate Daddy", sending Blossom's, Tiger's (the dog and the cat), and his "fondest" love. "Have you played lacrosse yet and how are you getting on with netball darling? Perhaps I could make a post and a net for you to practice in the holidays—it's jolly exciting to think you'll be home again then."

My father's work kept him busy, and he travelled round the country to various naval air and sea bases as well as commuting between Whitehall in London and Portsmouth dockyard. Only now, in retrospect and through re-reading his letters, is it clear he was taking time and effort, trying to repair his fractured marriage and perhaps his damaged relationship with his daughter.

Darling Katharine,

3rd October 1967

It's my turn to write and I have just time to finish a letter and catch the Sunday post if I drive this down to Haslemere.

We arrived back safely from Cornwall late on Friday night after a very enjoyable week. Gillan, the place we stayed was about ten miles from Culdrose where I did some helicopter flying each day. Mummy used to drive me to work and then spend the rest of the day driving round various beauty spots we used to know before we were married. Of course she couldn't resist going in just about every antique shop in Cornwall! Then Mummy used to collect me at Culdrose about tea time when we did a bit more sight-seeing before going back to our hotel for dinner.

The place we stayed was very nice and the beach, river, sea and cliffs are all only about a three minute walk away. We are seriously thinking we might go there for our holidays next Summer. We would hire a motor boat for a whole week and keep it in a little cove just at the bottom of the hill. We could then take a picnic lunch each morning and spend the rest of the day until supper in our boat. We could swim, fish and explore the creeks and coves in it. Do you think you would like that sort of holiday darling?

Look after yourself darling, we are dying to hear all your news. We all send our fondest love.

Your affectionate Daddy

My father *was* trying hard to make amends (we *did* go to Cornwall for a week, sometimes two, every summer and he did hire a boat every year, insisting their joint initials were painted on the bow of the boat along with the exact number of years they'd been married).

It was during this time that my mother formalised her love affair with antiques.

The most exciting headline appeared in the *Times* and *Telegraph* on Thursday. It said "A Leader fetches £850". What that means is that a picture by the same artist as my painting was sold by auction in London (Sotheby's) for £850. Can you believe it? Don't you think Mummy is very clever? Now Leader has the publicity it means the prices of all his pictures will go up—not that I'm going to sell mine! Must go now to paint my nails and have a rest before the party.

Lots and lots of love to you from us all,

Mummy xx

In addition to Chapel and letter writing, other Sunday activities included hair washing, a walk in the extensive grounds, a one-hour siesta after lunch when we were expected to read in silence on our beds before then changing our sheets—well, of sorts: one clean sheet to replace the top sheet which was then in turn moved to replace the bottom one, thus rendering only one dirty sheet to go to the laundry.

Spare time, the little we had, was spent in the house room, in my case Grenville, which was shared by around thirty girls from Lower, Middle, and Upper IV. A healthy trade in girls magazines existed: bartering and swaps between *Jackie*, *Honey*, and *19*. There was a television set encased in a wooden cabinet and a Dansette record player—both for limited use, as per the rules—which was dominated and controlled by the girls from Upper IV, naturally. On Thursday evenings supper was a rushed affair, enabling all to get to our houseroom by 19:35 for the start of *Top of the Pops*, which simply everyone wanted to watch.

Sunday evenings were always depressing, particularly when we had Evensong and had to walk back from Chapel in the wet, cold, and dark, knowing another tedious unhappy week lay ahead. It was equally depressing, if not more so, being driven up the long hill back to school following a Sunday "exeat". (All these years later, I still get a sinking Sunday-evening feeling, made no better by the current early-evening TV offerings which truly don't seem to have changed that much, apart from *Songs of Praise* having finally been shunted to an alternative slot.)

Each term you were allocated three exeats, which allowed parents to collect their daughters and take them out, usually home for the day, unless, of course, you'd been given a Conduct Mark for bad behaviour which meant one exeat would be docked as punishment. A lesser evil would produce a Careless Mark but three of those added up to a Conduct Mark and the net result was the same: one exeat removed. (Over the years, I seemed to collect rather more of these bad marks than seemed reasonable, so, over time, I had to instigate my own custom-made plans for escaping school!)

Saturdays were marginally better, but only after we had got through two or three hours prep with an extra hour in the classroom if you had detention. Some afternoons there would be a classic feature film in the assembly hall: *The Guns of Navarone, The Sinking of the Bismark, The Inn of the Sixth Happiness, How to Steal a Million* ... a few come to mind (weirdly, to this day I have a penchant for old war movies). Invariably the film would take up more time than anticipated as the cine-projector had a habit of going wrong, usually with the film slipping off the sprockets causing further unravelling from the other giant spool. Whoever was on film-monitor duty received boos and taunts whilst their hands trembled trying to thread the film back through the projector and back on to its spools.

If you were in a school sports team, you missed the film as Saturday afternoons were taken up with matches against other reasonably local schools and whether home or away, they both took up the whole afternoon. But it was swings and roundabouts, as some of the films were dire (*The God of Creation*); but then again, so were many of the matches, as the RNS teams had a habit of losing.

My end-of-term reports over this time were mediocre— generally B for "Achievement" and B+ for "Effort". I was, apparently, generally considered at that time to be "a pleasant and well-behaved member of the form although a little unhappy and forlorn at times".

The Punishment Fits the Crime(s)

Looking back, it's interesting that so little attention was paid to my health. I was far from being a healthy child during school term time, and I was always queuing at the sickbay to see the school sister, complaining I didn't feel well. I felt sick most of the time and was not eating properly. I often had a sore throat, tonsillitis, and numerous colds and stomach bugs; some of my ailments were all part of school life. "I still have my white spots and a sore throat and headache. I have been in bed for two days but if I'm not miles better, Mac and Sister say I can't come home on Sunday."

There were the endless problems with my period, or lack of, and then my alopecia:

> Found out I was going bald, got worried and saw Sister who said I had to see the Doctor and after I saw him he just gave me some ointment.

I was extremely thin, but no one seemed to think there was anything untoward. When I went home for the holidays, my parents noticed I was underweight and did their best to "feed me up" before the start of the next term, and with some success, so my weight was merely put down to the "not very nice" school food.

I spent many stretches of time as a patient in the sickbay, otherwise known as HMS *Canada*. Depending on what was wrong with you and who was on staff duty looking after the invalids, you could have quite a nice time, but on the other hand it could be awful. A stomach bug usually meant just water and no food all day, apart from a dry Jacob's cream cracker, if you were lucky. Often there were others who were ill with you and, if you weren't too ill, it was possible to have a bit of a laugh, sharing jokes, books, or hanging out the window tipping jugs of water on your fellow classmates as they walked beneath the window three floors below.

I didn't get into much serious trouble during my first two years but when I did, the headmistress, Mac, always dreamt up a unique form of punishment to match the crime. During a stay in Canada, I had been regaling my fellow inmates with saucy extracts from a Harold Robbins book, *Stiletto*, unaware that Sister was listening outside the door, probably enjoying every minute of my recital. On recovery and discharge from *HMS Canada*, I was summoned to see the headmistress. Sitting behind her large desk in her grand oak-panelled office-cum-drawing-room, with her gin and tonic and cigarette, she opened the book at the page I had been reading out loud in the sickbay.

"Leppard, stand over in that corner and read to me what you read out loud to the other girls in Canada."

I sobbed and choked as I tried to enunciate the lurid description of a woman holding a throbbing erect penis, rolling down a Durex from the tip to the base in readiness for penetration … and then of course, all that and more.

"Leppard, I can't hear you, speak louder … what, girl? … shout it out … and again!"

The headmistress' summary on my end-of term report reads as follows:

Katharine has shown an early taste for salacious literature. In her desire to share her finds she read it aloud so that those in adjacent rooms in her recent stay in the San might share in her finds. However, she professed strong disinclination to read it aloud to her parents, so I may have gently arrested her taste for such matters.

Another occasion I was summoned by Mac was after having been caught "stealing" a loaf of sliced bread (Mother's Pride) from the dining room at teatime to feed the horses who roamed in a field down below the lacrosse pitch, just outside the school grounds. Mac had sent an order for me to go to her room at "7 o'clock sharp", the exact time of the school supper bell.

Shaking with terror, I knocked on her door and entered. Immediately it became apparent what was in store for me. Housed in the large bay window stood her quite substantial oval dining table, which was set for two, one place-setting at either end. On seeing a lone plate stacked with a whole loaf of sliced white bread, it was obvious where I was to sit.

Through the open oak-panelled door appeared one of the kitchen staff wheeling in a trolley with a three-course dinner for Mac, who stubbed out her cigarette, pulled up her chair to her end of the table and proceeded, in an exaggerated manner, to slurp her soup. "You, my girl, are not leaving this table until you have finished eating that entire loaf of bread." I chomped away as best I could but after eight or so slices my tears and pleas commenced, finally culminating in some retching, which got me promptly ejected from her room, and the jaws of her punishment.

Having a record of my life in the form of diary entries (1967 to 1973 and beyond) and extensive letters, I can conclude that I had a relatively "normal" first two years at boarding school. Writing a diary or journal at such a young age is a very different process from writing one now. I mention very few emotional worries and write mainly about events: "I did this ... I did that ..." There are a few notable brief exceptions, illustrating the naivety and innocence that goes with that age but with just a smidge of opinion creeping in:

> 5th June 1968 – Awfull about this Kenneddy man being shot and he died.
> 1st July 1969 – Watched the Investiture of Prince Charles – it was very boring.
> 4th July 1969 – No lunch because of Christian Aid Week and the starving Biafreians. Super that Ann Jones beat Billie Jean King in the finals but we weren't allowed to watch it.
> 20th July 1969 – Three men landed on the moon. Nice supper, then played tennis.

Some entries are rather more understated than others! A bit like the secret codes I invented, thinking no one would understand ... "managed to bring back some fdydags and we went to the woods and smdydokdyded them." I did start smoking at thirteen but, happily, not habitually, and therefore managed to avoid being caught during my first two years at boarding school. However, this was going to significantly change in the years to come as I entered a very naughty phase, building up to being extremely bad—a ringleader and rebel. Interestingly, this was a badge I would wear with pride.

But in those first two years, still in the relative flush of innocence and youth, end of term always culminated in a midnight feast—about the most exciting occasion, made even more thrilling by the risk of getting caught and all our food and drink getting confiscated. We'd plan the feast at least four weeks beforehand, drawing up a list of who was responsible for getting what, then bribing the "day bugs" to do some shopping for us. Dairylea triangles, packets of jelly, Chipples, Jaffa Cakes, Coca-Cola, and even grapes were on the menu.

On the last day of term, in bold letters at the top of my diary page it usually said: "HOME SWEET HOME". I was so excited to be going home to Mummy and Daddy, to my bedroom and my "stuff", to good home cooking, to Tiger and Blossom—our cat and dog—and four weeks with no school.

Sadly, underneath that excitement and longing was dread and the fear of what lay ahead at "home sweet home": long nights of terror; screaming and shouting; smashing of pictures and plates; and physical violence between dear Mummy and Daddy. During the holidays, with my father at work, my mother took her rage out on me. The anger and resentment my mother displayed as she went about her household duties was truly frightening.

"Remember what your father was doing on your eighth birthday ..." or "Poor little rich girl", she'd shriek as she proceeded to instruct me in the household chores of cooking and cleaning, washing and ironing—but to her *very* exacting standards—which "every young girl should learn from an early age".

To make matters worse, all this while my brother gets off scot-free. Even drying up the dishes is considered "not a suitable job for a boy".

3

Singapore Revisited

There was much I didn't know about my father, and to this day one of my regrets is that I never talked to him, on his own, over a glass of wine or two. On reading his obituary in *The Telegraph* a few days after he died in July 2016, one day before what would have been his ninety-second birthday, I cried and felt guilty. Why had I not indulged him, encouraged him to talk about his flying experiences, especially during the latter period of his significant successful thirty-five-year career in the Royal Navy, not to mention his additional twelve-year stint working in civilian life?

The fact was that I'd been indoctrinated, from a child, to dislike my father, to refuse to give him the time of day, let alone listen to him. Fortunately, over the years, and especially as a mature adult in my fifties, things had improved, gradually and significantly. During the last ten years of his life we had a pretty good relationship. I did love my father, but not enough to listen to him talk for too long. I had just enough attention span to clock that his favourite aircraft had been the Tiger Moth and Spitfire, and that he was irritated by the glory heaped upon the RAF after the war: apparently, they got all the best planes but didn't have half the skills of Fleet Air Arm pilots operating from aircraft carriers at sea, landing and taking off in extremely restricted spaces.

Most crucially, I would have liked to have understood more about his relationship with my mother who, for over six decades, never allowed his side of the story, any of his stories, to be told. My matriarchal mother gained control; individually and as a family we became too scared to stand up to her. But—and this is the *big* but—we loved her.

The family continued to function, though in a very dysfunctional way. My father's job took centre stage, and his career path was manipulated, to the extent that she was able, by my mother. Perhaps some would say she "supported" my father's career, except it wasn't the usual sort of support. She would flirt with his bosses; she had the looks and out-going personality to get away with it. She was driven by success and wanted more. She was ambitious for herself and her children, which, of course, was not unreasonable, given her humble start in life.

Behind every successful man there's a …

My father was never allowed to talk about his career or tell his flying stories, even those from the war. My mother always shut him down with her infamous dinner-party joke: "The trouble with aviators is, they never know when to shut the hangar door", or, if she was simply brewing up, "Shut up Keith. No one is interested."

In 1969 a new role was offered to my father which suddenly justified sending me and my brother to boarding schools: he was appointed the Fleet Air Arm's Chief Staff Officer for Operations and Training in the Far East, based in ... Singapore! My father's chequered history in Singapore included having spent his twenty-first birthday in 1945 as part of 882 Squadron celebrating VJ Day (Victory over Japan); then, forward twenty years to his trip on HMS *Victorious* in 1963–64 and the affair with the Whore in Singapore; and now, only six years later, he found himself stationed there once again, but this time along with his hell-hath-no-fury-like-a-woman-scorned wife and his two children.

Big new challenges lay ahead for my father ... and that was *before* he'd started the new day job.

The preparations for moving to Singapore started in the summer of 1969. The first thing was to find tenants for the family house. Naval base accommodation would be provided for Mum and Dad but, this time, rather more was required than the lowly "married quarters" they had been accustomed to when stationed in Lossiemouth and Haverfordwest. This job came with a five-bedroom house, a large, gated garden with a sweeping circular driveway, a cook and a housekeeper, and two guard dogs!

Much of the expat and military residential communities lived in the north of the island, a couple of miles from the village of Sembawang. A grand, wide road—King's Avenue—flanked by palm trees, with a monsoon drain either side (when it rained, it really rained), housed many senior naval personnel, including the admiral, whose house at the bottom of the hill had a wonderful swimming pool (it was a real treat to be invited to visit). But if you continued up to the top of the hill, there, boasting the best view of HM's Royal Naval Dockyard below, sat 124 Kings Avenue, our new colonial-style whitewashed home for what was to be the next two years.

If naval salaries were considered poor, then perks surely went some way to help bridge the gap. My parents' moving expenses were paid for, as well as the house and the staff who went with the job and, into the bargain, the Navy picked up the tab for their children to fly out for two of the three annual school holidays. For summer and Christmas holidays, British Overseas Airways Corporation flights were booked and paid for by the Navy; but for Easter holidays, Mum and Dad would have to put me and my brother on a waiting list and, if successful, pay for what was known as an "indulgence fight", courtesy of the RAF.

The BOAC airplane came with all the usual advantages of the latest jet engines, and, of most interest to me, these included a free large tin of BOAC sweets for children under sixteen. There was always a chaperone to escort us from the terminal onto the plane, helping with check-in and readiness for the eighteen-hour flight and the three refuelling stops.

Over the course of two years, my brother and I notched up twelve return flights to Singapore. I hope it pleased my father that I took such an interest in the various types of aircraft, as I wrote in a letter to my parents after a return flight (12th January 1970):

I did not find any difference at all between a VC10 and a Boeing 707 only that the 707 was better at landing and taking off. And, guess what, when we arrived in London we got a bit held up due to the Jumbo jet coming in for the very first time and we saw it land—it was on the News.

Once a year, for the Easter holidays, we had the rather different experience of an RAF flight—usually a twinned-propeller plane, a Britannia, carrying mainly freight, with most of the seats stripped out and replaced by various enormous wooden crates and huge metal items of machinery. Quite often, as few as fourteen seats were available and these, following RAF safety protocol, were back to front; that is, you took off looking to the rear of the plane, which meant that when you landed you were thrust firmly into the back of your seat.

The good news for my parents was that the cost of the flight was a mere £8 each way—you only paid for the food! The even better news for me and my brother, and other military "indulged" children, was that you got to sit in the cockpit with the captain and co-pilot for hours and hours, headsets on, conversing with them and admiring the extraordinary views during the day and the night. There was no shortage of time; the flight took up to forty-two hours from RAF Brize Norton in Oxfordshire to its destination of Singapore, including three refuelling stops at RAF bases en route.

Sometimes I flew with my brother, sometimes alone; there was little advantage to flying with him as all he did was eat, sleep, and moan "Are we nearly there yet?" He would also cramp my style, as, according to my diary log, he clearly did on one trip …

> I was so surprised when Pete F came and sat next to me and I'm sure I sounded stupid the way I said 'hello' cause I was so surprised. I wish Andrew had not been sitting next to me cause I could have smoked and talked to Pete far more freely. I felt so juvenile what with my teddy and then spilling my orange squash. Both Andrew and Pete fell asleep and I was left stuck in the middle of them. I lit a fag out of pure boredom and just sat there.

I was generally terrified of take-offs, landings, and turbulence, feeling sick most of the time and only able to eat the sweets out of my BOAC tin (when I wasn't smoking—yes, really!). There was always a minimum of three refuelling stops, regardless of which plane you were on, and, occasionally, an overnight stop was necessary due to extreme weather such as a severe thunderstorm. I would count down the last few hours on the final leg of the journey, scared of the landing but so excited to be arriving in Singapore.

Far-Eastern Fun

When we disembark from the aircraft on our very first trip, it's dark, and a wave of extremely hot and humid air hits me full in the face—it smells like an old damp blanket that hasn't been washed for a decade. That first overwhelming sensory experience of the tropics has stayed with me ever since—funnily enough, I now crave and seek out that smell, that humidity ...

Sat, 13th December 1969

HOME HOME HOME SINGAPORE! ARRIVING SINGAPORE!

Stopped early in the morning at Tehran. It was not very interesting but the scenery was pretty, snow on mountain tops and clouds. Felt sick taking off again. Later on in the morning we stopped at Bombay, it was really very very hot and I was almost stifled. Back on the plane. Time again dragged by. Lunch was served but I only had a snack and so did Andrew.

Travelling still until we stopped at Ceylon, Columbo. Very hot here too. Rather a posh lounge to wait in. Bought Mummy some Ceylon tea. Back on the plane. The last hours seem to drag by, then at last we landed. Saw M&D and drove home and saw the dogs Suzie and Sam for the first time. Took them for a walk and had something to eat.

Mum and Dad are as excited to see us as we are to see them after three months and 8,000 miles of separation, eager to share in the delights of our new regular holiday destination and home. The "guard dogs" turn out to be simply adorable—Suzie and Sam. The size of Labradors but very much plain old Singaporean "pye-dogs", crossbreeds rescued from the streets by the previous occupants of the house, Suzie and Sam are huge fun and very playful. Sam could get a little boisterous, being very much the alpha male, but both, without doubt, earned their keep as reasonably reliable protectors of the occupants of 124 Kings Avenue.

Sun, 14th Dec NB: OC = Officers Club
Woke up very late and felt very refreshed. The look of the garden and all the windows open, well no windows in some places, heat etc etc made me very happy. Breakfast was pineapple and toast. After Andrew had wakened went down to the Officers Club and stayed there for lunch. Swam a lot, Andrew did not much. OC lunch.

Had another swim after lunch and lay in the sun until I could not bare it much longer. Went mid afternoon and had tea at home. When it had cooled down, we all had a game of badminton. Came in had a drink went to OC for another swim. Supper—roast chicken (yumm). Took the dogs round the block. Had a shower.

So, my brother and I, at the ages of eleven and fourteen respectively, begin our privileged period of Far Eastern holiday fun and new experiences, albeit heavily interspersed with the continued arguing and physical fighting between our mother and father. They could only contain themselves for the first twenty-four hours of our first holiday. And it is soon to get much, much worse.

Mon, 15th Dec
Was woken up by Mummy and Daddy quarrelling and

carrying on. After breakfast we went into the village and did some shopping. The heat was fantastically hot. At last we came home to a cool house. Bread and cheese for lunch.

Coming from England in December made the change in temperature seem even more extreme. It was *so* hot. Most afternoons it would suddenly pour down, often accompanied by thunder and lightning but with rain so heavy we'd never seen anything like it. Just as quickly as it started, it would stop; the sun would come out and the roads and gardens would steam before drying out completely—all in the space of less than an hour.

The "black and white house on stilts", built in the 1920s, has a high-pitched roof and is large and airy, with very little glass. Through the front door to a substantial hall with a cloakroom, the stairs lead up to the main house on the first floor. The sides of the house are largely open due to the huge overhanging eaves to protect against the tropical winds and rain—no need for windows or, indeed, air-conditioning. All the main rooms have shutters or bamboo blinds with ceiling fans that are exceptionally high, due to the extreme pitch of the roof. With cane and mahogany furniture, softened by coverings and cushions in batik-style fabrics, it feels like a step back in time, and quintessentially colonial.

My brother and I each have a huge twin-bedded bedroom with en suites. The beds are almost four-poster in style, surrounded by a frame from which to hang fitted mosquito nets. "Chi-chaks" (referred to by my brother and me as "chit-chats") roam the ceilings, mostly at night, to feast on the mosquitos that have escaped the fumes of the "mozzie coils" that smoulder away in various corners of the rooms. It's explained to us that these lizards have suckers on their feet to enable them to hang upside down on the ceilings; occasionally, one will fall on someone's head, getting stuck in their hair, causing huge shrieks of panic and general hysteria. I think it wise to always keep one eye on the ceiling directly above my head.

To the rear of the house, down a flight of stairs from the kitchen, is a small bungalow which houses the family of our Chinese amah, our cook and housekeeper, Ai Ing. A petite, dark-haired, attractive, but quite formidable, fifty-something, her husband and two teenage children answer to her instructions to maintain the smooth running of the house and help with the cleaning, the washing, and the gardening.

Ai Ing has worked for senior Royal Navy officers for many years, and, for at least the last five years, she and her family have occupied the living quarters at the back of the main house. She appears to be extremely experienced in the etiquette that accompanies the extensive dinner-party entertaining of senior military officers and their wives and is a superb cook; fortunately for her, we are only too happy to try as much traditional Chinese, Singaporean, and Malaysian cuisine as possible. So, it is a perfect fit—almost.

It soon becomes clear that there's only room for one dominant female resident in the house ... and it isn't me, and it isn't Suzie the guard dog!

Within a few months trouble is starting to brew between Mum and Ai Ing. Mum wants things done *her* way, in *her* house, and Ai Ing feels pretty much the same way. It became a power struggle, and it isn't difficult to see who, in the end, is going to win. But at what cost?

During the day, the arguing between Mum and Ai Ing increases. The sound of my mother yelling abuse emanates from the kitchen quarters on a regular basis. In the evenings, when Dad gets home and he and Mum are not entertaining "at home" or going out, there is yet more screaming and shouting, this time between the two of *them*. If it isn't about "the Whore in Singapore", it's about "the Chinese Bitch in the kitchen"!

Most days, either Mum or Dad deliver me and my brother to HMS *Terror*, the club for naval officers, their wives and children. The main attraction is a large swimming pool which we more or less live in. We become water babies—to the extent that the mix of the chlorine in the pool together with the sunshine causes an extraordinary chemical reaction on our fair heads of hair; we will both go back to school for start of term sporting bright green locks. Heads will turn in disbelief—all very pre-punk, and we just loved it!

Very occasionally, Mum would join us at the club for a few hours—never longer—to share some of the limited available "family" time. She even swam with us once or twice, but it all went horribly wrong one day when I asked her, as a joke, if she wanted me to duck her. Thinking I had asked if she wanted to race me to the other side of the pool, she said "yes", so I went up behind her, in the deep end no less, and put my weight on her shoulders and pushed her right under, new hairdo and all! After resurfacing, arms flaying (she was not a good swimmer), coughing and choking she managed to get a hand on the edge of the pool, where a huge scene erupted, and all heads turned in amazement. I don't remember ever having another mother–daughter swim-along.

My brother and I both make separate friends (as brothers and sisters tend to do at that age) and we improve our lung capacity massively with swimming races both over and under water, jumping off what seemed (at the time) like a very high diving board, ultimately building up enough courage to dive off the very highest board, driven by competition and "dares" from the other teenage kids.

Sometimes, we will be collected and taken home for lunch, only to be returned to the club in the afternoon for another session in the pool. We are, of course, only too pleased. Other times, we'll be armed with a book of "chits" (no doubt we confused "chits" with "chaks", hence our other name for the chi-chak lizards. Or was this my dyslexia?!). These "chits", or vouchers, can be exchanged for a sandwich and an ice cream, though in my case it will just be an ice cream ... or three!

My father, meantime, was busy at work ... naturally. Aircraft carriers coming into dock, others leaving, senior visiting naval or government officials to be welcomed and, of course, entertained. Hospitality plays a big part in naval life, as it does in the army and the RAF. I was conditioned in my teenage years to think that drinking at lunchtime as well as the evening was perfectly normal—and it certainly was—not that I drank more than a lager or a lager-shandy at this stage.

Andrew and I were often taken by Mum and Dad onboard the visiting ships and submarines when they had been invited to cocktail parties. Here plenty of "grog" was consumed by all. (One of the most popular drinks was a "Horse's Neck", which, can you believe was merely a mix of brandy and ginger ale?) We certainly weren't indulged in the partaking of grog, but instead were whisked off by some poor mid-shipman who had been ordered to give us a guided tour of the ship whilst the cocktail party was in full swing. I have to admit that a trip round an aircraft carrier was hugely impressive—drink or no drink—and certainly not a short walk.

Quite often we had a commodore or another captain from a visiting ship to stay at the house, and Dad would host yet another dinner party in order that the guest could meet with other naval Singapore-based senior officers and their wives. This meant my mother had to set dates aside for dinner parties at our house and liaise over menus with Ai Ing. As time went by, the level of tension between the two women grew.

One day, having already spent many a day down at the poolside, my mother decided that she wanted to branch out from "just being a naval wife", socialising only with officers' wives. She chose to take up bridge and joined a club, a forty-five-minute drive away in Singapore City. Through the bridge club, Mum met many well-to-do civilian expats; one of her newfound friends, an elderly wealthy "Lady" and author, invited us to stay at her private island retreat.

The island, or part of it, had been given to her, the "Datin" ("Lady" in Malay), by the Sultan of Jahor and was situated twenty miles off the East Coast of Malaysia and was reached by private launch. We visited well before tourism; in fact, even before there was electricity and mains water supplies. *Time Magazine* in the '70s named Pulau Tioman one of the world's most beautiful islands; and we had all been invited there—to this private villa hideaway in a tropical paradise by Mum's new bridge partner!

Over the next five decades, my mother would claim that, for many reasons, taking up bridge had been one of the best choices she had ever made—the benefits had been enormous, in terms of friends, skillset, and competition and, at the same time, exercising brain power. But in this instance, in 1971, my mother gained huge satisfaction from the fact that due to her taking up bridge and making new friends, we had received this impressive invitation—and it had absolutely nothing to do with her husband, the naval officer in charge.

She started to become a very accomplished player … and an accomplished shopper too! Singapore was, and still is, one of the shopping meccas of the Far East, if not the world. As well as loving jewellery and watches, Mum acquired a taste for silk dresses. Obviously, for entertaining she needed to look the part, so she embarked on the purchase of yards and yards of fantastic silks and having dresses made up—both long and short, for day and evening wear. The silks were utterly fabulous and, by Western standards, exceptionally good value; the work of tailors and dressmakers cost next to nothing.

So, having dropped her children off at the pool, she escaped the naval base and the officers' club, shopping, having countless dress fittings, and regularly playing bridge in the city. There was some threatening talk from my mother that she "might be having an affair". I don't think she was, but I'm confident it suited her for my father to have suspicions. After all, this was now *her* time in Singapore.

Mum occasionally dragged me and my brother along to join the shopping expedition. Robinsons Department Store and Cold Storage Supermarket were the two regulars, although as a treat we were taken sometimes to Change Alley, a market selling a diverse range of goods at bargain prices where you could barter until you dropped and then, when we'd had enough of that, we'd sometimes stop at a street food vendor and eat satay.

On a bad day, Mum would take me with her to the dressmaker. These were the outings I dreaded most. She would get measured up for both her evening and day dresses, taking ages, and then insist I be measured for a couple of "pretty cotton dresses"—dresses I just did not want. During the tense fittings—it was always hot and humid, which further stoked tempers—I did my best to feign interest, but what I really wanted were corduroy jackets and jeans, even though it was too hot to wear them in Singapore. Mum would lose her rag and scream at me. With persistent pleading and, to my delight, I did eventually manage to get a couple of sets of corduroys made to take back to England.

On the other hand, Andrew and I loved going down to the local village markets, mainly because we were able to go unaccompanied. There were many excursions to Sembawang and Chong Pang to buy joss sticks, Thai Silver snake rings (at a mere $2 each they made great presents to take back to my girlfriends), and blank cassettes. You could choose an LP in a record shop, and have it recorded for a mere dollar and a few cents, but you had to barter— that was the way in Singapore—for simply everything you bought. The Beatles' *Abbey Road* and the Rolling Stones' *Let It Bleed* were two of the first albums I paid to have taped, followed by the Beatles' *Let It Be* shortly afterwards.

It never occurred to us at the time that we were supporting an illegal "bootlegging" practice. It seems incredible to think it took the record industry another decade and a half to come up with their anti-home taping campaign. Ironically, years later, in the '80s, I was working for EMI, selling records. In the rear window of my company car—a red Ford Cortina estate, no less—I was obliged to display a skull-and-crossbones sticker reading "Home taping is killing the Music Industry". Luckily, by then I hated the inferior sound quality of cassette tapes. I'd become a vinyl junkie.

Most Sundays, we attended church, located, very conveniently, at the bottom of the hill and attended by many families from the naval base. I think Dad felt he had to be seen there, with or without Mum, as she often refused to go at the last minute. After the service, naval families would join forces and, only when one wasn't available to borrow from the HM Dockyard, hire a large outboard-motor launch and cruise the Straights of Singapore and Jahor, Malaya (as it was known then).

Dad was useless at handling a boat of any size and was the butt of endless naval-officer boat jokes, though, to be fair, he did have the excuse of being a naval aviator! Fortunately, it was always other fathers who physically steered and navigated the boat although Dad, the senior captain, still loved to give the orders, as long as there wasn't an admiral on board.

Cargo included booze and picnics hampers, aquaplaning board or skiing equipment, and even Suzie and Sam came along for the Sunday "Banyan" outing. We used to dive off the boat before lunch for brief swims—brief because we were terrified of the poisonous sea snakes and jellyfish, of which there were many. Throwing a left-over crust of bread overboard usually brought a sea snake to the surface almost immediately, whereas the Portuguese man-of-war just gently trawled a foot under the surface. It was certainly an incentive not to fall off your skis or the aquaplane board.

On occasions, an ex-pat civilian couple would join the seafaring party and bring their speed boat. The wife, a qualified ski instructor with a sense of humour would offer ski lessons but wouldn't tolerate anyone in the back of their speed boat being "helpful", and cracked a joke rather aimed at my father: "There are two things one doesn't need in a speed boat, one is a lawn mower, the other is a naval officer!"

We all had a go at skiing, even my mother who, keen to give it a try, went around the bay twice with her knees fully bent sitting on the rear part of the skis, unable to stand up whilst at the same time too frightened to let go of the tow rope for fear of what lay just below the surface. Unfortunately, already hugely embarrassed by her inept display, worse was in store for her.

Immediately after reboarding the still-lunching launch, she became doubled up with severe stomach-ache—sitting on her skis had produced an enema! Luckily there was a WC in the cabin below deck where my mother stayed for the remainder of the day's outing, suffering from pain and the indignity of it all.

Most Saturday nights we went down to the officers' club for the weekly film night. Most of the films would be "family friendly" and if, by any chance, they were too "adult themed", the teenagers would be given the usual fare—a Coca-Cola plus a packet of crisps—and sent to amuse themselves in the club's grounds. And amuse ourselves we did—the irony being that it provided my first experience of sexual encounters with boys.

This was relatively harmless activity, conducted behind the pool maintenance shed while sharing a cigarette—a bit of kissing and groping—but it was the start of something completely new and potentially quite exciting, leaving me curious and eager for more exploration, although rather nervously, as I knew it was "wrong".

It took a couple of school holidays before I found good new friends, always daughters and sons of other naval families. I had two best girlfriends, Brigitte and Sue, who both had elder sisters; we were envious of them because they were always out in the evenings with boyfriends at parties, unlike us, stuck at home with no television and parents who, when they *were* in for the evening, would try to teach us to play bridge!

The three of us girls were still only fourteen, so our parents kept strict control of us when it came to boys. We accepted it to start with, but bit by bit, as we met more boys in the swimming pool and at the officers' club, we started being asked to parties, and we desperately wanted to go. In the meantime, at least once a week, the three of us were allowed to have sleepovers at each other's homes. Whilst our parents were out for the evening (as too were Brigitte and Sue's sisters), we learnt, with much practice, to inhale cigarettes and make our own unique cocktail mixes from our parent's overflowing booze cabinets. That's not all that overflowed—we were violently sick on many occasions.

I guess the Singapore setting was bound to enable us to mature more quickly, but even so, when we finally started going to local parties on the naval base our curfew time was usually 23:00, with the exception of 01:00 on New Year's morning—"No boys around until we had our swimsuits on when we swam at the stroke of midnight" (diary 31st Dec 1969). There was no escaping the pre-agreed collection time by the parent who'd drawn the short straw to do the party pick-up run.

The colonial-style black-and-white houses built on stilts had huge basements, except that these "basements" were at ground level, directly under the house, surrounded and supported by many concrete pillars—fantastic for parties, plenty of room for "disco" dancing, with the numerous wide pillars perfect to hide behind to have a kiss and grope with whoever one had "got off with" that night.

Joss sticks were burned, many cigarettes were smoked, and I don't remember anything other than soft drinks and beer; but that was fine, as it was the boys who were the main attraction for us three curious and keen teenage girls.

This was all pretty normal teenage behaviour, albeit in a privileged Singapore services setting, but Mum and Dad suddenly decided after collecting me, Sue, and Brigitte one evening, that it had not been a "normal" party. Despite it having been held in another naval officer's house, they had suspicions. The three of us giggling on the back seat, the smell of joss sticks on our clothes and hair; this meant – well, of course, it *had* to mean—that we were on DRUGS and that BOYS had been taking advantage of us.

Not To Be Trusted

So began the furious, and continuous, battle between me and Mum and Dad which was all about them not trusting me. But sometimes Mum would disagree and say it was all about them not trusting the *boys* rather than *me* … "Your father knows what young men get up to, given half a chance", and the row would escalate from there, in front of my friends, and become exceptionally unpleasant.

My brother, being only eleven, lost out on the parties but gained in having very few fights with Mum and Dad. He was able to have a friend to stay overnight and visit his chums for stayovers. As he got older though, it became apparent to me that the parental rules for teenage boys were very different to those for teenage girls. (Perhaps it's still the same today, when parents overprotect and restrain their daughters whilst encouraging younger sons to have their full rites of passage.)

Although most of the time it was too hot during the day to play tennis, we were able to hit on the floodlit courts down at the officers' club. Sports-loving Dad (passionate about all ball games) would always be up for playing with me, but I hated playing with him. Although he was quite good, he had no style; he pushed, he poked and chipped the ball around the court, making me run like crazy.

The more annoyed I got, the worse my tennis became, so, in trying to be kind, he would call some of my balls in when they were miles out. I resented this and found it patronising, so would get angrier. I was a bad loser when I played against Dad, but I tried to justify it by saying I didn't want to play with him at all, but with my friends.

Dad was keen for my brother to learn how to play golf and Andrew was given a set of golf clubs for his first Christmas in Singapore. I'm not sure he was very thrilled to receive them—I was given a tape recorder and was extremely happy. The main purpose behind playing golf was no doubt father–son bonding. I think it was more successful than the father–daughter tennis equivalent!

Andrew and I would often play badminton in our tropically lush garden, though only when we were bored with nothing else to do. Dad would sometimes join us for a game after work; it was also cooler then and there was a brief period before total darkness fell at 19:00. I loved the smell of frangipani and was fascinated to see the flowers open in the moonlight.

Suzie and Sam always accompanied us when we were in the garden and if we were going out, they would run behind the car, down Kings Avenue, and still be sitting there on the side of the junction to greet us on our return, chasing back up the hill after the car—ideal pets, but perhaps not such reliable guard dogs after all.

An invitation to visit the admiral's pool was considered a great honour for Andrew and myself, though I think it was equally so for my father; the admiral was his boss, and my mother certainly didn't mind sitting poolside with a G&T and the boss's wife!

The admiral and his wife had a son, Edward, who was a year older than me. Over a period of several school holiday visits to Singapore we became quite friendly and developed a "girlfriend–boyfriend" relationship; that's not to say it was exclusive as other boys were on my radar and I didn't doubt the same for him with other girls.

By then I was fifteen, Edward sixteen, and it was all reasonably innocent—holding hands with a peck on the cheek (and a bit more at a party). How far the relationship was to develop would be strictly monitored by my father and mother, until it all went very wrong during a holiday trip to the East Coast of Malaya.

The week before the trip, Mum and Dad had been arguing more than normal and this led to frequent family meltdowns as everyone was hot and extremely bothered, made worse by lack of sleep due to the all-night fights. I had already started getting lippy as "I'd had enough"; so, too, had my brother, but we dealt with it in different ways—Andrew would go quietly to his room and stay there; I would rush out of my room screaming for them to shut up.

It is July 1971. Every day there is a diary entry. And nearly every day there is a drama …

Mummy was in a hell of a baite with me and I'm just getting rather sick of it, if she's not being bad tempered she's arguing with Daddy.

Mummy came back from the dressmakers and in front of the Campbells she blew me up for nothing and was a real bitch. I left with no money and no chits and went to Sue's house.

Had to play tennis against Admiral W. and his son. We both won one set each. Came home, had supper and another scene after supper. Was sent to my room". (NB: a different Admiral and a different son!)

Daddy drove me mad again, I could have hit him like he did me!.

We got back late and got into trouble for taking the piccolo boat back late. As usual Mummy lost her temper with me and gave me no supper—helped myself though and had an early night.

Mummy and Daddy were really getting on my nerves, M was getting on edge and being very unfair. Then went to the dress-makers to collect my beach wrap. Wow what a scene, it was all my fault 'cause it wasn't right. I was bloody furious with M—selfish bad-tempered bitch—she makes me sick every time I have a so called "family disagreement" (mildly put). I can't wait to leave home.

Mummy bought a black crocodile bag of which resolved into trouble. When we got home, Daddy was furious and hit Mummy and threw the bag at her and kept going on about how over-drawn they were (sorry—we are!).

These are extracts from a single week ... the week before our family holiday at the Tikit Inn, Kuantan, halfway up the East Coast of Malaya. Off we went ...

1st August 1971

D woke me up at 6.00. Christ what an effort to get up so early. Had a quick breakfast. Did not get off till about 7.10. Got over the Causeway to JB in Malaya (Jahor Bahru) okay. Had an alright drive to the Tikit Inn—there was mile after mile of rubber trees on plantations. The exhaust bust half way and had a 2 hour delay. Arrived about four. Went for a swim on the beach. Nice chalats except I am sharing with Andrew—a damn double bed too. Had some tea—messed around till supper and were all tired so went to bed. I finished my unpacking. Had a bloody awful night—Andrew tossing and turning and taking all the sheet.

2nd August 1971

We swapped the two chalets for a family chalet, luckily

I don't have to sleep in the same bed with Andrew. Had supper which was not v good. D&A went to watch for turtles but M&I wanted early night. I finished my book The Pearl.

3rd August 1971

Daddy thumped me—big scene, God sometimes I hate that man. Am missing Edward very much—looking forward to when I see him tomorrow I hope.

4th August 1971

All morning I was looking forward to seeing E and I thought of it all morning. It's very strange but I like him sort of, in a funny way, but I do like him. Went down to the beach again—still no sign of E and then I found out that he was not coming till tomorrow (my heart really sank), I now can't wait for tomorrow. Had supper. Played bridge.

5th August 1971

This morning there were great arguments as to whether to drive 110 miles up to Kota Terenganu (or something Kota). A & I did not want to but of course in the end we had to go. I was furious (partly 'cause I wanted to see E) … When we got back went to look for E. Found him, could not speak to him alone. Hardly saw him. Great disappointment. Supper. Bed.

6th August 1971

I'll never forget today in a hurry or shall I say evening.

Spent the morning on the beach and went for a walk with Edward. D followed us to check up on me—I was furious. After lunch stayed on the beach. Swam with E, Sue etc. This evening has been the final straw. A&M wanted to see turtles—I didn't. I had arranged to go for a walk with Edward. Daddy wanted to go or pretended he did and he would not let me stay behind on my own. As he was so nasty to me, I was determined not to go because I know he would not.

What made me so cross is he can't even leave me on my own for a couple of hours at the age of 15 just because he doesn't trust me. (He thinks we get up to all the dirty things he does or used to do!) So I stayed and D stayed too—he tried to beat me up like he does M. I had a real scream so everyone could hear. He would not let me go for the walk. I got really histerical. I had 5 mins to go and tell Edward I could not come. Poured out the whole thing to E. Poor bloke but he was very understanding.

7th August 1971
DADDY if you ever happen to read this go to damn hell (and stay there).

Luckily D had gone to the garage 'cause I was still furious from the night before (furious was not the word). …Then after supper—Christ after supper … we had the same scene as the night before. The arrangement was for me to go to E's chalet and then at the last minute, M&D would not let me go. I stormed out bloody furious, (no exaggeration). E was waiting outside and we went to his chalet. M came to fetch me back and E came with me to ask D a reason why we could not be together. (He's mad that man.) D couldn't think of one except that I was irresponsible. We (E&I) were privillaged enough to be able to sit in the bar till 10.15—wow! We tried to work out a solution but in vain. We felt we gained something through the argument but we weren't sure what.

8th August 1971
Got up at 6.30 or there abouts (didn't sleep well). We packed up our things and had a quick breakfast. D said good morning to Edward's father who is his boss and the Admiral ignored him—serve him right. Had an argument about last night's episode (M was on my side—our side) I got really hot in the car but the journey was not really too bad—no major crisis. Suzie and Sam pleased to see us but Sam has found himself a new girlfriend!

Perhaps unsurprisingly, that was the end of my relationship with Edward. As days went by, it became obvious that he was making excuses by being unable to meet up. The admiral had given his son orders. I'm sure that the whole incident didn't do my father any favours— it's never a good idea to upset the boss. As for me, I was left angry but not heartbroken.

Our two years in Singapore (six school holidays for me and my brother) were an education and a privilege, marred only by torrid parental turmoil. The family dynamics continued to change and become ever more polarised. Whilst we had exceptional experiences with wonderful trips and made new friends, it was an extremely unhappy time emotionally. Now, to help keep my head above water, I became even more angry; the rebel in me was unleashed—a default position which would stay with me for many years.

Ai Ing's Revenge

The angriest member of the household, the woman in charge—my mother—came, unsurprisingly, to final blows with Ai Ing when Mum fired her. She was told to leave almost immediately, which meant Ai Ing and her family had to pack up all their possessions and vacate the bungalow at the back of 124 Kings Avenue that had been their home for many years. Dad had no say in the matter; he knew that if his wife didn't get her way, his plans for career advancement would be going nowhere.

Having prepared, at my mother's request, a cold supper (a seafood *nasi goreng* and salad), Ai Ing and her family leave in the late afternoon. The four of us are sitting at the dining-room table, ready to eat. After three of four mouthfuls it becomes apparent that Ai Ing has been rather generous with the chili. A few more mouthfuls, in the space of what is probably only another minute, and we all experience a terrible burning sensation in our throats. A look of alarm is exchanged between Mum and Dad and suddenly we are all four of us running ... running to the loo.

We have been poisoned. Dad manages to call the naval base duty doctor who comes straight away and, after examination and assessment, tells us we are going to be okay but rather unwell for the next twelve hours or so. My father insists that the remaining *nasi goreng* is taken away and tested in a lab, only to have the results come back as inconclusive—they couldn't find the type of poison used in the rice dish. The Chinese are renowned for their skills in the use of herbal remedies; it seems they are also very good at brewing concoctions from poisonous plants that cannot be detected even under the strongest of laboratory microscopes.

Ai Ing had taken her revenge on my mother—though it was a shame it had to involve all of us. But, as usual, Mum had the final word by declaring she never liked the Chinese anyway, and they were definitely not to be trusted because they were "cunning and devious".

4

Expulsion of Officer's Daughter

THE ROYAL NAVAL SCHOOL

HASLEMERE, SURREY.

TELEPHONE: HINDHEAD √415

18th January 1971

Captain K.A. Leppard, R.N.,
124 King's Avenue,
Naval Base,
Singapore, 27,
B.F.P.O. 164.

Dear Captain Leppard,

Your daughter was one of a group of girls who were found by myself and the Senior Mistress smoking in one of the wash-rooms on Friday evening. They admitted so doing, and in consequence I have removed one of their exeats for this term. This means that Katharine will have three exeats this term instead of four - as Grenville House were awarded an extra one last term.

I am sure you will agree that this is a serious offence, and I hope that you will co-operate with me in discouraging such behaviour.

Yours sincerely,

Diana H. Otter.

Headmistress

B ack from Singapore to reality and school with a bang, sporting bright green hair! How I hated going back. Getting caught smoking within the first few days of term was far from clever. "I'm sorry but it was the first time this term and the last—please don't be too cross," I wrote to Mum and Dad.

Halfway through my "detainment" at the Royal Naval School, there was a change of headmistress. Mac "retired" (was she pushed, or did she jump?) and was replaced by Miss Otter. They were poles apart and I couldn't possibly have imagined that I'd look back and wish Mac was still in charge!

Miss Otter is young, late thirties, and has quickly climbed the teaching ladder, from headmistress of Putney High School to head of The Royal Naval School. Always booted and garishly suited, she wears heavy makeup, light-blue eyeshadow and brash bright-red lips, with black hair piled high in a tight perm. Unlike her predecessor, not a G&T or a cigarette in sight. Although appointed by the board of governors, it isn't long before parents, pupils, and staff guess she is a little out of her depth.

Her style is so very different to Mac's, particularly when it comes to punishment. Looking back, Mac had humour and took great delight in trying to fit the punishment to the crime—as she'd illustrated by making me eat a whole loaf of bread after the "stealing" incident; similarly, making me read out loud to her the very same porn I'd been caught reading to my chums in the San. Mac's unique style of punishment had really been quite effective (because I never repeated either crime); she was always clearly amused as she basked in the glory of her clever idea and, happily for the perpetrator, the matter was then put to bed.

But, oh no, not so with Otter, the "new kid on the block" (ha!) and looking to prove herself. I'm caught smoking within days of her arrival and so my card is most definitely and permanently marked. But much more is to come and, had she known it, she'd probably have invested in a Rolodex exclusively for Leppard. Less than four weeks later comes another letter from the headmistress to my parents …

16th February 1971

Captain K.A. Leppard, R.N.,
124 King's Avenue,
Naval Base,
Singapore 27,
B.F.P.O. 164.

Dear Captain Leppard,

On the 10th February a considerable quantity of herbal cannabis was discovered at the School. The Police were called in and it was discovered that the cannabis had been imported from abroad by two girls, who have since been expelled. Ten other girls were involved in varying degrees, and Katharine was one of them.

In my presence and in front of the Police officers Katharine stated that on 15th January she went out on the terrace with three other girls and that she smoked a cannabis cigarette (a reefer) at the end of the terrace to see what it was like. She claims that this was the only time that she smoked it, but that she knew from that day that cannabis was in the School but she would not inform against her friends.

I contacted Katharine's legal guardians, Commander and Mrs. Durell, and asked them to come and see me on Friday, 12th February, when I explained the circumstances to them. All the girls concerned in the case were suspended, and in Katharine's case she may return to School on Sunday, 28th February, at 6 p.m.

I hope that you will endeavour to bring home to her the seriousness of this whole affair. Charges could have been made against her, but in her case, through my intervention, the Police agreed to leave her punishment to me.

Yours sincerely,

Diana H. Otter

Headmistress

Dearest Mummy & Daddy,

Thank you for your letter, and I suppose all I can say is I'm very sorry. I don't know how much you have heard but by the sound of your letter you sound as if you have heard that I am a drug addict.

Well, I will tell you the whole story. At the beginning of term J. and H.M. brought the cannibis back from Kenya. They came back late, and on their first night back they had some. They asked me to go with them and me being stupid went with some others. I stayed with them for litrally five minutes and had 3 puffs and went. (To tell you the truth I did not like it). Then I had nothing more to do with it because I realised afterwards how stupid I had been, and I swear that I really did not have anything to do with it after that. I even tried to stop them and they did not take any notice, and I stopped being friends with J. and left her to it. I knew they were going to get caught and sure enough they did, and I was then dragged into it.

Luckily I was the one who was one of the least involved and I came back to school after 2 weeks. Others are coming back in four weeks and some next term, and some not at all. Commander and Mrs Durell were very nice to me and understood that it was the first time and I was trying it out and I would come across it some time in my life. I stayed a week with the Durells and a week with Uncle Don and came back. Everything is back to normal except for the staff, they are not very nice to me but I suppose that can't be helped.

I don't suppose its any good me saying sorry as the damage is done, and you probably wouldn't take it. I don't think there is much else to say on the subject, and if you will except it I am very sorry to have upset things.

I have been changed forms I am now in Lower V (1) instead of LV (2). I don't know why I have been changed, but I suppose it's because all my friends are in the other half (LV2), also moving form has upset my work, because this form is doing different things in some subjects, and when it comes to the exams I won't have done half the things this form has done. That is now everything.

Well, I must close now. Please try and forget what has happened, and please try and forgive me.

Lots and lots of love, Katharine xxxxoooo

My version of the "whole story" was, surprisingly, pretty accurate. The year before, I had become best friends with Jane and school life had begun to change for me. Jane was brainy, sporty, popular, and fun … and a little bit naughty. The fact she had chosen me as her "bf" elevated my status in the form—it also meant that she allowed me to copy her prep.

Drugs being found in a public boarding school for girls in the early '70s was considered a major drama, even though it was only cannabis, because it was deemed almost certainly "to lead to stronger drugs". The headmistress, with her limited experience and overwhelmed with the enormity of it all, decided to call in the expertise of the Drugs Squad. So, far from the incident being kept under wraps, word got out and within days there was a report in the local newspaper.

Twelve of us were interviewed separately, to check that our stories matched up; we were locked in separate rooms in the sick bay until the police had cautioned and interviewed each of us. I remember being told I would have a criminal record if I failed to tell the truth. I was terrified.

Jane and her older sister were expelled immediately, and I never heard from her again—we were forbidden to have any further contact. In total, five girls were expelled, five were suspended for four weeks, and two for two weeks. Being in a year lower than the other girls, I was in the last group. But that wasn't the end of it; more trouble was looming, post our suspension … and well beyond.

Grenville, RNS 13th January, 1971

Dearest Mummy & Daddy,

I hope you've cooled down after my last letter, and once again I am very sorry if I have upset you and I don't know whether you understand or not, but anyway please may we try and forget the matter, well as far as possible. By the way, did you get my last letter via HMS Mercury I sent it about a week ago because of the postal strike.

Since I've been back I had a miserable time. Everything that's gone wrong in our form I am blamed for. The last two preps there have been two incidents where there has been trouble and I am blamed for it. I met Miss Otter this afternoon and she said she's beginning to think that its me causing the trouble in the form. So now, I am swapping desks and going to sit at the front of the class with the so known group of "goodie goodies" (of my own free will) then any trouble in future will not be blamed on me because I'm going to keep right out of any! (and work hard!)

It sounds ridiculous but nothing has happened, It never does at school...

It's bedtime now, must go.

Lots and lots of love, Katharine xxxx

In truth, quite a lot happened at school, and digging dirt on school staff, especially the housemistress, was a useful foil for the constant trouble I seemed to attract.

There is a big scandal at the moment. The House Mistress is having an affair with the maintenance man—Mr B.—who is married anyway. Well as we are in HMS Lidesdale next to the House Mistress's room we see most things that go on. He goes in there every evening at about 9 am and comes out about 12 am midnight (or as far as we have noted not at all sometimes) and then we always see him either coming out or going in when she is in her dressing gown and slippers!!! Most odd, isn't it??!!

Until now, my behaviour at boarding school had not really deviated too much from the norm—a few scrapes with authority here and there—but the drugs incident meant that, along with the only other girl in my year who'd been allowed to return to school, I was to be picked on, watched, separated in class, and generally given a hard time. Any disruption in the classroom was put down to us, and often down to me.

Unlike the other girl, R., I wasn't remotely clever—indeed near bottom in most subjects and lagging well behind. The school's tendency was to concentrate on the brainy ones in order to boast in the school prospectus just how many places "our girls" had achieved at Oxford and Cambridge. Those who were mediocre or struggling were left to their own devices and at no time were offered encouragement or further tutorial help. Sadly—but hardly surprising—being good at tennis, netball, and lacrosse didn't count for much, although it *did* please my "sports mad" father. Had everything in our family been "normal", this would have been a good thing; but, in fact, it made me angrier than ever—by now I had been fully indoctrinated by my mother to avoid pleasing him in any way.

It was sink-or-swim time. I had completely the wrong set of pencils in my pencil box to help me rise to the academic challenges. Propelled by anger at the "unfairness of it all", I dug deep to find other ways of keeping my head above water; the problem was that while I was very unhappy at school I also dreaded going home to Mum and Dad for the school holidays, especially now that we were back from Singapore and in the family home again, just three miles down the road from school.

M&D had one of their inevitable disagreements and as usual I'm brought into it. Screaming and yelling went on, smashing and banging. I don't know how they go on and on the way they do, they don't seem to realise what it's doing to Andrew and I. Mummy spent all day in bed, then when she came down she started up again in supper so I walked out and slammed the door and that didn't please her too much to say the least.

Was woken up by Mummy who wanted me to do something, i.e. all the dirty work there is in cooking i.e. washing up and all the greasy tins etc. Fetching this and that and the other. Damn well ironing from 11.30—12.45—I hate ironing. M& D went out for drinks at lunchtime. Did nothing all afternoon except watch the box—The Beatles "Hard Days Night" was on. M&D had a row after supper. Although when I write this it may sound casual, well I get very upset by it all and don't know whether its best for me to yell too, run away or what.

I was furious with Daddy today—Christ I hate him—I can't change my manner towards him. I've been brought up by M to hate him. M&D argued most of the day. I hated M for saying she had read my diary—I nearly burnt all my diaries but I have now locked them up and hidden the key. I don't trust M or D, not one bit.

Feeling really depressed. I'm sick of M being so bad

tempered and getting on at me the whole time. She says it's D that makes her like that but how can it be when he's been away all week. I had to get out of the house somehow, I'm just so sick of everything at home, so I stalked out in a furious mood, or rather in a state of manic depression. Am terribly tired coz of these sleepless nights, I wish I could go to sleep straight away. Packed my trunk. God I can't bear school tomorrow.

Rebel Rebel

Over the next two and a half years I gradually became more rebellious. I didn't set out to be, not initially at least. I made a group of new friends, deliberately chosen outside the various dull "goodie-goodie" groups, such as my fellow in-the-woods secret smokers with whom I'd spend hours not just smoking but swapping and bartering No. 6 cigarette coupons so we could get free gifts from a catalogue.

There was plenty of group rivalry, including competition over choosing one's very own "gone-on" or "crush". This was a boarding school ritual where you chose a sixth-former to "worship" (every evening saying "goodnight", buying her a small present at end of term and offering to run errands etc.). At a young age it was easy to look up to, even idolise, a senior girl who was popular, brainy, and good-looking. Sexual attraction would not have crossed my mind, probably because at that age we were far too naive—well

I most certainly was. That's not to say there wasn't lesbian activity, but I only came across it several years on. Funnily enough, an affair between the head girl and the sixth-form house mistress comes to mind, but that's a completely different story!

Lagging behind in my work and, now that my friend Jane had been expelled, with no one's prep to copy, it must have been obvious that I needed extra tuition. But none was forthcoming:

> Katharine makes no real effort to understand what she is doing or to think for herself … Katharine would benefit from greater concentration and less vocal fuss in class … Katharine's progress has been rather erratic, she seems to have much ground to make up if she's to reach the required standard … a pleasant member of the form though can be too blunt at times … outspoken and not very helpful in her dormitory … Katharine can be pleasant and helpful but her manner is sometimes rather sullen.

I dreaded my reports arriving at home. Mum and Dad would go mad and shout at me about how I was wasting their money.

Being so far behind in my work meant I couldn't understand most of what was being taught in the day-to-day classes. Maths and French were my absolute worst subjects, and I was really scared of both teachers. I floundered more and more and became bored and depressed and increasingly, to cover this up, I became *angry*. I took up smoking on a more regular basis, while my eating disorder continued; most of the time I felt sick and generally unwell. My already quite regular visits to the San increased and though the nursing sister listened and said she'd help, none was ever proffered. I did, however, get prescribed more cream for my ever-worsening bald patches.

I was still writing to my parents, but only the obligatory once-a-week Sunday letter. I would occasionally walk miles across the heath to the nearest phone box and call home, especially when I wanted some sympathy, but it wasn't always sympathy I got.

> M was in tears. I am really worried because I don't think that M&D can go on living together much longer. M just won't be able to stand up to it. She sounded on the verge of a breakdown. Am really pissed off with everyone.

A total failure in attracting any positive attention—apart from in my sporting activities—I had, as the terms rolled by, quite inadvertently, proved very successful in attracting *negative* attention. I played the victim, then got angry, then incredibly badly behaved, and, later on, just plain *bad*. I would perform the "dares" that no one else would dream of risking. My peers (though, clearly, only the fellow hardcore "up-for-a-laugh" chums) were suitably impressed and this gave me a notoriety that, of course, encouraged me further.

Competition for the record player in Grenville House common room was fierce. Don McLean, Cat Stevens, Gilbert O'Sullivan, The Carpenters, and the God-awful

Godspell droned on, evening after evening, this being the majority's choice of music and style. It wasn't until I was in the Upper V that I was able to demand turntable-time and play my choice of 33 rpm vinyl albums: Pink Floyd, Led Zep, the Stones, Mott the Hoople, and Bowie—though not without difficulty as, un-bloody-believably, most of the others didn't appreciate my taste in music and the essential volume!

I would stand on top of the common-room table playing air guitar or use my tennis racquet as a prop, throwing my head back and forth, miming to the lyrics and generally being thoroughly annoying to the few girls who had still not vacated the common room. On one occasion, and completely unaware (no one gave me a "heads up"), the headmistress entered and stood behind me, watching as I gyrated on the tabletop. Outcome … not good.

In my diary, day after day, I rage, swear, complain, and moan about being bored or feeling ill …

Feel ill again today—it depresses me so much but I'm sure I imagine most of it. Went for a run eeeeek 2nd lesson, it nearly killed me and made me feel worse. Cherie pegged out. Had that terrible farting and pain again and felt sick.

Had a bloody fire practice at 6.30 am. Got French dictation results back—I got 49 mistakes—terrible. Miss P. confiscated my signet ring.

Worst day of the week—Geog, Maths, French, Biology (double), History, English, Maths, Lax and then Lax practice. Felt in a hysterical mood tonight.

Had masses of prep to do, couldn't do Maths. Lax match against Guildford High—god I hate that school, we lost 14-0. Had a bloody headache and a bloody backache.

Feeling rather depressed. Miss P. got on to me about taking prep—she blew me up and went on and on at me, I felt like thrashing her. French dictation—64 mistakes, she told me I was not trying, oh God!

What a hell of a drag today was, I turded around with Cherie all day. Got depressed, not unusual and the food was terrible. Bored stiff.

Maths results, I got 1/20. Christ—puke puke—Miss P. blew Cherie and I up in Maths lesson, it makes me really mad. Mr B. practically accused me of cheating coz I got 20/20 for my Geog test—charming! I felt I wanted to give up altogether. French results 4/20 bottom—depressing.

Terrible weather. Had French dictation—tres terrible. RI (Religious Instruction), he talked about divorce and we got really mad—DGW slammed the door in his face and broke the glass and was very rude to him. L. makes me puke, her and her stupid ideas. Otter was mad about prep taking and I had to see her after supper.

Bilge test was so-so. Got Maths results 0/20 great. Bloody fucking Miss A. marks so unfairly. Lax practice was gastley—had to beef round the lax pitch 6 times. Miss P. confiscated all my work books in the bedroom.

Got sent out of RI—he got in a real bait about nothing so I was rude and slammed the door but didn't break the glass.

Morning dragged by. Had French test, no comment! After lunch had a careers lecture from Otter who was trying to make RNS's 6th form sound appealing. In netball I felt a migraine coming on. In RI (test) I felt ill—I didn't do the test and went to bed.

Had a close shave in RI—I wrote a pornog letter to Daph, really bad telling her my feelings and talking about me going to bed with the right bloke etc. Griff caught it. With some sucking-up managed to get it back. Lost my pocket money from where I left it in Grenville—someone pinched it. S. B. told me off for being rude this evening!! Bloody cheek—I nearly throttled her.

After waking up at 3 am I felt grotty. Boobed up my turn at being radio monitor for the news at breakfast— god it was embarrassing! Went to the doctor about my curse i.e. not having started it yet, eek he gave me an internal—it was embarrassing with Sister there too. He gave me some pills. Low and behold after feeling ill all morning, ended up in in the San—feeling depressed and had temperature of 102.

As time, and terms, passed, so reality and mock O-levels loomed:

The nearer it gets to mocks the less work I'm doing but I'm getting so worried. With everyone fussing about mocks, it's making me nervous. I must work, MUST starting from tomorrow.

There are days and days in my diary given over to "madly revising" and showing my state of anxiety:

Revising Keats like mad … I'm so worried about not passing coz I really want to do well in History … I had this sudden pang to do well, another one! I went to early Communion this morning.

Perhaps I was thinking God would help! And before I knew it:

Last minute cramming in History, the exam was hell, I could only answer 2 out of 5 questions but I answered them quite well. Maths multiple choice, I just made pretty patterns, hadn't a clue how to do anything … I made such a mess of Eng Lit, I didn't do the right ones and the right number. I'm so cross with myself coz I could have got a good mark. Puke. I'm so worried I'm not going to get any mocks. I revised History madly all afternoon.

I do remember having one marvellous teacher, Mrs K., who taught English language and literature. She was Burmese, and rumour had it she was a princess. Small-framed with dark black hair, and a little older than the other staff, she was certainly by far the most experienced and qualified, with two MAs from Oxford. No one misbehaved in her classes because she was so interesting and encouraged all levels of ability. She wafted in, always smiling and wearing black M&S slippers, her black gown billowing behind. Just after the mock exams, she wrote on my report:

> Katharine's lively personality has made class-work enjoyable for us all. I do hope her difficulty in comprehension will not stop her from success in the examinations.

My revision efforts didn't deliver in either the "Mocks" or the real-deal O-levels three months later. During the summer holidays the dreaded results arrived:

> Friday 25th August, Christ OL results arrived. I was bloody upset only got two, Eng Lit and RI. Failed History and Eng Lang. M was furious and told me to get a job as a shop girl. D was not too bad. I don't know what's going to happen now. M&D still not speaking to each other.

The plan for my further education, based on getting at least four O-levels, had been to go to another public school and join the sixth form for two years to take my A-levels. This was clearly no longer an option.

Having decided that I was going to be a journalist, I suggested to my parents that I should go to technical college to re-sit some exams whilst taking a course in journalism, an idea that was immediately quashed by both parents. In agreement with each other, for once, they claimed that I'd be dealing drugs within weeks if I went to tech college. Terrible arguments ensued and two days prior to the start of the autumn term:

It has been decided for me to go back to the Naval School. How mortifying it's going to be. I can't stand the people and O's all over again. I am really fucked off—them deciding what's good for me.

So, on 12th September 1972, back to RNS I go.

It's so mortifying being back, the people, the school etc. In a bedroom with xxxx, xxxx and xxxx, ugh!

Weds, 13th Sept: Woke up before the bell sweating about today and work etc. Squill [the only other pupil who flunked her O's and had to go back] and me were told to move apart and I to come to the front of the form—sick!—by a new staff who knew my name straight off. I was really mad. Staffs faces fell when they saw me back.

Thurs, 14th Sept: General studies in this establishment is such a bloody waste of time—it's really bad. I was so bored, we did nothing all day, nothing worth doing. I want to do an Eng Lit AL so I can get out of the General. It's so petty and bloody boring this place. Otter read out the OL results only down to 3 luckily. Prep for the first time was a bloody bore.

My life at boarding school continued from there, and I hated it. I became even more fed up, angry, and, in turn, disruptive. As my pocket money—or my "allowance", as it had now become—didn't stretch very far, something had to give. Mars Bars and chocolate bars of all sorts, purchased from the tuck shop, had to be severely reduced, though that's not to say a little bit of "nicking" didn't occur in order to get by. My cigarette consumption had increased to at least ten No. 6 a day, so this necessitated another cost-cutting exercise ...

Bought £1's worth of tobacco—have decided it's nicer and cheaper to roll my own fags. Have also decided to make fags and sell them to make a bit of money.

And a few days later:

Had to keep going outside to sample my cigs which are at last perfected and should be selling soon.

Marketed as Blue Line (with a ruled blue biro line down the side of the Rizla paper), they could be bought individually, or there was a small discount for a purchase of five or more. To make the tobacco go further, I mixed the Golden Virginia with dried leaves from the woods. My recipe was a well-kept secret.

Thurs, 21st Sept: Otter makes me sick—her preaching to the school on "Ott on the Spot" telling us not to panic about the hair nits. "Even the best of us could get them, even me"!!! My cold was really bad today and I felt so grottie and depressed. Daph phoned and I had a long chat with her.

Fri, 22nd Sept: I think I'm going to have nervous breakdown at this place, I just can't stand it. I wouldn't mind if M&D were reasonable and understood but being unhappy at home and school is too much. Keep breaking into fits of depression. My cold again bad today and I have almost lost my voice. I had to go to a lax practice and I'm in the team—I'm so bloody cross and tried to get out of it but no go.

Sat, 23rd Sept: My bloody voice even worse today but actual cold was not too bad. Tried to work as usual in prep but I get so easily distracted. Had early lunch to go to Ascot (all the way to fucking Ascot, St Georges!) to play lax. Moaned and groaned all the time to try and get out of the lax team but negative and we lost 6-3 for a change! Finished rolling ciggies tonight and have fulfilled all 1st orders, making a small profit.

Weds, 27th Sept: That bloody R. woman tried to give me a black mark—she gave me an essay to write instead,

"The Importance of being Mannerly", bloody cow! RI with Otter was bad. History re-take was insufferable and so was Classics. Am so worried about my hair coming out, it's getting worse. Was turding around this evening and Ott the Grott walked in and blew Squill and I up. Typical—it would have to be us two.

Fri, 13th Oct: Bloody tired this morning but fuck me if I didn't get a lot of work done today. I keep thinking how near OLs are—all over again but the more I'm pressed to work the less I can. Civics was a real farse. Griff caught me with fags and went berserk, absolutely mad. It was really funny. No letter, no phone call—it's all so boring and monotonous. Had a bath and washed my hair.

My father had changed jobs again and was now commanding officer of a naval air station in the West Country. The advantage of this was that I could go out for the day (each term we had three exeats) but not home (it now being too far away). One of the three exeats could be an overnighter (as long as one hadn't been docked for bad behaviour), which meant I could sometimes stay with my best friends, brother and sister Daphne and Philip, the son and daughter of my comparatively liberal-minded guardians who lived locally.

As far as my parents and the school were concerned, weekend exeats were approved, and all was above board. But it really wasn't! Philip had recently moved into a shared flat in Islington and had new male friends all taking part in the same management training course at the iconic Heals department store on the Tottenham Court Road. Well, of course, this was perfect for Daphne and me. We had a riot on our weekend visits to London. As the parents of my best friend and her brother were good acquaintances of my parents, ("terribly nice family") and mainly due to our fathers both being naval officers, my parents' suspicions as to what I might get up to on an overnight in the big bad capital city were largely allayed.

Sat, 14th Oct: God knows how I found Phil's flat but I did—took the train (£1.94) then the tube (15p). Had a great time. Went to a Mott the Hoople concert—really good. Some friends came round and we tried Mandies and Tunals—VG.

Sun, 14th Oct: After sleeping with Paul, or rather not sleeping but … We got up about 11.00 and had a late lunch. Then went to bed for 2 hours with Paul during another trip, not bad. Time went so fucking quickly before I knew where I was I was back at school. Came back on the train with Phil, we were still very numbed.

Mon, 15th Oct: I was so bloody tired today- went to bed for the first two lessons and slept. Triple English—I couldn't keep my eyeballs open. Geog test—what a shag. C. and I tripped about 3.30—it didn't have as much effect on me as yesterday but it was good. We went for a walk. During prep I kipped down on the library floor and fell asleep. Shagged out tonight.

Now aged sixteen, I seemed to have accumulated a number of interested boyfriends; not to say that I wasn't interested in them myself, because I was. Although I'd slept with Paul—oh, and Mike—I hadn't actually lost my virginity, technically speaking. Paul was London, Mike was Somerset, and Crispin, David, Tim, and Tony were Petersfield ... and then there was the new boy on the block from Farnham, Ewan. Squill and I met Ewan and Tony at a sixth-form dance hosted by their school that November and from there the four of us started to meet secretly out of school, and totally "out of bounds"!

The main attraction to Ewan—being honest—was that he had a car and money. And not just any car, but a red convertible Triumph Vitesse. This was certainly a notch up for us and his car helped facilitate several clandestine meetings and pub crawls. Squill and I would slip out illegally and Ewan and Tony would pick us up, hiding the red sports car down an obscure track just off the access road to the school.

On a Saturday afternoon we could just "sign-out", saying we were walking into town to do some shopping; we'd ask a trustworthy chum to sign us back in if we weren't back by the 18:00 curfew, so enabling us, unofficially, to stay out later. It was rare for the book to be checked as members of the sixth form were considered more responsible.

There was no question that "perks" were to be had in sixth form. A separate building, "High Rough", a very large rambling Victorian house, a ten-minute walk from the main Stoatley Hall, was home to the upper and the lower sixth; providing the luxuries of tea- and coffee-making facilities in a basically equipped kitchen, there was also a TV room, a common room-cum-library and a bike shed (we were allowed bikes and mopeds, but the shed was also handy for smoking if it was raining!).

The central staircase led to various different-sized characterful bedrooms sleeping between three to five and, if you were lucky enough to have grabbed one, a couple of twin-bedded attic rooms. There was a payphone on the landing (and always a queue).

Although "lights off" was officially 22:00, this was rarely observed and if you kept the sound down (including portable record players and transistor radios) you were pretty much left to your own devices. This meant we could even sneak having a fag out the bedroom window! The old building was full of nooks and crannies and the rooms leading off several corridors were serviced by two or three back staircases—it was easy to play "low profile" and be somewhere else.

> Fri, 24th Nov: Today was another drag. Squill and I phoned Ewan and told him we didn't like being fucked around—he says he'll talk to us tomorrow when we meet up. Had a beauty session tonight—face pack etc. Tried on my eyelashes, they looked okay.
>
> Sat, 25th Nov:

This page remains blank with no further diary entries for 1972.

Crash!!

On that fateful Saturday, Squill and I are otherwise occupied … we are, as it turns out, going to be admitted to, and detained in, Farnham Hospital.

Ewan, whilst driving us back to school, and showing off, loses control of his red convertible Triumph Vitesse, rolls the car on a sharp bend and hits a tree, with disastrous results, made all the worse by the fact that the soft-top canvas roof is down and there is no rollbar. We are about to be "caught out"—though saying that is something of an understatement. Caught out we most certainly are … but lucky, it seems, not to be dead.

After an hour of lying upside down in the front passenger seat, I will be cut out of the car by the fire brigade. (This was a time before seat belts were mandatory, but I guess it was in my nature—as you may probably by now agree—to be contrary: I was, in fact, wearing a seatbelt.) Ewan, Tony, and Squill have been thrown clear as the car rolls over and will be ambulanced to hospital ahead of me; their cuts and bruises will be attended to. Ewan will find he is missing an ear.

The three of them are still in shock and, having thought I was dead, are relieved when, sometime later, they hear me shouting down the hospital corridor from the inside of an A&E cubicle: "Get your fucking hands off me!" Such delayed hysterical behaviour after an accident can be caused by trauma and amnesia, I'm told. Strange, as I'd been perfectly calm and had cheerful conversations with members of the fire brigade during the hour they'd worked hard to release me from the overturned car.

Apparently, whilst strapped into the front passenger seat, hanging upside down, with blood dripping from the wounds in my face from the shattered windscreen and hot oil from the gearbox seeping all over me, my major concern had been the damage to my new black velvet jacket and platform boots. (I will find out, over forty-five years later, that the fireman I was in conversation with that night was the uncle of one of my oldest friends and was on duty with the Farnham Fire Brigade that night!)

Fortunately—and even to this day—I remember nothing. I also "miss" the first few days of my two-week stay in the intensive care ward. Broken jaw, broken nose, with over 200 stitches in my face and the backs of my hands. I look like a monster.

So, it's little surprise that when my mother sees me, she faints and then suffers deep shock; so much so that she is kept in hospital overnight. When Paul and Phil come to visit me a week later, Paul will faint at the end of the bed, and Phil say he feels sick and has to leave, swiftly and tactfully, trying not to hurt my feelings.

Both my parents are shocked, Mum to the core. She takes it badly, as far as I can work out: her daughter scarred for life; in turn, it seems to emotionally scar *her*. Realising that she's nearly lost her only daughter pulls her up short … and out of her ongoing marital problems.

With tears in her eyes, she gives me a small, plain, but perfectly lovely, gold bangle—the bangle is so small that to get it on over my hand and knuckles is a struggle, extremely difficult and painful ... but when it is on it is a perfect neat fit. It'll come to represent a sort of "bond", staying there on my right wrist for several decades ... until the day I have to wrestle, both physically and mentally, to remove it.

I remember dealing, at least on an emotional level, reasonably well with my "new look"; there was a bonus in being the centre of attention everywhere I went, as my notoriety was boosted even further. During the period of convalescence at home, generally whilst sitting watching TV, out of the corner of my eye I'd be aware that Mum was staring at my face, often with tears welling up. I remember asking her to stop doing this as it was making me self-conscious.

The trials and tribulations as a result of the car accident went on for years: multiple visits to specialist surgeons, two plastic surgery operations, and the legal wrangling in order to claim enough damages to pay for my operations and hospitalisation. All that and so much more, but still, come January 1973, I had to go back to The Royal Naval School; yes, BACK AGAIN, to resume studying for my O-level retakes. I'd been lagging so far behind that it wasn't clear if it'd be possible now for me to pull out the stopper and deliver on results. This was the big question in my mind—and everyone else's—probably tinged with a small dose of optimism.

Mon, 8th Jan 1973: Back to RNS for 11 weeks and 3 days.
Back and last-minute panic. In bedroom with Squill (goodie and as planned). Pissed off with school. The

same faces for yet another term. Noticed how everyone was looking at the scars on my face.

Within a few days, I had been summoned to the headmistress's office. I knew there was a lecture coming, though thankfully she didn't punish me further for last term's AWOL as she seemed to consider my injuries to be sufficient punishment.

Digging Out The Mole

The life of tedium and of trouble resumed. Many of my friends had left after O-levels the previous term, choosing to continue their further education elsewhere. My friendship with Squill (aka Caroline), 'Chenda (Richenda), Moira, and a new sixth-former, Sandra, along with a couple of others in the lower 6th, helped me get through, in a matter of speaking, the classroom bit!

So did Grateful Dead, Cream, Deep Purple, Pink Floyd, Focus, Yes, and a host of other bands. I was mad on Floyd and our after-lights-out-treat was to play "Echoes" from the album *Meddle*, a whole twenty-three minutes of sublime music which helped me drift into sleep just as the needle was playing the final chords and the arm of the portable turntable clicked gently off. (Fifty years on, "Echoes" remains as perfect for sleep induction as it is, indeed, for early morning yoga!)

Apart from *Top of the Pops*, the other two "must watch" TV programmes of the time were *Monty Python's*

Flying Circus and *Colditz*; the common room was always packed to the rafters for both. Squill and I came up with what we thought a cunning plan to catch the "snitch" who clearly existed in our form. We had been caught smoking by the sixth-form house mistress, and although we were not punished at the time, it became clear there was some jiggery pokery going on ...

> Thurs 1st Feb: Ott on the Spot—she talked about cigs non-stop. I'm mad, I found out from Miss S. that Otter says that it's me and Chend who have been giving the juniors fags. I'm bloody furious—I wouldn't give a squitty junior a fag! It's a bloody drag having to now go across the road for a fag.

We knew someone was feeding intel to the head girl who in turn fed it to the house mistress. (Sadly, at that time, we didn't know the two of them were having some sort of affair!)

So, whilst the sixth form tries to watch *Monty Python*, Squill and I play up by performing silly walks, accompanied by equally silly noises, marching back and forth in front of the TV, pretending to be out of it. We're thrilled with ourselves ... "pretended to be tripping—really funny how gullible they are".

Three days later, Squill and I are summoned to Otter's study ...

> Otter accused us of having acid (our point proved—it didn't take long for reports of our acting-up to get to

her—3 days). Had a general bloody time with certain people.

After all that, we were no nearer to finding the mole and, into the bargain, we were in BIG trouble. I couldn't see any way out other than to phone my mother and explain (in part!) what had happened, swearing on my life that the accusation was just not true, that we had no LSD and never had. I obviously couldn't bring myself to tell her how the accusation had come about.

Fri, 16th Feb: M&D went to see Otter and got things sorted out. From what I gather, M seems to have talked Otter down. Hee hee!

On this occasion, I certainly benefitted from my mother's anger: she had, in no uncertain terms, told Otter that she would report her to the board of governors for daring to suggest that her daughter had LSD at school with "ABSOLUTELY NO PROOF". So that was that—except it significantly reduced the likelihood of me making it to the end of the school year at RNS.

I do, however, make it to the next term of summer 1973. There was always plenty to share, and catch up about, with your friends at the start of a new term, and that May I had some significant things to share. First, I went back proudly armed with Pink Floyd's brand-new album, the seminal *Dark Side of the Moon* and, to make it even more special, my copy was a limited-edition American import.

And, having gained a precious new album, I had lost my virginity … and had details to spill.

The "no-sex-before-marriage" kind of girls frowned on the idea, but *my* friends were extremely curious and excited, though somewhat nervous, by the possible opportunity of losing their virginity quite some time *before* their big wedding day.

M. and a couple of others in my form also claimed to have lost their virginity during the Easter holidays and, inevitably, question marks were raised as to whether we REALLY REALLY *had* … or was it just a false brag. I had difficulty relaying the intimate sexual details of my experience, as, to be honest, it had been a real let-down. I couldn't possible say that; it had to have been AMAZING. My peers were suitably impressed.

The third big thing to share on that first day back was my elevation to captain of the school tennis team, as well as having been made first couple with my doubles partner. I was chuffed to bits and encouraged by the realisation that at least my games teachers liked and supported me.

The summer term gained pace; I was on the tennis court at every opportunity, between smoking on the heath and doing a little light revision for my two remaining resits.

Mon, 7th May: What a great day. Stayed in bed til 10.25 (the morning after the boozy night before). Skipped triple English AL. Stuffed at the Tuck Shop and smoked. Read on my bed all afternoon. Tennis practice with Mills. I've decided I must get down to some work.

Then, on the Friday of that same week, the 11th of May:

Things sure warmed up today!

Fire, Fire!

Squill and I have skipped the last class of the week—Music Appreciation—thinking we were not going to be missed. We're off to our usual smoking place on the edge of the heath, tucked away behind trees, just across the lane and only a few yards from the sixth-form building, High Rough. Although early May, it's cool, but bone dry underfoot, so we're wearing our cloaks.

Somehow, not taking care, not paying attention, the lighted match I think has gone out as I am shaking it and letting it fall to the ground amongst the dried bracken, hasn't, in fact, been properly extinguished. Within seconds the bracken catches light. I instantly (and, in my opinion, quite heroically) whip off my cloak and try to smother the flames, but in doing so, inadvertently spread more sparks further afield.

In the space of a couple of minutes, greedy orange flames are licking at the trees twenty feet up. Completely "freaked out", we realise we're in deep trouble; the increasingly alarming fire, now truly out of control, is being fanned by a wind—a wind that is blowing in the direction of the school. We run for it, leaving my cloak burning in the embers in the bracken.

We rush back to the school and into the library, where we

gather ourselves and stick our heads in our books to appear to be swatting; but on looking out of the window we realise, in horror, that the flames are fast approaching High Rough. Even more quick thinking and, weighing up the SERIOUS SHIT we could be (are certainly) in, "yours truly phoned 999" (as my diary, sometime later, insouciantly recalls).

Three fire engines race up the hill to deal with the blaze while the whole school turns out to watch, transfixed by the dramatic scene. And thus it transpires that Kathy Leppard saves the day, and the school building, having spotted the fire and having, oh so promptly, called the fire brigade. Well done, Kathy!

Except, not everyone was so convinced. The teacher who took Music Appreciation has clocked that neither Squill nor I were in her class and has reported it to Otter, who was pretty sure who had started the fire, in spite of our earnest claims to have been studying in the library. Her problem, and our saving grace, is that she has ABSOLUTELY NO PROOF and, most fortuitously, there is no evidence: my cloak has gone up in smoke. The remaining ash has been scattered to the winds.

I didn't feel smug for long; ten days later the next piece of shit hit the proverbial fan.

Tues, 22nd May: Otter caught Sandra and I on the heath after dark—blew her top—stupid bitch. Has forbidden mopeds til next term—will sell mine.

Tues, 23rd May: Things really moved today. Otter threw me out of prayers for talking then yelled at me for walking on the grass! Then wanted to see me about last night and implied she was going to expel me. Had a migraine and went to bed. Phoned and explained to Dad. Mum phoned me this evening and said she won't have me back home. Lost my temper—the whole thing really upset me. Daph phoned, I asked to go for Half Term there and then. Dad said I couldn't and wasn't going to get out of it like that.

School's Out

```
            THE  ROYAL  NAVAL  SCHOOL
                 HASLEMERE, SURREY
              TELEPHONE: HINDHEAD 5415

                                     22nd May, 1973

  Captain K.A. Leppard, R.N.,
  Reedley House,
  Podimore,
  Ilchester,
  Somerset.


  Dear Captain Leppard,

            In confirmation of our telephone conversation this
  afternoon, I could see you at 12.15 p.m. next Thursday, 24th
  May to discuss Katharine's recent behaviour.

            Last evening at 9.45 p.m. whilst walking on the
  heath with my dog, I caught Katharine and Sandra ████████
  returning home after coming across Hindhead Common on their
  mopeds.  They were out of bounds;  out without permission,
  and out after dark and after locking up time at 9 p.m.   I
  was unable to get a satisfactory explanation from either of
  them.

            The School Rules state that anyone doing this is
  liable to immediate suspension.  Obviously they cannot flaunt
  School discipline and go unpunished.

            My immediate reaction is to send Katharine home
  forthwith.  She is not making the best use of her time here,
  and on many occasions is breaking rules, because as she says,
  she "does not think".

            Possibly, a compromise solution would be for her to
  leave immediately her "O" Level retakes are over.

            Yours sincerely,

                 Diana H. Otter

                 Headmistress.
```

109

For the next two weeks I did my best to keep a low profile and to study; but I made up for it by going to London for a weekend with Daph and staying in Philip's Islington flat. I was able to get away on a Friday as I had an appointment in Harley Street to see a plastic surgeon about my pending operation. On the Saturday,

Floyd concert at Earls Court—amazing. Bubbles on the brain—didn't go to bed.

On the Sunday,

Slept til 1.00pm. Went to a Wimpey Bar. Party. Bubbles.

And then,

Watched the box, hitched back to school.

I was lucky to get a weekend away when I did.

5th June, 1973

Captain K.A. Leppard, R.N.,
Reedley House,
Podimore,
Ilchester,
Somerset.

Dear Captain Leppard,

        This is to confirm our conversation on Sports Day that I am prepared to keep Katharine until her last "O" Level examination has been taken, provided that she does not infringe the school rules any further. I have told her that if she does the latter she will be sent home straight away. I have withdrawn all her exeats from her. She may go out on Saturday afternoons, but she may not go out on Sundays or away for the weekend. I hope that this time Katharine will learn to be more co-operative.

        Could you please let me know when you intend to collect her after the examinations are over.

Yours sincerely,

Diana H. Otter

Headmistress.

Sun, 10th June: Tried to do some work this morning after the goddamn Service. Chenda did a fake faint, Squill and I took her out hoping to miss the rest of the Service but got sent back in. Drat!

Mon, 11 June: Felt so fed up this morning. Upset with my English essay result after so much effort. Worked in prep. Otter want to see me this evening and had my three fags on her desk but she was really nice. Knew about M&D etc. Talked for 45 mins.

Tues, 12th June: Tired, so tired. Still felt slightly more inspired after talking to Otter. I for the first time feel some respect towards her. Worked in the bedroom listening to Floyd. Had a bath and washed my hair.

Fast forward another nine days to my last OL re-sit and my last night at RNS ...

Thurs, 21st June: Biology exam not as bad as I expected. Started to pack. Celebrations ... everyone was so nice to me this evening, they made me a super cake and gave me some flowers. Learnt something about Sandra.

Little did I know then that the "something" I had learnt from Sandra on that last night at school was soon going to profoundly change the rest of my life.

And on my last day, unbeknownst to me at the time, Miss Otter had written yet another letter to my parents ...

Fri, 22nd June LEAVE RNS FOR GOOD

Bloody Miss S. made us go into breakfast. Finished
packing. Very casual morning. Phoned M—she had a
letter from Otter accusing me of something else! Christ.
M&D came up to speak to Otter. I hate that woman.
Everyone came to say goodbye. We drove back home.
I'm already so bored.

On the plus side, it had turned out I wasn't the most
badly behaved girl in the school, and I had gained another

3 O-levels, taking my grand total to five. But my report was hardly flattering ...

Katharine never really seemed to enjoy or settle down to Sixth Form and found it difficult to conform and abide by the rules. This naturally led to endless trouble and reprimands. If only she would channel her energies in the right direction and apply a little more self-discipline, she could become a capable and responsible person.
Miss G.S., House Mistress

Katharine has a strong personality, many ideas and considerable charm. She took preparation reasonably efficiently. She is apt to feel aggrieved and criticised instead of using it to help her. She never really settled down to Sixth Form life. She has the ability and a certain charm of manner and could do well if she put her mind to it.
Miss D.M.O., Headmistress

Very much on the minus side, Technical College and a course in journalism was out of the window. Secretarial college loomed and my kicking and screaming was to continue.

5

The Hangar Door ... and More

Dad's last flight, Royal Naval Air Station, Yeovilton

Funny how things can sometimes turn out. I got the opportunity to go to college in Oxford and, can you believe, I didn't want to go ... to secretarial college that is! I had no choice in the matter as my parents declared it was their final and only proposition for my further education.

It was made crystal clear that after a year's tuition in all matters secretarial I would have to support myself and, "make no mistake", I was to knuckle down and get the required results.

It wasn't unusual in the seventies for those girls who didn't go to university—and many didn't—to enrol on secretarial courses and, indeed, many of the smart-arse Oxbridge girls from RNS went on to do a secretarial course after their degree.

On my aggrieved behalf, and as they were paying, Mum and Dad enrolled me. It was like being shoe-horned into a pair of stiletto shoes three sizes too small rather than a comfy pair of Doc Martins. I didn't fit in with the twinset-and-pearls brigade from secretarial college, even though I did wear long Laura Ashley skirts and dresses, which were prone to tears and smears of oil from my moped.

I did, initially, attend some of the "staircase parties" held by the Oxford undergraduates (nearly all men)—some of the dullest experiences in my social outings, including the one summer ball I was invited to, which topped the lot. I wasn't interested in their intellectual discussions, their various tedious tea parties in their halls of residence, or what I, at the time, considered to be their other lame pursuits. Ironically, I made a new group of friends at the Oxford Tech. Visits there on Friday or Saturday nights to attend numerous gigs meant I was able to stretch my wings socially and share in the spoils of someone's latest drugs score!

School holidays have been replaced with college breaks at home, now in Somerset where my father has been

Dad and HRH

appointed Commanding Officer, Royal Naval Air Station, Yeovilton. The hangar door was certainly wide open now and "at home" entertaining was to become more frequent and to reach new levels. To my dismay, if a guest cried off at the last minute, I'd be asked to attend the dinner so as to make up the numbers and balance the seating plan.

At one point, I am actually asked if I'd like to attend a dinner with the then Prince Charles—yes, indeed, HRH himself—when he was posted to the air station to master the art of flying helicopters under the tutelage of, amongst others, my father. It was a non-starter all round, but my mother was avidly keen that I meet him; she would bang on (and insisted on doing so almost to her final day!) about how I had my chance to be married to him! "Think Darling, it could have been you, the Queen of England." Yeah, right!

Naturally, with the new house come staff: naval ratings from the station, a cook and a steward—more when required for a dinner, cocktail party, or an event such as luncheon on the day of the annual air show. The role of commanding officer of this air station is the pinnacle of my father's career so far, and he loves it. This clearly annoys my mother, and my father knows that he must continue to tread carefully to keep her on side.

A dinner party that cannot be forgotten is when the First Sea Lord and his wife come down from London, escorted by two suitably high-ranking officers from the Admiralty, plus another two captains from the air station. At the last minute, one of their wives goes sick, so I am asked to attend the dinner. On my best behaviour, I sit politely, only speaking when being spoken to. (Needless to say, I don't have to talk much!)

We've finished dessert; the gold-crested bone china plates and cutglass wine goblets have been removed; the two stewards are standing to attention in front of the mahogany sideboard waiting for my father to give the nod for coffee and brandy to be served. We are approaching the moment of the after-dinner etiquette where the men will be offered a cigar, and the women will politely ask "to be excused" so that they might "powder their noses".

Men to men, women to women—this is the time when

I am more than ready to escape to the security and privacy of my room, my records, and my fags. The stewards are still waiting to serve, and my father is too polite to interrupt the in-full-flow conversation (such a bad decision); the men continue to reminisce about their various postings in

Mum, the captain's wife

Singapore serving on aircraft carriers during the sixties.

I suddenly hear my mother's voice cutting through the chatter: "Oh, Keith has lots of stories from Singapore, tell them about 1964." My father smiles awkwardly but goes pale and my mother carries on: "Yes Keith had a great time in sixty-four, he fucked a whore in Singapore, didn't you Keith?"

I want to crawl under the table and curl up; it is truly awful. After a moment of complete silence—as if breath is being held—there are guffaws from the men and nervous giggles from the women. The stewards look at their feet. The wives politely get up from the table and escort my mother (who clearly needs prompting) out of the dining room and upstairs to the "powder room". I slink up the back staircase to my room, not meeting the eyes of any of the curious, and slightly astonished, guests.

Driving Lessons

Reedley House dominates the village of Podimore, which is tiny, though it does have a church … and a pub. The imposing white Georgian house, partially hidden by a high old stone wall with a gated entrance, leads up over gravel to a central circular driveway where visiting guests are dropped off at the quite impressive entrance: three steps centred by two Georgian pillars leading up to the double-width white glossy front door with bevelled glass panels.

Although the house is only two miles from the air

station, my father is provided with a car: big, and black, and with plenty of shiny chrome and a fluttering flag on a stunted staff pole crowning the bonnet. Sometimes he drives himself to work, other times he has a chauffeur, but the car is for his sole use and not to be touched by his wife (and certainly not by his daughter who has started learning to drive).

The family Hillman Avenger, tucked away in the double garage, is used by my mother for local expeditions and occasionally by my father to give me driving lessons—on the airfield no less! On these occasions, I put my foot to the floor, careering down the runway, driving as fast as I can … because I can. He'll yell at me to slow down and suggest that I concentrate on my three-point turns; I'll retort that he might be able to fly planes, but he certainly doesn't know how to drive a car! This is rude of me, but true; when he's driving, we're all extremely nervous passengers: he drives as if he's flying a plane, looking out of the windows left and right, as if he has all the time in the world, but not actually looking at the road in front of him.

One memorable afternoon—memorable for all the wrong reasons, of course—my mother has a major meltdown. I'm lolling around in my bedroom to escape the shouting downstairs (thankfully the cook and steward are off duty) and I hear the sitting room door slam, then the front door.

It goes momentarily quiet, and I go down to investigate, to find my father in the sitting room, head in hands, looking utterly miserable. Suddenly, there's an almighty crash, and we rush to the front door to see my mother sitting behind the wheel of the Hillman Avenger which she has just smashed into the back of my father's black limo—and, from the evidence of the damage, she's done it at some speed.

Revving the engine, she reverses the car twenty feet then puts it into first and shoots forward, ramming the back of my father's car for a second time. Dad, in a frantic state, rushes out onto the drive and tries to stop her but she's locked the car doors and is unstoppable. She now reverses down the drive and then, with the car in high revs, shoots round from the other side of the circular section, gaining even more speed as she does so, finally smashing into the front of his black limo.

Glass shatters and oil and water spew out over the driveway. To my added horror, I catch sight of a dozen or so members of the village standing, with eyes on stalks, at the entrance to the drive, having come out to see what all the noise is about. My father, thinking the damage done, and not wanting to make the scene worse by confronting my mother in front of the village spectators, then goes back into the house through the front door.

I think my mother is about to go in too, but she's stopped by the side of the front steps, bent down, and is struggling to pick up a large piece of rockery which she then hurls, with all her might, at the passenger-side window of the already wrecked limousine. What sounds like the wail of a demented banshee accompanies the noise of shattering glass.

As if that isn't enough, she proceeds to pick up another three rocks—one at a time, and slowly, as if checking each for appropriate weight and shape. She then does the same to the remaining three windows. A final flourish: as she walks past the car towards the front door, she pauses momentarily in front of the bonnet and, as if as an afterthought, grabs the flagpole with both hands and snaps it in half, leaving a very limp Royal Naval white ensign draped on the bonnet.

Shaking, scared, I can't believe that this embarrassing, out-of-control, very public display on the part of my mother is really happening. I retreat to my room, where I remain frozen in shock.

I'm sure you can, by now, appreciate that I am desperate to get out of the house whenever possible. Although I don't have my driving licence, I do have my moped (with L plates) which allows me some escape. I don't have friends to visit (they're all in Sussex and Hampshire) but my two wheels are certainly useful for holiday jobs. Fruit picking in the summer is the pits—back-breaking and sheer physical hard work for very little reward—"picked strawberries for two hours (never want to see another) and got 30p—big bloody deal."

Eager to save up enough money to replace my portable Dansette record player with the latest hi-fi music centre, I secure a part-time job at the local Little Chef, on the main A303, for which I'm paid thirty pence per hour. On a good day, I fry eggs on the griddle, fry chips in the basket-fryer, and then wait on tables. On a bad day, it's solid washing up after having cleaned the loos and mopped the floors of the ladies' … and the gents'.

This is a holiday job, and this is what teenagers do to earn themselves some holiday money (including the "captain's daughter"). But my parents seem to be embarrassed by it, nervous of me being spotted working at this roadside greasy spoon by any of the ratings working on the air station or at the "captain's house".

"It just is not appropriate, Katharine," I'm told, when I ask why they're so worried. Similarly, I am forbidden to meet our cook and our steward for a drink in the local pub. I feel totally justified to scream at them that they are "hypocrites and snobs". All part of teenage rebellion, I guess, but I still feel that their attitudes are ridiculous, and quite offensive.

Who is to say whether the ongoing daily rows that took place were due to "teenage rebellion" or were due to my mother's bad temper brought on by her unhappiness with my father and their toxic relationship? My diaries are full of such rows, accounts of doors slamming, of me staying in my room, or of my mother going to her room and staying behind locked doors for the whole day.

I have to be grateful for the countless times I was *not* at home during some of their worst rows, although I did get to hear most of the details when speaking to my mother on the phone. There was an understanding that I had to telephone home to report back from college at least twice a week (by now the use of the phone had become more normalised and regarded less as a luxury). It was easier to listen to details of their latest dramas than it was to be there in the middle of them. So, I listened …

At one point, my mother relayed a scene that shocked me deeply and haunted me for many years. In fact, I still struggle to think about it, and still find myself incapable of forgiving my father.

It seems that one Sunday afternoon, the vicar, passing the house, decided to pay a visit, perhaps hoping to be asked in for tea. My mother was in her dressing-gown and had taken "some pills" after "a few lunchtime drinks". My father answered the front door and asked the vicar in, but my mother confronted him in the hall and "apologised", saying it was not convenient for him to stay, she was having a row with her husband. My father seems to have thought that this was more reason for the vicar to stay, to see if he could help, but Mum was having none of it and "excused" herself as she made her way upstairs to the bedroom.

My mother recounted the terrible scene between her and my father that took place after the vicar had left. Omitting details of the physical and verbal abuse which, without doubt, would have been played out, she told me that my father had then called the air station's duty doctor and asked that he and an ambulance attend immediately. On arrival, two naval medics and the duty doctor were asked up into the bedroom where my father ordered them to put his wife in a straightjacket.

Triggered by hearing about this awful episode, one of my worst nightmares remains one where I'm being restrained against my will, I'm trying to explain I'm not crazy—"You've got this all wrong"—but the more I plead, the crazier I sound, and this makes me even more hysterical.

The utter outrage of it.

I can imagine how terrifying this would have been for my mother, her fear heightened by booze and pills;

I can still hear her sobs, her pleading to be released. She demanded her own doctor be called but my father took no notice; he had given his orders to his staff, and it was very much "Yes, sir." Instead, he phoned some long-standing friends, a naval couple who lived nearby (the wife was my godmother) and asked for them to come straight away so they could see for themselves "the state of my wife and what I have to live with", as my mother claimed he said.

On recounting the events, my mother delighted in telling me that my godmother, on walking into the bedroom and seeing what was going on, immediately turned to my father and said, "You should be ashamed Keith, get her out of this jacket, send your staff packing and call her GP right now."

I already hated my father, but now, on hearing this, I utterly despised him.

For the Sake of the Children?

Every Christmas since 1964 had been incredibly unhappy—the festive season seemed to bring out the worst in my parents; their behaviour became even less restrained, and they made no attempt to pull back for the sake of their children's mental well-being, never mind their own. In fact, every Christmas Day Mum would announce they were getting a divorce, which had the desired effect of winding Dad up even further and upsetting my brother and me. The nearer we got to the big day, the more the family dynamics ratcheted up:

Fri 21st Dec: Woken up by M&D carrying on. M made D leave for Xmas—he went to stay with Nana. M & I & A went to Yeovil to buy a stereo for A. Then we went to Bournemouth to buy a portable typewriter for my Xmas present!!! Mon, 24th Dec: M phoned D yesterday to ask him home and he arrived at lunchtime. Went out to visit the Clarks (cycled) and came back to find M in a mood again and gone to bed for the entire Xmas. Tues, 25th Dec: Happy Christmas! Great coz of M & D (say no more). We didn't go to church. Watched tv most of the day, "Far from the Madding Crowd" was on.

Although not reported in my diary, I remember this Christmas Day well as it was my turn to out-perform *them* by ramping up the volume and the violence a couple of notches in a desperate effort to get them to shut up.

Mum had come down to the sitting room in her dressing-gown, intending to further fan the flames between her and my father, drink in one hand and cigarette in the other. She picked up from where she'd left off half an hour earlier, and my father retaliated. So, I grabbed the top of the Christmas tree—not a huge tree, but certainly not insubstantial—and, with all my strength I pulled it out of its stand, jerking at the electric cord and pulling the plug out of its socket.

I then swung it round my head two or three times, a bit like a cowboy's lasso—only slower, as the tree was quite heavy—before finally releasing my grip and sending it flying into the wall, smashing the fairy lights and all the delicate decorations that had adorned the branches.

This worked well. There was complete silence for what must have been a few seconds before they started on their remonstrations, at which point I yelled "Just fucking shut up and pleeeaaaase get a divorce!", running out of the room in tears.

There's only so long one can keep repeating the mantra "We're staying together for the sake of the children." Young as I was, I knew that my parents had crossed the line of acceptable behaviour at least five years earlier. The point of no return was way behind them.

Thurs, 27th Dec: Stayed in bed. Watched the tv. Did my thank you letters. Watched tv. Fri, 28th Dec: Got up at lunchtime. Watched tv. M&D went mad—really wild. Bed early. Sat, 29th Dec: Stayed in bed. Watched tv. Had a carry on with M. Watched tv for a change.

Sun, 30th Dec: Stayed in bed. M&D still really mad. It really upset me to find M had gone thro' my things— found tobacco and papers and accused me of being on drugs. That's IT as far as I'm concerned. Mon, 31st Dec: Well yet the end of another unhappy year. I wonder when things will begin to look brighter for a) the family and b) myself. Let's see what 1974 brings ... Stayed in and watched the box.

Small mercies, but at least the start of the spring term didn't mean going back to school; instead, back to "college in Oxford" (I've played on that many a time over the years). To make up for disliking the course intensely, I made sure

I had a pretty good social life as, for the first time in my life, I had relatively unsupervised free time. My allowance from my father was £5 per week for food and transport, for everything really, so I decided to get an evening job for two to three nights a week working at the Cherwell River Boathouse, a popular up-market restaurant-bistro on the river just off Oxford's main Woodstock and Banbury Roads.

Prepping veg, waiting on tables, washing up—standard restaurant hard work, but certainly a level up from a Little Chef. I'd get back to my shared room at my digs at around 02:00. I was dog-tired most of the time but not too tired to prevent me from going out and spending my hard-earned cash, meeting friends in various pubs or at gigs at the tech. The extra money gave me opportunities to make new friends and to start to have more fun. I had at last truly escaped from the confines of "home life" (or so I wanted to believe).

I completed the one-year secretarial course in July 1974, managing to scrape through my "secretarial duties" exam and, despite having struggled hard in both skills, gained Pitman certificates in shorthand (80 wpm) and typing (38 wpm). Whilst not great results—certainly down in the second half of the class—they were decent enough to add to my tally of six O-levels (if Aural English counts as one) and appear on my very first CV.

It seemed that putting that CV together was done just in the nick of time; it turned out that, with the ink on it still drying, I had to find a job, urgently.

One of my last diary entries, written at home, reads:

26th July, Fucking Goddamn rows and heavy scenes—
really pissed off. Want to get out. Made up my mind
I'm not staying at home longer than I have to.

And that was written before my bedroom had been
searched (yet again) by my parents who, on that infamous
occasion, found three months' supply of "the Pill".

And that was the occasion on which this desperate
eighteen-year-old's final straw snapped.

6

She's Leaving Home ...
With a Police Escort

Maybe I'm slightly stoned or maybe still recovering from the after-effects of Saturday night's Mandrax or Tuinal, but boy oh boy, do I feel a sense of gloom descend as I drive down the high street of my childhood home town. My father's two years stint at Yeovilton is up and my parents have moved back to Haslemere, from where Dad commutes to the Ministry of Defence in London each day and where I, expelled from school and now having finished my brief secretarial course, am now living.

Pondering the meaning of life and questioning at what stage the modest trappings of privilege outweigh the cost of emotional damage, I grip the steering wheel with cold sweaty hands, weighed down by the prospect of a Sunday evening back at parental HQ.

The price of living at home, apart from obeying the general house rules, is to accept the cross-examination about who I've been with, and exactly what I've been up to with them, for the last thirty-six hours. Can I make it match with what I told them I was intending to do when I left? There will, no doubt, be the obligatory *Songs of Praise* droning on in the background, plus the family meat-and-two-veg, all before I can escape to the privacy of my own room. Very limited privacy as it turned out.

Little do I know that there is far worse waiting to greet me on my arrival home.

It's late summer, 1974. I'm eighteen, driving home from London in my pride and joy, my first-ever car, a fourth-hand Wolsey Hornet. These wheels of freedom were eagerly purchased for £150 with the spoils of my Post Office savings certificates and the income from various modest holiday jobs. With leather seats, a walnut dashboard and fin-like back wings—some would call it a glorified Mini, and, indeed, it is—but I am a chuffed and proud owner.

I've been to a party the previous evening—I can't remember how rock 'n' roll it was but anything up in London was many times cooler and more fun than the alternatives available in the Home Counties; full of the offspring of stockbrokers, city commuters, and, I hasten to add, a smattering of naval officers. Up in the Big Smoke there was an abundance of cheap drugs and lager. Popping pills wasn't a regular occurrence but toking on joints was. The turntable revolved through the night, mostly playing Pink Floyd. Quite definitely there had been no sexual activity because I didn't have a boyfriend and although I'd lost my virginity the year before (what a disappointment that had been—the act not the fact), I hadn't slept with anyone else since.

My parent's house is two miles from the town and just over the Surrey border into West Sussex. They'd always been proud to live in a "private road" and even more pleased with themselves (in hindsight) that it only cost £3,500 when they bought it in 1962, although the purchase was mainly driven by my mother's desire and determination to own their house. My father, "no good with money", according to my mother, not only had to take out a twenty-five-year mortgage but also a loan for the required minimum deposit.

Little Holt, c. 1963, photo taken from the air by Dad. On the back of the photo in my father's handwriting: "Taken over the main road. Katharine is in the centre of the top lawn with Mummy waving something white!" (I was too young to know it at the time, but the "something" was ... her knickers!)

Little Holt was not a big house—three bedrooms and only one bathroom at that stage—but it gave the impression of being grander than it was as you rolled up the gravelled drive, bordered by well-established rhododendrons and evergreen trees completely obscuring the house from the road. Set amid over an acre of garden and built at the turn of the twentieth century, it was solid-looking and well-proportioned—nothing hugely special, but it did possess those black square leaded windows set in chunky oak wooden frames—nice from the outside, a little oppressive from within.

So, I sweep up the drive in my nippy little motor, tooting as I park up. I can hear Marty the family guard dog's short, sharp, and slightly hysterical bark—quite impressive for a long-haired miniature dachshund. I retrieve my overnight bag from my dinky boot and in through the back door I go. "Helloooooooo …"

My father appears as I go into the house, through the utility room into the kitchen. "Katharine, your mother and I wish to talk to you in the sitting-room, now."

"Really, now … this minute?"

"Yes, NOW!"

I sit on the large, old, but soft settee covered in faded gold damask, my mother in her armchair to my right, my father in his occasional chair opposite. They start to give voice. It seems that while I've been away overnight, they've decided to look through my bedroom drawers and cupboards in search of contraband—drugs, cigarettes, booze, I guess.

What exactly have they found? Buried at the back of

my knicker drawer they have uncovered three month's supply of "the Pill".

"We thought of other people's daughters doing this sort of thing but certainly not our own," my father yells. My mother is even more hysterical and lights another cigarette. Within a minute, a full-on row has erupted. Is the Pill Affair going to trump Expulsion-Gate?

I am furious. In a mixture of already bottled-up frustration and simmering rage, I too let rip, as is the family way.

Neither of them is interested in what I have to say, and they simply will not listen to my explanation: that my GP has prescribed a three-month course of the pill to help regulate my periods and boost my underperforming hormones.

Mum and Dad have now started rowing between themselves. I announce that I am leaving home and am told, in no uncertain terms by my father, that I most certainly am not. Mum and Dad ramp up their rage and there ensues an even bigger row, with my mother declaring, "Let me tell you something Katharine, when I married your father, I was a virgin." With a dramatic pause and a sharp intake of breath, she screams, "and by Christ do I regret it!"

I resist the urge to laugh, remove myself from the sitting room, and proceed to pack. I have to pull the loft ladder down from the ceiling above the upstairs landing in order to slide my old, not-so-long-ago-stored school trunk back down the wobbling metal steps. Meanwhile, screaming and swearing is coming thick and fast from downstairs.

I don't really have many clothes or a life collection of "stuff" to pack as, I guess, one doesn't at eighteen. What I did have all fitted in the trunk, including my music centre and vinyl collection which, in those days, only amounted to about thirty LPs, but each one is a much-treasured possession.

An hour later I am packed. Emotions are still running high.

I slide the heavy trunk down the carpet-covered stairs with considerable difficulty, having to retrace my steps to collect a couple of plastic carrier bags filled with makeup and bathroom essentials, packed for relatively easy access.

My mother is in the sitting-room, by this time on the whisky, as well as chain-smoking. My father repeats that I am not going anywhere. I scream and say, "I am, and you can't stop me." He responds by saying he can. With my hand on the back door handle, he hits me—not very hard, but it's a warning blow—on my arm. Physical violence like this is no stranger in this household, but I'm shocked and run sobbing to the front door. But it's locked and the key is missing from the lock. I return to the back door, but by this time my father has locked the door and removed the key.

I scream, I shout about my rights as an eighteen-year-old, but my pleas and protestations fall on deaf ears. I threaten to call the police, but my father takes no notice. I rush up the stairs, leaving my father thinking I've gone to my bedroom to continue with my upset behind a closed door. In fact, I've gone straight to my parents' bedroom and, from their telephone extension, have dialled 999.

My father is incredulous when a police squad car parks up in the driveway and he has the embarrassment of having to fumble for the key to unlock the door to let the officers in. My father tells them it's nothing more than a good old family argument, "a heated domestic", but the officers ask to speak to me. I'm still crying but manage to explain to them what's happened, that I'm eighteen and want to leave home but am being prevented from doing so.

"Sir, your daughter is eighteen and has a legal right to leave these premises, and without any interference," says the officer, to my silent delight.

Stunned into silence, my shocked parents have no alternative but to stand there and watch me leave. The police officers help load my trunk onto the back seat of the car and the remaining carrier bags into the tiny boot. To complete my leaving home in style (which certainly had not been my intention at the time) the two officers insist on giving me a police escort to Haslemere and then on to the main London road. Though I am too upset at the time to think about it, looking back, the extra "icing on the cake" would have been if they'd used their blues and twos.

Still shaking from what's happened, I nevertheless feel a sense of validated victory as I drive up the A3 to London. But I'm also scared. I have nowhere to stay, no job or income and only fifty pounds of savings in my pocket, but a decent wodge at the time.

I am also deeply conflicted: terrified I've permanently damaged my relationship with Mum and Dad and am now on my own for good. It had been one thing to escape to London for weekend jaunts but totally another to find myself on my own, looking for food, shelter, and work; but, still seething at their efforts to control me with their sly underhand ways, I am propelled by my anger, and determined to survive and make my own way.

Feeling decidedly shakier now than on my earlier drive down from London, I suddenly remember an ex-school friend, Cherie, who lives just outside London on Richmond Hill. I stop to call her from a service station phone box; her mother agrees to let me stay a few nights while I find a job and a room to rent, which I manage to do within three days.

The work I land is secretary to the sales manager of a builders' merchant based above a supermarket in Putney High Street. A mere two miles away in Mortlake, I secure a room in a small terraced shared house for £8 which I get reduced to £7 per week on the grounds that there's no hot water or central heating.

This Baby Boomer is on a roll!

Leaving home ... with a police escort ... in the late summer of '74 coincided with an abrupt end to my keeping a diary—I guess the traumatic events, and suddenly being on my own, kicked in big time and I had far more urgent matters on my mind: survival—finding a job, finding somewhere to live ... My diary entries ceased—and so did contact with my parents. I didn't see them, or speak to either of them, for the next six months.

My first secretarial job, for the builders' merchant, didn't last long. My shorthand let me down badly. I was transcribing dictated numbers the wrong way round—entirely back to front; not helpful—exact quantities and dimensions are everything when ordering building materials for your clients. I was forced to move on.

Stock market figures became of slight interest in my new job, though not with any understanding on my part. Fortunately, I didn't have to transcribe any share dealings as such; that activity was very much under the table. I'd secured a secretarial role in an office just off Park Lane, in Grosvenor Street, working for several directors of a property management company. My main task was operating the switchboard, which was a nightmare to navigate. I never got it quite right. "Please hold the line" … "Hello sir, it's x from your brokers" … "Sorry to keep you waiting, just putting you through, sir" … and then promptly cutting them off.

Sometimes I was able to eavesdrop, which made it so much more interesting. I was completely oblivious then, but now I'd hazard a guess the "property management company" was a front for stock market activity with a little light money laundering thrown in. And since I mention laundry, it reminds me of all the extra demands—"Can you pick up my dry cleaning?" … "Can you bring me a coffee now and then bring four more for a meeting in the board room?" … "Can you go down to Shepherd Market to buy my wife some flowers?" This job was never going to last.

Time passed. My father's job had changed again, though he was still commuting to Whitehall, appointed Director of PR for the Royal Navy. My parents and I were talking now. I was back to phoning a couple of times each week, always speaking to my mother, who unloaded her latest marital grief; and visiting on a Sunday once or twice a month, like a good dutiful daughter.

My father suggested I get a "decent" job and clipped a "position vacant" out of the *Daily Telegraph*. I applied to Rolls Royce Aerospace in St James's Square, to be secretary to the VIP liaison officer, and secured the role, mainly due to being the daughter of a naval officer, and more importantly, of an aviator.

The VIP liaison officer's role was to put together a list of VIPs from Saudi and the Middle East to invite and then deliver the top military brass to Farnborough Air Show to help boost sales of big-ticket military hardware such as fighter planes—those sporting Rolls Royce engines, obviously. This "proper job" was a bit like going back to the Royal Naval School.

I coped adequately in the house in Mortlake. I never went out on weekday evenings as I didn't have the money, nor any friends who lived locally. When the Monday-to-Friday live-in landlady went to the country at the weekends, I did host the occasional "dinner party"—if you could call it that. The absence of any dining furniture meant up to ten people sitting cross-legged on the floor with one plate and one glass, but I still managed to rustle-up three courses: a humble prawn-cocktail, spag bol, and apple crumble come to mind. The novelty and freedom of my first London rented accommodation soon wore off and my chilly room and the cold bath water no longer held any attraction, especially as I was now working in Central London.

Then, out of the blue, my old RNS sixth-form chum, Sandra, who I hadn't seen since leaving school two years previously, got in touch and asked if I'd like to share a flat just off the Kings Road in Chelsea. She knew someone who knew someone …

And so it came to pass that we both moved into a one-bedroom basement flat in Royal Avenue, with the nearest shop being The Chelsea Drug Store on the Kings Road no fewer than 50 yards from our front door. The rent was cheap, it included gas and electricity, which meant we could saunter round the flat in tee-shirts whatever the weather.

With just the one bedroom, we decided to toss a coin and Sandra won, which meant I got the single bed in the corner of the large living-room—it was hardly the end of the world, all things considered. The galley kitchen was under the stairs, along with a large larder-cum-cupboard for our food which, from time to time, also housed a family of mice who feasted on the contents of our cereal boxes.

We even had a small garden, bordered by an end wall which we would shimmy up to jump down into Woodfall Street, the home of the Pheonix Pub. We'd landed on our feet. With me came my beloved Wolsey Hornet with leather seats and walnut dashboard, now displaying a shiny new resident's Royal Borough of Kensington and Chelsea parking permit!

Love and Affection

And then something happened that was to truly change the course of the rest of my life. In 1975, aged 19, I had an affair with Sandra.

It was a huge shock, and at first, I just couldn't get my head round it. I thought back to my last night at RNS, two years before, when I'd "learnt something about Sandra" and tried to join the dots; but I can honestly say I didn't see it coming—if I had, I'd have probably run for the hills.

I'd never ever questioned my sexuality; I simply fell in love, for the first time, with a woman and it bowled me over. It was to make a strong and lasting impact on me. I was intensely happy. For the first time in my life, I felt engulfed in love, understanding, and endless support. Sandra helped me cope with my parental nightmares and the unhappiness that had always accompanied them. However, unintentionally, we had now created a new level of potential, and shared, angst: about, horror of horrors, either of our sets of parents uncovering the affair.

Lacking self-confidence and disliking my job intensely, Sandra helped me get through. More importantly, she looked after me during recovery from my two plastic surgery operations and ongoing alopecia treatment. I'd never had anyone to truly lean on before. We laughed, we loved, we cried and, inevitably, we had lovers' tiffs. But it was a magical time.

To put this lesbian affair into some context, fifty years ago this was a BIG DEAL. I knew no lesbians; I'd never even knowingly met one! The derogatory term "lezza" was freely bandied around at school without foundation and could be brushed off as just a spiteful riposte. The irony is that it had never crossed my mind that it might apply to me in the years to come. Such ignorance (or innocence) could be explained away as a combination of my middle-class upbringing, my naivety, my age—but the bottom line was that I was—both of us were—deeply ashamed and terrified anyone would find out.

We cut ourselves off from our friends, making flimsy excuses. We rarely had anyone round for fear of giving something away that would lead to us being discovered. Even my oldest and dearest friends who I'd known since the age of eleven and were like brother and sister to me … I just couldn't bring myself to tell them. I was too scared they'd be horrified and drop me.

But frightened as we were, we *were* in love; I couldn't wait to get home every day from Rolls Royce Aerospace. I'd jump off the number 19 bus and run in my midi-skirt, tights, and heels as fast as I could back to our basement den so that we could be together.

One day at work, sitting at my desk in the office shared with my female boss, the VIP liaison officer, who was probably ten or fifteen years older than me, I made a grave error, misjudging the level of our camaraderie.

I'd been working for her about four months (a record in my secretarial logbook) and we'd got on quite well, up to a point. She kept an eye on my timekeeping, but on a Friday afternoon she'd allow me to leave fifteen or twenty minutes early, based on the week's achievements. She was quite tweedy and strait-laced but with a "jolly hockey sticks" personality and some days would compliment me on the outfit I'd struggled to put together as "slacks" were a no-no. Staying in the office for lunch, we would often share sandwiches and talk about our weekends and our favourite breakfasts, share hair and makeup tips and compare nail varnish colours.

Chatting away one Thursday lunchtime, I let my guard down and opened my big mouth too wide. Brimming with effervescent happiness as I was, I proceeded to confide in her that I was having an affair with my female flatmate.

On arriving at work, on time, the next morning, with no sign of the VIP liaison officer in our shared office, I found a memo on my desk asking me to report without delay to Personnel where I was handed my P45. I was told "with regret" that the VIP liaison officer did not find my work "up to the required standard" and that I was to go and clear my desk and then "leave the building forthwith".

Clearly feeling uncomfortable with the situation, the two suited men from Personnel attempted to put a kinder spin on it but floundered as I sat in complete shock trying to digest what they were saying ... "These things can happen ... personality clashes can occur ... it's not necessarily a reflection on your ability but very unfortunate ... we have a cheque for you, your salary owing, and, out of goodwill, we've added two extra weeks' pay."

Once I'd put this harsh reminder of blatant homophobia to one side—though I continued to feel betrayed and hurt, and, yes, even more ashamed (now, as I write this, I just feel outrage and anger)—I was elated to have the rest of that Friday off, plus two weeks' money. And I was even more thrilled never to have to go back to that hateful job.

The following week I trawled the Kings Road and found myself a full-time position in a shop. "Shop girl"—I could already hear my mother's predictable, sarcastic, told-you-so put-down. But I didn't care because it was one of the most enlightening, "educational" … and fun … jobs I've ever had. I learned almost everything I know about sales from Doug, an extraordinary eccentric character, the proprietor of what became the famous western boot shop, probably the longest surviving independent retailer on the Kings Road, "R Soles" (say it out loud for maximum benefit!).

Rolling out of bed, throwing on jeans and a pair of cowboy boots, walking four minutes to work, rock-and-roll playing all day on the sound system, meeting all sorts: from punks to cool fashion trendsetters, to mother and daughter Sloane Rangers and loads of characters in between. It was a hoot!

If my father had been in his element running his air-station he equally loved being in charge of PR for the Navy; but he and my mother continued to fight, even though he tried to toe the line at home and play down how much he enjoyed his job. She didn't like "it" taking over. Unfortunately, the phone rang frequently, during the evenings, at weekends, with enquires from leading journalists wanting the latest response from the Navy about their involvement in any tactical movements by air or sea.

But it wasn't all about military logistics. My father was, at the time, also in the role of aide-de-camp to the Queen, making him the link for any official royal visits to naval air bases and docks, whether for ship launches or for the meeting and greeting of overseas dignitaries and fellow royalty.

The project that really captured his interest and kept him most busy was the fly-on-the-wall BBC series *Sailor*— it was he who'd persuaded the Admiralty to agree to it being made—about life on board HMS *Ark Royal* on six-month deployment in North America. Despite serious misgivings at the highest level, the series was a huge success, gaining a cult following and excellent viewing figures.

The theme tune was Rod Stewart's "Sailing", with a choral backing by the ship's company. The single went to number one in the charts and Dad claimed that Rod Stewart had him to thank for its success, adding, "what a shame that Mr Stewart couldn't get himself a decent hair cut."

Although I constantly got the low-down from my mother (how selfish he was, how she'd had enough, how she didn't trust him etc.—same old same old), thankfully, living in London, I didn't have to witness the rows in person nor, thank goodness, did I have to watch the whole series of *Sailor*!

My parents were fiercely competitive, both in private and in the company of friends and naval colleagues; they both needed to be the centre of attention. Perhaps sharing the birth-sign of Leo didn't help, but the fact was my father's job made him feel important and it made my mother feel very much less so. When lions go to war, as they are inclined to do, you know it's going to be drawn-out and messy.

During the spring of 1976 I had my second of two plastic surgery operations and the summer that followed was long and hot. Who could forget "The Summer of '76"? Water from the street standpipes, no baths permitted, and only flushing of the loo a couple of times a day. People sat outside until midnight and beyond—all because it was so hot; tempers frayed in the streets and bus queues, but it was a summer like no other. Sandra and I were in love and made plans for our future together.

Sandra was born and raised in the West Indies—Grenada and Barbados—and was permitted to stay in the UK for her further education: two years at the RNS and then a further two-year permit was granted for a course in business studies at a private college in London. The UK Government gave no work permit extensions, and it was made clear she had to leave the country once her course was over.

With limited career prospects in the Caribbean, she (and her parents) decided she would be better off going to Canada with her newly acquired qualifications to explore a career in hospitality and catering. After contemplating various scenarios, it seemed the only way we could stay together was by me going too! "R Soles" was not a long-term career position, the experience and fun had run its course. Still terrified any of our friends or family would find out about our relationship, Canada seemed to offer safe distance and space for us to continue being together without being "caught".

For the best part of the next nine months we went back and forth between home and the Canadian High Commission, dealing with passports and permits, references and guarantors (fortunately, I had an aunt living and working as a teacher in Toronto—my mother's "brainy sister"), at the same time giving notice on our Chelsea flat and me my job at "R Soles". My parents were amazed at the news of my emigration, but I dressed this major move up as "great experience for a few years but definitely not for good" … "and how great to have Mum's sister there just in case" … etc., etc.

Naturally, it came as no surprise to Sandra's parents; it was what they'd planned, and they were only too happy their daughter was going to be joined by an old school chum and London flatmate so they could both share a new apartment in a new country and have each other to lean on. Ha! So far, so good.

We booked the flights for autumn 1977 but had also decided on a farewell European tour in the summer before our departure to North America. So off we went by car to Greece, via France, Germany, and Italy and then a ferry over to the Greek mainland, taking two weeks to get there, camping on the way. We arrived in Athens and stayed a night with a Greek ex-boyfriend of mine (I think he sussed us) who offered to look after the car for two months while we swanned off to discover the Greek Islands via the numerous ferries, with our backpacks and a very tight budget. We had an idyllic time. Those were the days when you could sleep on the beach at night, get by on very little, but have so much. We lived on Greek salads and bread, with the occasional warm moussaka as a treat plus constant supplies of beer and retsina … and smokes.

In the meantime, my father had received bad news. After over thirty-five years of successful service in the Royal Navy, he was informed he was not to be promoted to the next rank of admiral. This was a huge blow. However, softening the news considerably was the announcement that he was to be awarded the CBE in the Queen's birthday honours. My mother pivoted from initially being vaguely complimentary to being not at all impressed: "It's your consolation prize for not making the next rung, it's the equivalent of a 'gold watch' ..."

Sandra had a flight booked to Grenada to visit her family for a couple of weeks prior to us departing and meeting in Toronto; I was to leave from London. Our return journey from Greece was much quicker than the journey there had been.

We are unaware of the nasty surprise waiting for us ...

After dropping off Sandra at the airport, I drive back to my parents' house where I'll be staying for the next two weeks before leaving for Canada. As soon as I walk in through the back door, I can smell tension in the air. Mum and Dad ask me to go to the sitting-room: they want to talk to me. "Oh God," I think. "What's coming. Been here before. Surely not again. Not now ... at the age of twenty-one?"

My mother does the talking:

We know you've been having an unnatural relationship with Sandra, and whilst you were away in Greece we wrote to her parents and informed them of this situation. As a result, they phoned us from the West Indies, and we have had a lengthy conversation. We're both equally shocked and appalled and agreed that this way of life is not what we want for our daughters. When Sandra arrives home tonight in the Caribbean, her parents will let her know that they know about your unnatural relationship and of our communication with them but, they were absolutely adamant that they would make Sandra give her word that she will never see you again.

The bottom falls out of my life. I am devastated. Anger and rage and "How fucking dare you" follow. I cannot be consoled. Immediate emotional turmoil is followed by a longer-term downward spiral of depression, and a subsequent sexual identity crisis, that will last for what feels like a long, long decade.

Having given up my flat and my job in London, and despite my plans with Sandra being in tatters, two weeks later I get on a plane to attempt a fresh start on my own in Toronto. There's nothing to stay in England for and, as far as I'm concerned, my parents can go fuck themselves, especially my mother who'd headed up the devious dismantling of my relationship. Though I'm now twenty-one, I feel as if I'm being sucked back in, treated like an adolescent, bullied and dominated; struggling to break free, come hell or high water, I am getting on that plane.

I have an awful time in Toronto. For the first two nights I stay with my aunt, my mother's sister, "the brainy one", who turns out to be very large and very eccentric. I had no idea. I then go to stay with her daughter, my cousin, and her husband and, make no mistake, she is completely round the bend. They live on the eighteenth floor of a two-bedroom high-rise apartment block and she and her husband fight like cat and dog. One night I lock myself in the spare bedroom whilst they brandish carving knives, threatening to kill each other—it is a repeat family drama.

After struggling to deal with employment agencies, I finally land a job—a dull secretarial role. I am deeply unhappy and can't stop myself crying as I sit at my typewriter. I stick it for three weeks before giving my notice with some flimsy excuse and profuse apologies.

Before I do, though, I've been contemplating taking on the lease of a twenty-second-floor studio apartment. Going down in the elevator after the viewing, and seriously contemplating a dramatic leap from the twenty-second-floor balcony ("That would serve them all bloody well right"), with tears cascading down my cheeks, I am befriended by a guy who saves me—literally!

Steve asks if I'd like to share his two-bedroom apartment, and I gingerly but gratefully accept, on the understanding there are "no strings". I can honestly say, apart from his immense kindness, his *pièce de résistance* was introducing me to the music and lyrics of Joni Mitchell … and his weed grown on his balcony in the sky. "I am on a lonely road and I am traveling …", "Oh, I wish I had a river I could skate away on …" and "He saw my complications and he mirrored me back simplified".

I can identify with these songs, and they hit a deep but melancholic chord that is profound. Through the agony and equal ecstasy of the music, I can keep two feet on the ground; plus, the help of my new platonic friendship with Steve … and his home-grown grass.

I met up with Sandra once during that time. I travelled by train to London, Ontario, where her parents had helped set her up in an apartment and on a trainee hotel management course. I spent the weekend with her. I think I sobbed almost all the time. And I think she was quite shocked at my fragile state.

We talked endlessly about alternative options so that we might continue our relationship: the only realistic course of action would be to turn our backs on our families and disappear into the sunset. I'd already half done that, but, unlike me, Sandra adored her parents, came from a very large and happy family, couldn't let them down.

We were both paralysed with fear, and still, it must be said, suffocated by shame about being lesbian; there wasn't yet any coherent community that might have supported us, and we were without friends in Canada. Was our relationship strong enough to take the plunge and leave everything we knew behind? Were we old enough, at twenty-one, to make such a major commitment?

Despondently, and tearfully, we agreed there was too much at risk. And that was that … sort of—for the next ten years we wrote intense emotional letters to each other. That was how long it took me to get over Sandra.

Work, Play ... and Property

So back to England I go, in pieces. Contrary to my original fears, my good friends are there for me, with plentiful support and the help I need to get myself back on my feet. I have no money, no job, and nowhere to live, so, initially, I go back to the family home. Mum and Dad—particularly Mum at this stage—bend over backwards to be nice to me, probably (I like to think, now) because they feel wretched at seeing the emotional state of their daughter because of what they considered to be a "well-intentioned" intervention in her life choices.

My mother has just started a small antiques business, buying silver, china, and small items of furniture at the sale rooms and then, after a little "sprucing up", she sells them from her stall in a high-street shop made up of market-style concessions. She invites me to join her business venture, and we even open a joint bank account!

I accompany her to the sale room several times, having been instructed in the dos and don'ts, although my role is very much to keep quiet and learn. She explains that you have to do the viewing beforehand thoroughly and write in the catalogue's margin your maximum bid to avoid getting carried away when the auctioneer takes bids from the floor.

But nearly every time she gets into the bidding, she'll ignore her "maximum" rule, bidding higher while I try to whisper discreetly in her ear that we don't have enough money in our account to cover her bid! Until she loses her temper with me and that's that … "DON'T YOU EVER DARE TELL ME WHEN TO STOP BIDDING."

I think we lasted four weeks and by then I'd made plans to sofa-surf and take refuge with some chums in London.

I'm off again.

It was just as well I left when I did. Things were brewing up to a new level of dysfunction at Little Holt. My father had by this time finished in the Navy and was "at home" (for the first time ever) and in search of a new job. At fifty-three he was too young to retire, and it certainly wasn't financially possible on the income from a lowly naval pension; he was being "helped" (read, pushed) by my mother towards the sort of job she thought he should be applying for. Unsurprisingly, they didn't agree. Yet bigger storm clouds were gathering.

Around this time my father was invited to Buckingham Palace to receive his CBE; his immediate family were invited to join him. My mother was adamant she wouldn't attend and, in turn, forbade me to go. I didn't argue: first, I wasn't over-keen to support my father; second, I was still acting out the "anti-establishment rebel"; third, I didn't really appreciate the immensity of the occasion. On the big day, my father was accompanied just by his son. The family fault-line was being fractured still further.

From sofa-surfing in London I graduated to my own room in a shared flat in Islington, the home of an ex-boyfriend, Tim, and his girlfriend, Karen. By this time, I had come clean with most of my friends, spilling the beans about my recent relationship with Sandra; part of me was unable to keep the secret and part of me desperately needed support.

In addition, I needed to dispel any fears that Karen may have had, just in case she thought I had ulterior motives regarding her partner Tim. They were both incredibly supportive and helped me refloat. We had loads of laughs, parties, endless pub crawls and games of snooker, and plenty of people came to stay. Saturday nights were a highlight: the midnight movie at Screen on the Green where you bought chocolate brownies in the foyer and then piled into the auditorium with your pre-rolled joints to smoke during the film.

At the same time as my father was applying for jobs, I was too. I had, by now, been persuaded that the name of the game was "to get in somewhere" as a secretary and to them climb up; but "somewhere" had to be in a field of "something" that would inspire me, and I couldn't think of *any* career path that remotely interested me. Then a penny dropped: I was reminded of my passion for music and for my vinyl collection and from there the idea was hatched to apply for secretarial jobs in record companies.

After several months of applications and interviews (plus inside help from someone who knew someone) I secured a position as shared secretary to the sales director and the sales manager at EMI Records. I was chuffed to bits and set myself a time limit of six months to climb up and out of secretarial work, without at that stage understanding what "EMI" really stood for. I was to find out, to my cost.

My father, too, secured a new role around the same time. My mother was delighted; it was one of the jobs she had pushed for (having noted the perks that she could take advantage of), and, in turn, the Institute of Brewing was delighted to have at their helm the services of a relatively young but retired naval captain CBE as their secretary and director general.

A non-profit industry organisation, their offices were situated in Mayfair; the position came with use of a penthouse flat and included first-class travel to brewers (and distillers) all over the world (nine times out of ten this would include my mother) plus a reasonable salary but with an exceptionally generous pension. My father's role at the IoB also warranted a secretary—in fact, he got his very own personal assistant—but this aspect of the new job was, inevitably, not going to please my mother.

Despite my tedious secretarial duties at EMI, I was in my element. I knew this was my sort of place. No longer in skirt and tights but jeans and sneakers and no "Please sir"— everyone was on first name terms. From Tamla Motown to reggae and all the chart hits, an eclectic mix of loud music emanated from every office ... along with the odd waft of herbal smoke.

A full-time job, with potential under my belt, aged twenty-six, it was time to "get a foot on the ladder" and look for a flat as I was now able to secure a mortgage. This was made possible by the £5,000 waiting in my building society savings account for this event—it had taken nearly ten years, two operations, and a long and protracted legal battle post my car accident to finally receive the damages due in an out-of-court settlement. Of course, had all this happened in America, I wouldn't have had to work again ever, so I was told!

Whatever level of property you buy into, there are compromises to be made, many more on a first-time purchase. After much research and many viewings, I found a very small one-bedroom ground-floor flat in Battersea, with shared garden, tiny bathroom with shower tray and plastic curtain, and a small galley kitchen. But I loved it.

My mother insisted on having a look before I made an offer "just in case" I was making a "grave mistake"; after all, she reminded me, she had six months' experience of working as an estate agent (until she'd been fired because she demanded the same pay as her male counterpart negotiators). She came, she looked, she hated it. The problem, as far as she was concerned, was that it didn't have any central heating, and in the bedroom there was a six-and-a-half-foot-high platform with just enough room for a mattress (so as to maximise floor space underneath). No matter how much I explained to her that this was the best I could get for my down-payment and mortgage offer, she refused to understand and told me not to buy it.

I bought it! With my very own sanctuary for the first time in my life, I was in my element. I had no money for going out, no washing machine, no heating, no furniture (that's how it was then, but yes, I had a foot on a rung), and I just adored the freedom I'd finally gained.

Despite my meagre financial resource, an essential flat-warming present to myself was a Technics stacking sound system and two Acoustic Research 100 watt per channel speakers (for which I had to buy stands to stop the awesome base reverberating through the floor and around the Victorian three-story building which housed six flats). I had arrived in *my* new bolthole, big time!

At EMI, I finally got the breakthrough I was so desperate for: that of no longer being a secretary. I wore my boss down by repeatedly asking for a chance to "go on the road" and sell the month's new releases. The nationwide sales force, split into twenty-five territories with a rep for each territory, "all trained and experienced", didn't include an opportunity for a woman—let alone one with no experience.

But week after week I pursued my plan of attrition; in a moment of utter frustration, I guaranteed I could sell more records than any of his "trained experienced" male reps, if only he would give me the chance! That did the trick and landed me in deep water without a life raft. I was told to pick up a "pool car" on the coming Monday and get out on the road, covering for a rep who was on extended leave. His area was the Surrey, Sussex, and Hampshire region. I was determined there was no way I was going to fail but at the same time, I was scared stiff. There was simply no way I could lose face or this opportunity.

For the next month I work my arse off. I really have no idea what I'm doing but what I do know is that I have to sell … and sell. I leave home at six in the morning to visit a minimum of eight shops a day, with my routes planned (no satnav in those days!), armed with a map of the Home

Counties, a huge record-carrying case with around a hundred new-release albums—classical, MOR (middle of the road), AOR (adult orientated rock), military bands (yes, really!), and pop, including licenced labels (such as Island, Motown, Staxx, Fantasy)—and a "daily report sheet" pad.

This rep isn't taking "no" for an answer (I didn't, at that point, understand the nature of specialist shops). She feels as if she's failed if she hasn't sold one or two copies of everything. A few retailers start to phone in with complaints: "Get this woman out of my shop, she's being too pushy." But, after a month's trial, the net result is that I've sold more records than any of the other "trained and experienced" reps; the sales director piggybacks on that and claims he was right to give me the opportunity and how great it is that I sell so hard and how it exposes the laissez-faire attitude of the other reps.

My teenage bartering experiences in Singapore, combined with having flogged cowboy boots on the Kings Road, with an added dollop of determination utterly propelled by fear of failure, earned me a framed disc with an engraved plaque—"Sales Person of the Month". Deeply resented by the other twenty-four reps (men)—"she must have got her leg over"—I nevertheless secure a permanent job as an EMI rep. Forty-five years ago, I become the first female "sales person" in the UK record industry, finally kicking the industry norm of "salesman" into the long grass (where it has lain, and withered, ever since).

I am on a (natural) high, so it doesn't matter to me too much that I'm not very popular with my male work colleagues. I love the job, the Ford Cortina estate (red, no less), travelling around visiting different people wearing my red and yellow promotional "Toots and the Maytals" bomber-jacket and gathering an ever-better collection of vinyl as well as expanding my knowledge and love of music.

The Island Records roster and catalogue is simply outstanding and, looking back, I feel extremely fortunate to have discovered so many profoundly exciting, diverse, and brilliant artists: Bob Marley, John Martin, Grace Jones, Robert Palmer, Nick Drake, Marianne Faithful (her astonishing comeback album of '79, *Broken English*), Ultravox, U2, the B-52's ... and so much reggae—which I still love: The Wailers, Burning Spear, Black Uhuru, Third World, Steel Pulse, Toots ...

After six months of working the counties, I will be promoted to West End rep, which means calling on the big retail accounts as well as the wholesalers: one day in a smart outfit taking the head buyer at Harrods to the café for an iced bun and coffee just before my new release presentation (mainly classical and MOR); the next, in my Toots jacket visiting a wholesaler in Harlesden, sharing a spliff in the back room as we listen to my reggae releases through booming sub-woofer speakers.

As you can probably gather, I am bursting with pride at my achievements; as you can probably anticipate by now, my mother is less happy and does her best to prick my bubble. "We did not send you to a private boarding school and an Oxford secretarial college at such great expense to have you become a common rep." I am gutted (but not surprised) by her put-down; in my view, promotion from secretary to rep is a triumph, a significant career achievement, and one that breaks through the glass ceiling into the male world.

Predictable as my mother's response is, I am, nevertheless, angry that she still can't even recognise, never mind salute, my achievements because they are *so* different from what *she* wants for me. Her ability to get under my skin, to undermine me, my pride and happiness, is boundless. However ridiculous I know her plans are for her daughter to become a PA to the CEO of a leading blue-chip company in the City (and then marry one), she can still reduce me to feeling like a disappointment and a failure.

My father makes no comment.

Although I'm still extremely confused about my sexuality, having buried it almost entirely, I end up falling into another relationship with a woman. During a monthly sales visit to Harvey Nichols, the female record buyer makes a pass at me; I decide to take the plunge. I go with the flow. I reciprocate.

The result is a happy and fun-filled two-year relationship with a woman sixteen years my senior. (As if making up for lost time, I'll then go on to have another two-year relationship with the ex-girlfriend of my ex-girlfriend—a bit messy, I admit, but forgive me, I'm still finding my lesbian feet!)

All the while, my mother and father are in the dark, though my mother is clearly suspicious. I religiously continue to visit on a Sunday at least once or twice a month and just gloss over what I've been up to, though I do make sure that I take pride in updating them on my position in the EMI sales league table. Having always been bottom of the class at school, it's novel now to be at the top. I notch up another two or three platinum discs for "Salesperson of the Month", and proudly show them off.

My father's second career is going well too and there are frequent visits to the Far East, Australia, and New Zealand. My mother makes sure that she goes along. In between the overseas trips, Mum comes up to London on shopping expeditions and stays in the penthouse flat above Dad's office. Still harbouring the same bitter resentments, she is nevertheless able and willing to run up sizeable amounts on his credit card by frequent trips round Harrods and Harvey Nics.

The spending sprees and visits to London will further escalate when she starts to suspect that my father is having an affair with his personal assistant. Based on no evidence whatsoever, other than the fact that Dad takes her for a drink on a Friday once a month, it is clearly more about my mother's total lack of trust in her husband.

Dad's PA is in her mid-thirties and, in fact, engaged to be married later that year. My father thinks it perfectly acceptable to show his appreciation for her work by taking her out for a drink and a sandwich at the end of each month. My mother (of course) thinks otherwise. Staying overnight in the apartment on one of her trips, whilst my father is asleep, she goes downstairs to the office on the ground floor and proceeds to search through desk drawers, both of her husband and of his PA, until she finds … a phone number! His secretary's home number.

My mother starts to call her at weekends and often during the middle of the night, usually after a few whiskies, making all sorts of vile insults and accusations, not to say sinister threats. Mum continues to stir things up, involving the chairman of the IOB and other office staff, and doesn't rest until, two months later, Dad's assistant, who has by now become a distraught and nervous wreck, resigns. The intense mental anxiety caused by my mother's behaviour also leads to the breakup of her engagement.

While this is going on I'm preoccupied with my job and with exploring my newfound freedom. After five years at EMI, having been turned down four times for various junior positions in the marketing department, the Personnel manager, a woman, takes me aside to tell me, in confidence, that there's no chance "they" will accept a woman in that department. Didn't I know what EMI really stands for? It's "Every Man for 'Imself!"

Furious at the unfairness of it all and adamant that they won't carry on benefitting from my hard work and sales skills, within three months I find myself another job—as an advertising executive selling space for the music industry trade weekly in Covent Garden, where, over the next eight years, I will climb the greasy pole to become publisher.

Shortly after starting my new job, I tell Mum, in no uncertain terms and not for the first time, that I've had enough, that I just can't cope with her despairing phone calls about her ongoing unhappiness with Dad—"He's done this, he's done that, he's a liar and a cheat, remember he fucked a whore in Singapore": the same old broken record. Nevertheless, I continue to visit the family home on a regular basis and phone twice a week out of a sense of duty: I recognise that Mum is depressed and vulnerable, and I feel a responsibility to try and improve her mood.

I outgrow my first flat and have enough confidence to upsize to a two-bedroom flat. Yet again, my mother refuses to be left on the side-lines and, with spare time on her hands (though her antique business is still doing well), she insists on accompanying me to a day of viewings. Due to good luck, being in the right place at the right time, an offer on my first flat, and a vendor in a contract race (and, I have to admit, through my mother's tenacity and an ability to spot a great bargain), I am able to leap-frog to a two-up two-down railwayman's cottage, still in my Battersea stomping ground.

The move happens quickly and within weeks I'm in my new home. It needs plenty of TLC and modernisation but, with all monies totally spent, improvements will be piecemeal. Treating damp patches and basic decoration will be first on the agenda.

Just as I'd outgrown my first flat, I'd also outgrown my last two relationships, each having lasted a couple of years. Neither affair had been unhappy and neither had an awful acrimonious ending; they'd just run their course, sort of petered out. I was still, even then, not clear about my sexuality. I needed time for reflection.

Sensing that I'm once again "unattached", my mother

wants to get more involved in the project of my new house. While I certainly don't mind accepting some of my parents' surplus-to-requirement items (i.e. stuff from their loft) to fill the gaps in my new-found space, I really don't want my mother imposing her vision of interior décor. I want to create, and have, something of my own.

During the run-up to Christmas 1985 I get a builder in to sort out the damp patches and, after blow-drying them with the fan-heater for several days, I start decorating like a mad woman, after work every evening until the early hours and again at weekends, making significant progress over the Christmas break.

January of the following year, 1986, is about to see the start of the next, and most significant, period of my life. Again, my mother is going to be very far from happy about it. And, yet again, she is going to do everything within her (not inconsiderable) means to try to change the direction of my life.

7

The Third Woman

Over the years, I had had many a tempestuous row with my mother but the one that started in the spring of 1986 almost led to a final parting of the ways. I hadn't seen or spoken to my mother for six months: she had refused point blank to accept that I was in a new and significant relationship with a woman I'd "allowed" to move in and buy into my house, the two of us making a new shared home together. Trying to explain to my mother that this was a demonstration of "long-term commitment" made it even worse. She was furious. So too was her daughter, now aged thirty but still battling hard to shake off her mother's dominance and be in control of her own life.

Suzanne and I had met a few years before we actually "got together" in '86. Introduced to her at a garden barbeque in West London, I immediately fancied her like mad. At that time, I was living with a girlfriend in her Chiswick flat where socially we hung out with a small group of other lesbians, playing regular badminton and visiting local pubs for some quite serious drinking sessions. Suzanne, too, was living with her partner; we were both reasonably content in our relationships.

There was no "hanky-panky" (as my mother would have called it), not even flirtatious glances. If the truth be known, we seemed like very different women—attraction was one thing, but we weren't sure how much we liked each other. I tended to be rather loud, rebellious, and a bit of a talker; Suzanne came across as quite serious and slightly aloof. Well, we know what they say about "opposites".

Fast forward two years, my Chiswick relationship over and I am back in Battersea, busy doing up my new house. My job is going well, I have plenty of good friends, and am generally pretty satisfied with my lot in life. (It would be remiss of me not to drop in at this stage that I had decided I wasn't really gay and that my next relationship was going to be with a man, though I was in absolutely no rush.)

Around this time, Suzanne's three-year relationship came to an end; we got in contact with each other and met for meals out to chew the cud. One night, after a good dinner at a curry house on Lavender Hill, and a bottle of wine, each, Suzanne was unable to drive home ... opposites do attract it seems!

We fell very much in love and fortuitously it turned out that we did have a great deal in common. We decided, quickly, that it was the right time in our lives to make a commitment, to each other. Although Suzanne was three and a half years older than me, we had both suffered similar "life" experiences: the "coming out" crisis; the heartbreak after the finish of the first ever lesbian love affair; and both of us had had two subsequent live-in relationships.

We knew, through meeting older women, that one of the common patterns in lesbian affairs was that they could be just that—"affairs"—and they would last, on average, around two years. When the going got tough (the honeymoon period being well and truly over), the tough (the less committed) would get out. On the prowl for new passion, no number of shared cats would be sufficient for the relationship to continue.

This two-year cycle could last for a couple more decades until you found yourself in your sixties without having experienced the benefits and security of growing together in a long-term partnership. Neither Suzanne nor I wanted this; that was a major factor in our commitment.

So, we celebrated with a small party and were showered with champagne and presents; a toaster, a decanter, and a Black & Decker drill come to mind! You could say we were ahead of the game; it wasn't for another eighteen years, in 2004, that civil partnerships were recognised in British law, never mind same-sex marriage, which took another two years.

We settled into our new lives together in our small, but cute, two-up two-down Victorian railway worker's cottage in Battersea. We both had cars, and both drove to work (these were the days when you could drive across London and, with perks of the job, even have an allocated parking space). I sported a red Ford Capri company car, courtesy of the trade music magazine I worked for (though I was a bit sniffy about the "Ford" badge); Suzanne had a rather stylish maroon VW Scirocco and drove to Thames Television at Euston where she was climbing the production ladder. We worked hard, we played hard. Life was good—except when it came to … my mother.

I'm extremely nervous of revealing the big news to my parents—indeed terrified (and that's not an overstatement) of my mother's reaction, but it can't be held off any longer. Suzanne, unintentionally, regularly answers the phone to my mother and feels rather awkward (and, at the same time, angry about, and frustrated by, my lack of courage); my mother, inevitably, is rather perplexed and, indeed, suspicious. Suzanne has to pressure me (and rightly so) into "fessing up". The shit is about to hit the fan, big time.

The phone call is awful. I spell it out; my mother spits back at me. Extremely vociferous opinions are exchanged. Awful things are said. In spiteful fury my mother yells: "If you continue down this path, you are not my daughter and I don't want to see or speak to you again", and she hangs up. I'm devastated. I so want, and need, my own life and independence, but I can't face it being at the cost of losing my family—highly dysfunctional as it is.

(Thinking about it now, it wasn't so much my family that I was afraid of leaving behind—my mother was making sure that I still couldn't stand my father, and my brother and I weren't close, because of the family divide. What it really boiled down to was the prospect of separating from my mother—the mother who held me in terror and in awe; the mother I'd stood by and defended against my father for the last twenty-four years; when it came down to it, the mother I loved.)

169

I was torn up inside—hurt to the core, frightened, angry, confused, conflicted.

Over the course of the next several weeks my father phones a couple of times to "keep in touch" and to ask how I am and generally show concern at the situation to see if there is any chance of him brokering some sort of reconciliation—at least a truce. He asks me to meet him for lunch near his office in Mayfair, but I decline, saying there's no point as I'm not about to end my relationship with Suzanne to satisfy Mum.

A six-month period of silence ensues between me and my parents until one day, unexpectedly, my father phones and suggests that Mum and I meet up for a drink over lunch on neutral territory to chat things through. I agree and a date is set. The meeting point is a Harvester-style eatery just off the A3—a halfway point for both of us. I prepare and learn my lines.

We have a glass of wine each. There is food on the table, but I don't remember eating any of it. It is tense. It is awful. There are tears and Mum leaves abruptly after paying the curious but bemused waiter on her way out. I stay a while longer. I order myself another glass of wine to help process my response to my mother's blatant efforts to stay in control.

She'd pleaded with me, again, not to "continue down this route"; she'd gone on about how having children was the single most important achievement in her life, and she didn't want me to miss out on the experience. And, if I were to carry on my relationship with Suzanne, she didn't want to see me again. As I sat and drank my wine, it occurred to me that the most significant thing she'd said was that there wasn't room for a third woman in the relationship; me being with another woman was denying her the possibility of an ongoing mother–daughter relationship.

This was a bewildering attitude, but, I guess, quite typical of her generation. (Funnily enough, a few years later, Princess Diana was to say something similar, but at least she was referring to another lover, not her mother!) I think Mum's contorted, but deeply conservative, vision of a mother–daughter relationship involved me and her in the kitchen preparing Sunday lunch whilst gossiping and moaning about our husbands, who'd be chatting over a beer and watching sport in the next room. And, as I'm sure you'll have by now realised, there was no way that was going to happen!

In response to my mother, I put forward three options. First, I tell her, if, just to please you, I end my relationship with Suzanne, I'll end up resenting you for the rest of my life; second, if I don't agree to end the relationship with Suzanne, losing you will make me incredibly unhappy; but, if we can both dig deep and respect the differences between us, I can assure you that an ongoing mother–daughter relationship is possible, in spite of me being in a relationship with a woman. I admit that it's going to be a long haul and will involve huge effort on both our parts. I say that we'll both need to maintain boundaries and understanding—or there really is no point in us trying.

I can't count how many years of doing that digging deep then followed until we got to a point where things started to feel even just a bit okay. For the next two, three, or possibly four years, I tried incredibly hard to please Mum, being extremely sensitive around her when Suzanne was with me. Sometimes I would visit her and my father on my own; sometimes Suzanne would come too; all was fine, polite, if a little strained. I never showed any affection towards Suzanne in front of my parents, either physically or verbally. I really did everything I could not to make Mum unhappy; to the contrary, I probably became a daughter too eager to try and please.

I overcompensated because I still felt *guilty* about being gay; in my mind, my sexuality now became the reason for my mother's deep-seated unhappiness and disappointment, her depression, her dysfunctional marriage. Desperate for her understanding, her acceptance, it seemed that I was taking the blame for *everything*.

In retrospect, I recognise that my mother *did* try hard, and our relationship progressed slowly, if not exactly surely. A breakthrough came when Suzanne received her first birthday card and present from both my parents—unprompted by me—which, in turn, gave way to presents at Christmas.

Suzanne was always very good with Mum and Dad and appeared to get on with both of them—she was a dab hand at polite chit-chat. But when it came to her chatting and laughing with Dad, Mum didn't like it one bit; she liked to control group conversation, which in her case usually meant dominating it. "Oh Keith, do shut up, you're boring everyone," she'd shout if my father was talking for too long.

One Sunday afternoon following a dog walk, the four of

us got split up, only because Mum and I walked faster than Suzanne and Dad. When the two of them finally caught up with us, Mum snarled at Suzanne: "Don't think I don't know what you're up to." We were dumbstruck. This was just one of countless occasions when she demonstrated utterly inappropriate, almost deranged, jealousy; she resented Dad getting any attention whatsoever.

Clearly a throwback to my days living at home, Christmas was (and still is) one of my least favourite times of year, which is why Suzanne and I make it our preferred time to leave the country and go on holiday: Mauritius, St Lucia, America, India, Barbados, Trinidad, Hong Kong, and on to Australia to visit friends—we've had some exceptionally exciting holidays. These trips meant we avoided spending too many unbearable Christmas Days with Mum and Dad (and my brother), although every second or third year we did bite the bullet and "do" the family day—alternating with Suzanne's family—but there would always be a flare-up when we did.

One Christmas lunch—memorable for all the wrong reasons—my father has just finished carving (slowly!) the turkey (the tension building up whilst he is doing it; "For Christ's sake Keith, just get on with it")—we're sitting at table—with the best silver laid on a white linen cloth, the homemade bread- and cranberry-sauces, red-berried holly twined round the Georgian candelabra, the perfect table centre-piece, the red napkins, the gleaming wine and water cut-glasses—when, out of the blue, the subject of Prince Charles and Princess Diana comes up.

Heated discussion follows about the royal marital rift, which ultimately boils down to which of us is on whose side. My mother doesn't hold back …

"It is simply outrageous Charles should have another woman, a mistress, and he should be thoroughly ashamed of himself."

Perhaps my father's pre-lunch wine has affected him, but boy, does he blow it.

"Having a mistress when you are heir to the throne is nothing new in the Royal Family and Diana should have known and accepted it or she should not have agreed to marry him."

All hell is let loose.

"Yes, your father knows all about having a mistress—the Whore in Singapore—don't you Keith?"

Suzanne and I are appalled. Furious. (I struggle to understand how I managed to stop myself from grabbing that hefty, Georgian candelabra that graced our festive table and …) Within minutes, we are on the road back to London. We leave the dirty dishes—and the wreckage of yet another family Christmas bloodbath—behind.

In 1990 I make a significant career move … and my mother approves! After eight years at *Music Week*, I resign from the trade mag. I've been told that I have to *prove* myself in my new role of publisher (which I've been doing for six months now) before I can receive a pay rise that is not only paltry but very much less than the man I have taken over from had received.

I'd quietly been sniffing around for a new job, and, to my

amazement and glee, I am offered a managerial role, with a significantly better salary, at the newly formed London radio station, Jazz FM. Equally exciting is being able to select my BMW company car, which means finally ditching the company Ford. I am thrilled with both the job and the car!

I join the day of the launch, when Ella Fitzgerald visits the station to cut the ribbon, so to speak, and perform live on air. It is exciting and scary at the same time; I find myself immediately well out of my depth, organising live outside broadcasts and playing an A&R role in selecting the band or performer, plus producing CD recordings to promote and sell on air.

There's also the upmarket merchandise to commission and oversee; the design of T-shirts, sweatshirts, joggers, and polo shirts, to market and sell to the Jazz FM audience who, hopefully, are going to be trendy and in the high-spending ABC1 demographic to please the advertisers. The poorer, older "Jazzers" are largely overlooked and complain endlessly that their more "trad" style of music is not being aired—in fact it is, except that it's very late at night or in the early hours of the morning.

That same year my father retires from his second career position at the Institute of Brewing. This means Mum and Dad are going to be stuck at home together 24/7 and very much without the luxury escape of a Mayfair flat. There's bound to be more trouble, whatever new arrangements are made, but my mother is one step ahead and lays down the rules: a) they get a second car, a new second car, that is, of her choice, for her use; and b) my father has to join a golf club and play a minimum of three times a week. Mum plays bridge two or three afternoons a week. The other bit of essential planning is to make sure that when Dad is out, Mum is in—and vice versa.

To a point, the new arrangements work quite well, but it doesn't give me any respite from my mother's repeated evening phone calls complaining about my father.

"He's so lazy and doesn't do anything around the house … all he does when he gets home from golf is sit and read the paper, stuffing his face with tea and cake and he can't even be bothered to take his dirty plates to the kitchen."

Mum would get home from bridge at around 6.00pm and, without fail, no matter how many times my mother had told him not to do it, he would be sitting there with the paper, early evening news on TV, and yes, in front of a teacup and saucer and dirty cake plate. She'd go mad every time. I don't know why Dad didn't get it—you'd think he'd go for the "easy life" option, but sadly not.

Or maybe he felt that after forty-five years of working, he deserved a break. Perhaps he was right, up to a point.

My mother's mantra (which she coined from her grandmother)—"Mummy is always right! She once thought she'd made a mistake, but she was wrong"—ran and ran through the decades; sometimes it was used as a joke, sometimes not.

Another regular protest from Mum was that "he expects me to wait on him hand and foot and I'm just not going to"; this would result in her withdrawing her excellent cooking skills and, thus, there would be no evening meal. She could go on strike for days, or sometimes for weeks.

Dad couldn't even boil an egg, coming from the era when men were men and women were in the kitchen, although he did have one kitchen role, that of "washer-upper"; he was very good at it and spent hours and hours, over decades, at the sink. I suggested many times that, "like most people these days", they invest in a dishwasher, but my mother would say firmly "no", that it was a waste of money when she already had a "washer-upper" and, as that was the only thing Dad did, she wasn't about to let him off.

My father *did* garden—indeed, they both did, and needed to with over an acre to maintain, although in later years they paid a local to come in for three hours a week to help with the heavier work. Dad mowed the grass and did the edging, weeding, some light manual work, supervising the clearing up and the bonfires whilst Mum did the "snipping", as Dad called it. They even argued about that: Mum would always be "cutting right back, because it needs it" and Dad would think differently and shout out, "What the hell have you done?"

Dad wasn't good at DIY around the house; he had to be asked several times before he attempted repairs or changed a light bulb. My houseproud Mum, however, couldn't sit still and, with a fag hanging out of the corner of her mouth, she would endlessly go round dusting and polishing her silver, porcelain, and antique furniture, hoovering up her ash as she went, to ensure the house looked perfect—all this in spite of them having a cleaning lady come in once a week.

Back in London, crisis had struck—I'd been made redundant and was now treading water, wondering where my working life was going. Although I'd been earning revenue as commercial manager for Jazz FM Enterprises, it turned out the core business was haemorrhaging money (the published RAJAR [Radio Joint Audience Research] audience figures highlighted this, demonstrating poor reach, with the result that the advertisers departed in droves). Back to the drawing board for the music programmers (who had clearly misjudged their audience). For me, significant panic and a serious rethink.

After so many years of full-time employment, I was now on the proverbial scrap heap, or so it felt at the time. It was the middle of the recession of the 1990s—a worrying time. I had no qualifications, other than my experience, with which to apply for any serious job where I would be able to command the seniority and income to which I'd become accustomed.

Supportive friends bolstered me with "all the best people get made redundant and quite often something better comes along." And, indeed, it did! It took a while to get into gear, but what followed was twenty-five years of self-employment in the music industry; freelancer, consultant, event producer, sales director. Based at home, I worked to survive, and, gradually, I secured a handful of high-profile long-term contracts, some of which I enjoyed.

Suzanne's TV career was on the up; by now she'd gone from production assistant to researcher. She was out of the house five days a week (more when on location filming); I was at home behind my desk in a newly converted bedroom-to-office. We had moved a mere half mile from our cute railway worker's cottage to a four-bedroomed

Gothic-style Victorian house, "twixt the commons" in estate agent lingo, more latterly known as "Nappy Valley". This was to become our home for more than thirty years—but without a nappy in sight!

The Woman of Many Hats

Just before our trip to Zanzibar in 1995, I decided to shave off my hair, that's to say the little hair that I actually had left. In fact, it was my hairdresser who suggested she shave my head, thinking that I wouldn't feel so self-conscious on the beach, as there'd be no one I knew, and it would give me an opportunity to get used to it. This was an excellent plan, but still traumatising; I was unable to look in the mirror as the clippers hummed and my hair fell to the floor. I had it shaved off on the morning before leaving; the only problem was that I was asked to remove my hat at passport control, and I nearly died of embarrassment as members of the long queue behind looked on.

My alopecia had, over the years, worsened considerably and I looked a bit like a diseased cat, with multiple bald round patches all over my head. It wasn't a good look, with straggles of hair hanging down beneath the hat in an ad hoc manner; my hairdresser insisted I was young enough to carry it off, though I vehemently disagreed.

Where we did agree was that I would look much better in all sorts of funky hats, especially if I made the effort to wear bold makeup, jewellery, and clothes and stepped up to the challenge of walking into a room in a *bold* manner, rather than cowering, feeling hideously unattractive and freakish. I've never minded attention but have struggled when it's for negative reasons; it took many years' practice until I was able to walk in to a room full of strangers wearing my latest hat without even thinking about it. I recall a number of challenging occasions though; from being asked if I was having "treatment" (i.e. chemotherapy) to a derogatory comment from a male delegate, at the drinks reception for a weekend conference I'd produced, who asked me bluntly in front of a group of work colleagues why I felt the need to make myself noticed by wearing hats. After a pause, feeling myself prickle and a rush of hot blood to my head, I looked him in the eye and told him I'd been given six months to live. That shut him up!

But my mother couldn't shut up and she *did* think about it and was, of course, very opinionated about how her daughter should look.

Some years earlier, my father had taken me to one side and told me something incredible. He shed some light on a possible contributing reason for my hair loss. For over twenty years, since the start of my alopecia at boarding school, I had sought a remedy and, via a host of specialists and dermatologists, I'd tried every treatment under the sun, including drug trials where I even had to sign a disclaimer form should I drop dead because of these experimental treatments. From lotions and burning potions (photographic developer fluid being one) to radioactive acid, to steroid pills and creams and injections in the head: I'd tried the lot.

The problem at that time was that the experts thought

they knew the cause, but they couldn't find the cure. I even tried "alternative" therapies—acupuncture, faith healing, Chinese herbal medicine—to no avail. Alopecia, it seems, is a disease that persuades your immune system to mistakenly attack a part of your body—in this case, the hair follicles—and shuts it down. And the cause? Predominantly, severe stress, but researchers also believe that it can be genetic, that is, the condition tends to cluster in families: if you have a relative with "patterned hair loss", this also appears to be a risk factor for developing the condition.

And so, my father proceeded to inform me that my uncle—on my mother's side, one of the three uncles I'd never met—and his son had alopecia and had had it for years. I was gobsmacked, and even more so when Dad told me not to let Mum know that he'd told me. Apparently having to deal with the scars on my face (that *she* had to deal with them, as well as me, was utterly typical) had made Mum even more ashamed that it was her side of the family that could be partly to blame for my hair loss. She couldn't face telling me herself.

I never told my mother what Dad had told me, mainly because I was so angry with her; I was frightened that any outburst from me would provoke even more extreme anger and, probably denial, from my mother. (This was very much how things worked—or rather, didn't—with my mother. She remained firmly in control, and I was paralysed by the fear of the consequences of speaking out.)

I felt guilty, too. Not only was I gay; I couldn't even fulfil her vision and need for a daughter who was feminine and pretty. Another thing for sure: if she'd found out I knew,

Dad would get both barrels, which, in turn, would blow the whole thing up into a monumental family melt-down. The good thing that came out of Dad's revelation was that I concluded that my hair loss was not *my* fault—"Sod it!"—and I could put a stop to worrying whether it was because I was eating too many dairy products, or too much chocolate or coffee, or too many glasses of wine, cigarettes, etc. I also decided to discontinue all treatments; nothing (permanent) had worked over the last two decades and there was still no known cure. I had a wonderful sense of liberation. I was about to become the Woman of Many Hats.

But … hold on! Not so fast! Mother thinks otherwise!

As a child, or even a young teenager, one needs and expects guidance from your mother on hair, clothes, and general appearance; even if you don't like it, it goes with the territory of growing up under the watchful and caring eye of the mother who "wants the best for you".

Into your twenties, thirties, and the subsequent decades, it becomes a bit more difficult, if not problematic. "Darling, I really don't think that colour suits you", or "Whatever you're wearing, it looks awful", or "Those shoes look like you've worn them through a muddy field", as I visit wearing my new, designer, light-grey and silver crushed-velvet trainers which have just cost me 120 quid! Or when I arrive sporting my top-spec, brand-new, varifocal, transition, tinted glasses, "Oh darling, those look like they've come out of a Christmas cracker."

And now we have the additional battle of the head gear.

I've tried, hard, to get on with wearing wigs. My friend Michele, a hair and makeup artist, gives me a variety to try, partly for fun, partly to see what colour and style suit me but mainly to see how I feel wearing one.

Rather than sweat in a natural-style but itchy wig, trying and hoping no one will spot the lifting edges around my temples or the riding-up at the nape of my neck, I consider having some fun by investing in some top-of-the-range but completely different styled wigs—an Annie Lennox look, perhaps Tina Turner, even a David Bowie cut. I really don't want to make a bad job of *pretending* to have hair; I've also overheard derogatory remarks by, amongst others, my mother (no less): "Oh look at her, she thinks no one knows she's wearing a wig."

So, I try wigs, but the bottom line is, even with the best quality, they itch like crazy, they are tight, hot, and sweaty. And I want to be me.

My acupuncturist informs me that her client, Tina Turner, is totally bald, having lost all her hair after her torrid time with Ike and although she wears a wig on stage and in public, she's relaxed at home—so much so that she answers the door for her acupuncture sessions in her natural bald state. That lifts my spirits hugely.

I stick to wearing hats from my ever-increasing collection. For family occasions, mainly to please my mother, and certainly on her birthday, I wear my natural-style wig, which also comes out for a few work-related bashes like the BRIT Awards, when I want to meld into the background, thinking none of my colleagues will recognise me. But they always do.

My freelance work continued to go well, and I was able to turn down clients and contracts I didn't fancy. Mainly producing events in the record and radio industries, at the same time keeping my sales hand in by flogging sponsorship and advertising space, I was busy. I always believed the secret to self-employment success was gaining high-profile annual contracts and keeping them, and the only way to do this was to give one hundred per cent. So, that's exactly what I did.

Mainly driven by the same old survival instinct and fear of no income, I kept nearly all my clients on through the twenty-five years of my freelance career. I was busy, but that didn't mean to say I couldn't find time during the weekdays to visit my health club for two or three games of tennis every week, as well as yoga classes more latterly.

As time passed, my parents showed interest in my work and, on the whole, were very supportive, Mum particularly so when I started producing an annual classical awards event. My first year's ceremony was quite a low-key affair but, over the course of a decade, grew in stature and became quite a big deal, jointly produced with the best boss I ever had, culminating in being broadcast by ITV. Presented by the late Jill Dando, live performances and appearances were from the likes of Roberto Alagna and Angela Gheorghiu, Kiri Te Kanawa, Andreas Scholl, Mstislav Rostropovich, Yo-Yo Ma, Simon Rattle, Bryn Terfel, Sir Paul McCartney, the London Symphony Orchestra, and—the one that topped them all, in my mother's book, as she was such a huge fan—Luciano Pavarotti.

Although I didn't manage to get Mum an introduction

to Pavarotti, I did get my parents invited to another client's annual event, the Classic BRIT Awards at the Royal Albert Hall. Suzanne and I sat in a box with Mum and Dad, happily scoffing and slurping on the corporate hospitality. They just loved it.

So I became officially known as a "career girl". Around the bridge tables of Haslemere my mother suddenly had a daughter to boast about, using my career to justify to her friends the reason her daughter hadn't married.

Twin Nieces (and Grandchildren) ... and Family Hols

Then something happened that altered the family dynamics significantly. My brother, a hard-up, but talented, artist, now aged thirty-five, decided to expand his artistic ambitions by going to Bali, to live and paint for a while. Within a year, he'd become a Hindu, married an Indonesian Brahmin, and, by the time he's unveiled this news in a letter to his extremely stunned parents, his wife is pregnant with twins. No doubt he presented my parents with a *fait accompli* because he knew that, had they been offered the chance, they'd have interfered in the most forcible of possible ways.

(The Indonesian narrative belongs to my brother; I only touch on it when and where it's relevant to my story and our shared family experience.)

In December 1993, Suzanne and I decided we'd extend

our holiday to the Philippines and Thailand and visit my brother Andrew in Bali to meet my baby twin nieces for the very first time. Natalie and Melanie were about ten months old and simply adorable. A blend of Balinese and English, they were beautiful. They moved—and danced—even at that stage, in an exotic, even though slightly stumbling way; their Balinese dance genes were already strongly present.

However, we quickly sensed all was far from harmonious between my brother and his wife, Dayu, so the six of us spent limited time together. Instead, my brother enjoyed taking us round his local areas of Bali and explaining its unique Hindu culture, showing us stunning waterfalls, picturesque villages, and jaw-dropping views of terraced paddy fields. Very much an artist's paradise.

Meanwhile, back at Leppard HQ, Mum and Dad were still reeling and, of course, fighting over whose fault it was that their son had carried out this act of complete stupidity and defiance, as they saw it.

"I will have nothing to do with half-caste grandchildren," screamed my angry mother, whilst Dad was very much more reasoned. Suzanne and I enjoyed the irony—Mum had a lesbian daughter who had not had any children and now her son had become a Hindu and delivered her "half-caste" grandchildren—a far cry from her dictatorial efforts to propel her children in what she regarded as being the "right" direction.

A very long story short: my brother returned to the UK with the twins a few months later—as a "single parent". After a sixteen-hour flight, my brother and my father (who'd flown out to Bali to help Andrew return home with the children) rounded the final corner from behind the frosted-glass customs area and into the arrival hall at Heathrow, where we were anxiously awaiting them. Andrew pushing the double buggy, Dad behind, pushing the luggage trolley, they both looked exhausted; the twins were clearly dazed and dishevelled.

I saw a strange expression on Mum's face that made me think of a wounded animal, eyes wide open with a fixed shocked gaze. We all exchanged welcome embraces, except my mother, who didn't touch the children or look at them again until we arrived home, when, quite suddenly, her practical motherly instincts kicked in and she couldn't help herself. Her jet-lagged son looked on as she took over with bathing the twins, putting them into night clothes with clean nappies, then feeding and putting them to bed.

A short time later, Suzanne, Andrew, Dad, and I, relaxing in the sitting-room downstairs, couldn't believe what we were hearing coming from the spare bedroom upstairs—Mum singing nursery rhymes to the baby twins! She stayed upstairs with them for ages.

If my mother had felt there was no room for a third woman in our relationship, she certainly found plenty of room for Natalie and Melanie in her life. She fell in love with them and took on a double role—that of both mother and grandmother—and she did so brilliantly, as did their equally supportive grandfather. My parents stepped up bigtime to help their son and their twin granddaughters. Love, money, advice, and guidance about manners and standards, rights and wrongs … indeed, all the way up to their further education and beyond, Nat and Mel benefitted from enormous input from their doting grandparents.

Finally, my parents had grandchildren, and in circumstances that allowed them to get involved to the max over many years; perhaps this went some way to make up for their eldest daughter not delivering in that department. Not that it was all plain sailing for them. It was, inevitably, hugely complicated. But it meant that Suzanne and I could, and did, step back. With the family spotlight now firmly on the well-being of the twins, we could travel guilt-free a bit more, especially at Christmas; Mum and Dad had their hands more than full with son and grandchildren—but that's not to say they didn't relish it.

My relationship with my parents improved over the years, particularly my relationship with Dad. The distraction of the grandchildren had a lot to do with it. My parents were totally in love with, and preoccupied by, Natalie and Melanie, which enabled Suzanne and me to further our lives with little interference.

There was only so much room at parental HQ for family gatherings, so it was a win–win situation. Summer holidays were different and happily from time to time Suzanne and I were able to join the small family ensemble. Mum and Dad continued to be drawn to the West Country, with renewed vigour now they had grandchildren to indulge, so they took to booking a cottage or house for a two-week period in the summer holidays. Nearly always Cornwall, usually with a stunning view of the sea, a four-bedroomed holiday home would be rented, and Suzanne and I would be invited to join them for a couple of nights.

This worked well for us: two or three nights' stay was considered the perfect length by all, *almost* short enough to ensure we would not be part of the usual holiday family blow-up—tensions could rise after an over-long day at the beach and over-tired twin girls; or Mum and Dad would have an everyday set-to; or even my brother, under the weight of repetitive parental instructions on how *not* to bring up his daughters—"only trying to give helpful advice"—might lose it.

My pride-and-joy car at that time (and over fourteen years) was a third-hand 1984 turquoise Mercedes 280 SL convertible; to drive down the lanes of the Cornish countryside, amongst the high, pretty, pink-flowered hedgerows, in the sunshine, with the roof down—this was seventh heaven. After our couple of nights' stay, we usually left following breakfast, sometimes lunch, to break the back of the five- or six-hour journey, to be home in London before the sun went down. As soon as we were back, the golden rule was to phone Mum and Dad to say we'd got home safely; this rule was always adhered to and went on for a lifetime as my mother claimed she was still traumatised by the memory of my car accident all those years ago.

On one occasion, having just arrived back in London, I phone to say we are home safe and sound. My father picks up the phone, sounding very tense, and reveals that Mum is in a black mood and she and Andrew have had a row. My brother had asked his new girlfriend to accompany him and his girls on the family holiday.

Mum and Dad had agreed and were happy to extend their invitation to Kate. Apparently, Kate had unwittingly overheard a conversation between my parents in the kitchen, my mother carelessly saying far-from-flattering things about her. Kate was reduced to tears; Andrew was furious and wanted an apology from Mum; my father was trying to calm things down and, by the increasing volume in the background, he isn't having much luck.

Dad pleads with me to speak to Mum to get her to simmer down and suggest she apologises to Kate. I try and fail: Mum hangs up on me. My brother and mother ramp up the row, both insisting the other one should leave the house immediately and, in an act of defiance, fuelled by a whisky or two, my brother goes into mother's room and throws all her clothes out of the window; then, with a vengeful touch of added rage (as a true student of my mother's behaviour over the years) rips up several packets of her cigarettes and throws those out, too.

I have my mother on the phone again. By now it is late and certainly after an inch or three more whiskies; she is incandescent with rage but crying at the same time, wanting my support and telling me she is waiting for a taxi to take her to the nearest hotel. I don't, I can't, stop her. It's upsetting all round; but how thankful Suzanne and I are not to be still there, in the thick of it.

My parents went beyond the call of grandparent duty and felt the need to compensate for my brother being a single parent. As my mother always said, "The twins need a woman in their lives in the absence of their mother."

Natalie and Melanie adored their granny and grandad, and my brother was grateful for his parents' love, attention, and, especially, being a struggling artist, the financial support.

The money side caused some tension between my brother and Mum and Dad, who felt that, as they were "paying", they got to call the shots when it came to making plans for their grandchildren, and that my brother, being broke, didn't have much wriggle room.

Three adults supervising two children didn't leave much space for aunts to get involved; given the potential for conflict and the regular tension, this was fine with us. I always imagined our input would be better suited when they were older. Perhaps some guidance in the area of "sex, drugs and rock 'n' roll", when they became teenagers!

In 2004, Suzanne and I bought a converted barn in the foothills of the Mediterranean French Pyrenees. We'd missed the opportunity to buy a weekend country retreat in England due to rocketing property prices, so took the plunge in France, which offered affordable prices and much more adventure. The barn was modernised (to a degree) and split into two gites; it wasn't exactly what we were looking for but, as it turned out, was extremely useful for friends, family, and rentals. Two sets of front doors, with their individual living and cooking spaces, it had many advantages both for visiting guests and for us.

A couple of years after we'd bought the place, my parents, and Andrew and the girls, came over for Christmas. True to form, it was to turn out to be another family Christmas nightmare.

Before coming to the barn, Mum and Dad wanted to treat the twins, now aged twelve, and their father, to a few days in Barcelona, a mere three-hour drive away, just the other side of the border. Suzanne and I spent several days preparing for their arrival, paying particular attention to putting up the festive decorations my father had insisted on, me stupidly having let slip we wouldn't be having a Christmas tree.

Beds made and aired (electric blanket for Mum), fridge stocked, tinsel and holly and fairy lights: all good to go and awaiting their arrival. The calls from Mum and Dad's hotel in Barcelona started on day two of their three-day visit. Apparently, the girls only wanted to "shop to drop" and weren't interested in galleries and the sights; so they split into two groups during the day, with an arrangement to all meet up in the hotel at 7.00pm for dinner together.

But the girls and Andrew didn't want to eat that early, more like the Spanish time, around 10.00pm, and so didn't show up at the agreed time. In addition, both Andrew and Mum had decided, at the same time but independently of each other, to give up smoking and, to go one stage further, my brother had decided to get himself a new holiday look—he'd shaved his head, on a number zero clipper setting. The latest call from Mum was to tell me she was so upset with everything that she felt like throwing herself off her balcony … but only after she'd finished her whisky.

The following day, they arrive. Mum is still in one piece—physically—but boy, are things tense!

On Christmas Eve, Natalie and Melanie have a row and, out of spite, flush each other's mobile phones down the loo.

On Christmas morning, the twins are asked at 10:00 to get up and dressed for presents and Buck's Fizz, before going out to a local restaurant for a special, reserved Christmas lunch. They respond in sullen tones, from under the duvet, that "we don't do Christmas". Suzanne is told off by my mother whilst eating a few nibbles with her champagne— "You shouldn't be snacking now when we're about to go out to lunch." And then we go to the restaurant …

We arrive in two cars, grumpy and silent, at the small village auberge, only ten minutes from our barn. A huge smiley welcome from our friends and proprietors, Brigitte and Houcine, is met with forced smiles and a simple "Bonjour" from my family. Our hosts have prepared, at our request (at the insistence of my mother), a delicious traditional English turkey roast with all the trimmings, a first for Brigitte and Houcine.

There's only one other table booked—a mixed group of twelve, mainly English, who bowl in shortly after we've sat down. Suzanne and I know them and, of course, being Christmas Day, being France, it's kisses all round! This was the last thing my parents wanted and the atmosphere on our table was getting progressively worse. Granny is as black as thunder; we remain silent, anxiously wondering how much worse Christmas lunch can get.

Amongst the twelve on the adjacent table, there are two girls, a four- and a six-year-old, who are being extremely irritating and noisy, their mother and father completely unaware, laughing loudly and relaxing with their friends. While the wine flows, the girls wander over to our table, partly to show off their latest shiny plastic Christmas toys and partly to have a closer look at the exotic-looking dual-heritage twins.

Thick green channels of mucous flowing from both nostrils of the two approaching, squealing, girls, my mother tells Natalie and Melanie not to let them come any nearer, they'll be full of germs. But nearer they come, and Granny, unable to contain herself, shrieks extremely loudly at her grandchildren, "I told you not to let those revolting children come anywhere near you."

It's one of those moments when you just want to be beamed up. The auberge goes silent and the mother of the two young "germ-carrying" children has overheard and is proceeding to weep. There's the sound of chairs being scraped back in the expectation of imminent action—mainly on the part of the woman's husband, but luckily someone sensibly manhandles him back into his seat suggesting that "as it's Christmas Day" it would be foolish to make "what's already a bad scene" much worse, especially "in front of the children".

I could have killed my mother there and then.

My father swiftly pays the bill. We exit in tense silence. Some days later, I visit the couple as I feel duty-bound to sincerely apologise for my mother's outrageous behaviour, putting it down to various unfortunate but non-specific family circumstances. I say that I'm truly sorry. I am still livid with my mother.

The next day it's time to take Natalie and Melanie for their very first ski. We set off in two cars for the hour-and-a-half drive to higher mountain altitudes, Dad with Andrew and the girls, Mum with Suzanne and me.

I'm already driving at a snail's pace to suit my mother, when she asks me yet again to slow down; the next time she screams as we turn a corner, I pull over and tell her to stop it or we'll turn round and go back, making it clear that whilst her nerves might be shattered, mine too are very close to the edge. That works; the journey lightens up, considerably.

My mother likes to talk (especially when she's on edge) and begins to tell us a couple of stories, both of which make me almost lose control behind the wheel.

It seems that an admiral, living near my parents, had been found dead in a hotel in Brighton—in a leather bondage outfit whilst having sex with a woman. Mum thinks it must be awful for the man's wife; she'd had to ask the newsagent in the village to remove the newspaper placard that sat on the pavement outside the shop, displaying a set of sensational headlines and, if that wasn't bad enough, apparently there was a joke doing the rounds for weeks after his cremation: "Can anyone smell burning rubber?"

And one more tale to entertain us en route: somewhat closer to home and almost unbelievable, should anyone other than my mother have been telling it—"I never lie, and I despise liars"—she starts off by reminding us that my father has had prostate problems over many years.

On hearing all the talk of Viagra, he'd gone to his doctor to ask for some pills just to see if his "thing" still worked—male pride, she assumed, as it was certainly not for sexual activity with my mother (or anyone else, or am I being too presumptuous?)—this was over two decades ago and since then they had slept in single beds.

Dad came home with the prescribed Viagra. That same night he took the pills whilst getting ready for bed and told my mother, who retorted, "What do you mean, you've taken *all* the pills?" Oh yes, he'd taken all of them! She shot out of bed, told him he was a "bloody imbecile", and, with that, she stripped off her sheets and blankets and rushed into the bathroom, locking the door behind her. She stayed there all night and slept in the bath.

By the time we get to the ski resort the mood in our car has changed from nerves-on-edge to near-giggling-hysteria. Suzanne and I had just about controlled ourselves as our wide eyes met in a glance of mind-boggled incredulity.

The girls are already togged up in hired ski boots and skis, Andrew too. Mum, Dad, Suzanne, and I watch the girls for a bit, have a walk, have a drink and something to eat … and then my mother wants to leave.

It's only early afternoon, but Mum starts fretting about icy roads and the fact that it'll be getting dark; she is adamant that it's time to leave and she wants us all to leave at the same time. Andrew and the twins are not ready to go and want at least another hour.

Although Dad thinks this will be perfectly acceptable, Mum overrides him. Andrew digs in. Mum is fuming and instructs me to get the car "NOW" and insists Dad come with us on the return journey, denying him the opportunity of staying with Andrew and the girls. The second car and its three passengers will get back safe and sound, and before dark, but a terrible evening ensues.

The following morning, they drive back to Barcelona

to catch their return flight home. We wave them off and the car disappears down the hill and round the corner. Suzanne and I collapse into each other, sharing a mixture of relief and joy, plus a few expletives of pent-up emotion. We return to the beautiful solitude of our upper gite, where we promptly open a bottle and start on the big clean-up.

My parents did revisit, but separately.

Mum came with her niece; they drank whisky and chatted away non-stop in the lower gite.

Dad came, nervously, on his own, maybe with a little father–daughter bonding in mind; perhaps he still really wanted to try to make things better. He had a weakness for chocolate puddings. He was suitably indulged.

My brother and the girls have not been back since.

Fifty Years On

February 2006 was my fiftieth birthday. I didn't want a party, so I decided instead to hire a riad in Marrakesh for a few nights and invite a small gang of friends. We sight-saw, we shopped (of course!), we ate, drank loads, and sampled the local "Moroccan". We had a blast.

On the evening of my actual birthday, whilst enjoying champagne and various cocktails, presents were produced, some more serious than others. One of my friends, Cherie— the only ex-Royal Naval School mate I'd kept in touch with over the years—gave me an outfit that she insisted I put on there and then. It consisted of her old RNS summer dress uniform, including a straw boater, plus another hat-cum-wig dreadlocks Rasta style, topped off with some round, black-framed bottle-end-like glasses. Hysteria ensued, we had almost peaked too early and before the special birthday dinner!

That year was also the RNS fiftieth reunion where all who'd been in my class thirty-six years ago were invited to congregate at the school. Cherie and I were full of reservations about attending, but curiosity couldn't keep us away. The most interesting discovery about meeting school-friends of so long ago was that they were all pretty much the same, by which I mean, they looked older, of course, but were instantly recognisable; many of the characters had remained largely unchanged even by the rigours and challenges of life over three and a half decades.

The "goody-two-shoes" and the "brainboxes" came across just as they had when they were fifteen, only now some of them were wearing pearls. During lunch in the main school dining-hall, it was pointed out to me that our old headmistress, Miss Otter (now a Mrs Somebody), was in attendance and lunching on a staff table at the front of the hall. I couldn't help it, I knew I had to go and say hello, despite my ex-school colleagues trying to talk me out of it.

I had a weird sense of déjà vu and familiar panic as I walked down the main thoroughfare separating rows of tables to the right and left, my footsteps echoing on the worn, wooden, slightly sticky floorboards. I had no idea what I was going to say, I was just fascinated to see how she had turned out.

"Hello Katharine." She recognised me straight away.

"Hello Miss Otter, I'm so sorry I don't know your married name."

"There's no reason you should. So, Katharine, how have you been doing. No doubt you're married and have children?"

"No, in fact, I haven't. I'm gay and I've lived with my partner Suzanne for twenty years. How about you?"

"Katharine, if you're trying to shock me it just won't wash", to which my prompt reply was, "I'm not, you asked me if I was married with children."

This was another crushing reminder of the age we still lived in and of the boarding school where I'd spent six years of my formative life. Nevertheless, we ended up having quite a civil chat. She asked about my parents and "Are they still together?" (revealing), to which I replied "Yes, but they'd be better off apart."

I talked a little about my work and "career"; she tried not to show any reaction as I relished making the point, with great satisfaction, that I was just about the only RNS fifty-year-old still working to earn a living, despite being the one with less than satisfactory school results. She loosened up a bit and volunteered how young and relatively inexperienced she'd been when she took the helm as headmistress of RNS.

By now, feeling quite relaxed myself, and certainly feeling like a fully-fledged adult, I asked her if she'd like "to join a few of us girls for a fag and glass of champagne behind the bike-shed, purely for old times?" She declined, but with a wry smile said she had to get back home to prepare her husband's dinner.

Much in life had changed over three and a half decades; some things had not: my old school was still only three miles from Mum and Dad's. I remember popping in to see them after the reunion with my head full of depressing "I'm half a century old" thoughts and it made me think, momentarily, about my parents' mortality.

Dad was a fit eighty, and no man of a similar age could chase down lobs on a tennis court like he could. (Not to say he didn't have the usual old-age aches and pains related mainly to his back and his problematic "waterworks".) Competitive to the last ball, he played tennis well into his eighties and golf up until his ninetieth birthday; mentally he was reasonably on the ball, if not quite as "on it" as he'd been. Armchair sport was also his thing (much to my mother's irritation): rugby, cricket, athletics, football, you name it.

Mum wasn't sporty and never had been, though bridge kept her mind sharp; but physically, from her sixties, her knees started to give her gyp and, despite being offered knee replacements several times over the years, she declined for fear of the operation going wrong, which meant her critically arthritic knees just kept deteriorating. The BBC's tennis coverage of Wimbledon was *her* armchair sport, greatly enhanced when they were able to attend Centre or Court One for a day; nearly every year my father would be successful in securing tickets via the ballot.

One February morning in 2014, whilst Mum was coming down the stairs, her knee "collapsed" and she fell head-over-heels down the last few steps, hitting her head badly and breaking her femur. My father phoned to tell me, saying she'd been taken to hospital, but she was going to be okay, just in need of an operation, more of which he'd know the following day. There was nothing I could do but wait and worry ... but something else was niggling me.

Strangely, and only the day before my mother's fall, I'd removed the gold bracelet she'd given me after my car accident forty-two years previously and to this day I can't remember why I'd taken it off, which is strange as I've clearly remembered so much else, albeit with the aid of diaries, documents, and photos. It was small and tight fitting and I'd never taken it off, thinking of it as a special gift from my mother—her acknowledgement that she'd almost lost me after the car crash. I now felt sort of guilty (and slightly superstitious) that her fall and the removal of my bracelet had coincided, so—with difficulty—I squeezed the bracelet back on over my knuckles.

Unsurprisingly, my mother was a nightmare in hospital (this was to be the first of many in-patient stays, courtesy of the NHS). To be fair, it had been quite a bad break, and a screw fixation was required, followed by recovery and extensive physiotherapy.

I drove down from London to visit nearly every day, first to Guildford Hospital; then, after a week, she was moved to Haslemere's tiny community hospital for a further two weeks, where they offered fantastic rehabilitation support, particularly for the older members of the community.

"I shouldn't be here. I should be in a private room in a private hospital." She glared around the ward, paying particular attention to any ethnic nursing, catering, or cleaning staff, enquiring "Where are you from?" On the ward, I gather my mother earned the title of "Lady Leppard". Whilst most people would have been mildly put out by this branding, my mother relished it!

My parents had paid for private health insurance most of their lives but now, retired and paying thousands a year (£8,000 at the last count, with many exclusions to the cover being added every year), they decided, given Dad's very average pension income and no savings, that it was bad value; they would rather be more comfortably off and able to afford to fund their grandchildren's further education. So, the grandchildren benefitted from the money that would have paid for private care, and my mum had to benefit from the care of the NHS.

My mother was incredibly rude to many of the staff. I'd cringe (and still do) and ask her to stop it. She claimed that no one was listening to her needs and made my father smuggle in sleeping pills from home to top up what she was being given in hospital.

Following most operations to repair breakages, the rule of thumb is to get the patient moving as soon as possible, usually, of course, through gritted teeth and aided with painkillers. My mother wasn't prepared to grit her teeth … and most days she refused to do her exercises.

I was there one day when the physiotherapist asked her to get out of bed and, gently, make her way down the ward on her walker to the kitchen where they'd like to see if she could manage to make herself a cup of tea. "No thanks, I don't want a cup of tea," she retorted, "my hip hurts too much." "But Betty, that's not the point, we need to prepare you for going home and want to see that you can do basic tasks." "No thanks, I don't want to do it."

On another occasion, a nurse arrived with a lunch-tray and asked her to put on her dressing-gown so that she could sit in the chair at the end of her bed to eat. Mum refused, saying she was more comfortable staying in bed. The ward sister was fetched and made the same request, explaining at length that it was all about getting the blood moving to prevent bedsores and stiffening joints, particularly her repaired hip.

But still she refused. Sister had a clipboard with her, presumably with all the medical notes: "You are being non-compliant Betty, and I will have to make a note of this on your records." Mum replied that that was fine by her and proceeded to eat her lunch in bed.

Meanwhile, back at Little Holt, my father had instructions to get a chair stairlift fitted without delay. Dad was rather flummoxed; not only having to find a specialist company (no computers or internet in their household) but having to choose and pay for such a thing was a huge outlay for him. On top of that he was having to shop and try to feed himself, walk Leo the dachshund, and visit his wife every day in hospital, delivering her yet more items on her "must have" list.

I helped liaise with the occupational therapists who, in turn, supervised the fitting of raised lavatory seats, grab rails, provision of walking sticks and walking frame with wheels, all to be ready for her return to home.

There's no doubt that this fall took it out of both of my

parents both mentally and physically. Mum took ages to recover—not that she ever fully did. She suffered severe pain for months; I felt sympathetic and made allowances for what was, no doubt, a "pain-induced" bad temper. I knew she wasn't a hypochondriac.

My father suffered permanently from exhaustion and from being hen-pecked; for many weeks he climbed up and down the stairs, squeezing past the parked-up stairlift, waiting on his largely bedridden wife who would impatiently and imperiously shake her bedside handbell for immediate attention.

The tiredness and the additional strain were probably what helped to start Dad on a series of his own falls; either he stood up too quickly after bending over in the garden, or he tripped whilst walking in the woods with Leo, invariably cutting his arm or leg (and as we all know, with age, the skin thins and takes an age to heal, if it doesn't go septic first).

Dad started having regular visits from the community matron to change various dressings—he was always in the wars and his wounds didn't want to heal. Eventually Mum started getting up and spending more time convalescing downstairs but was forever on a short fuse, particularly irritated by the visits from the community nurse who was coming in to tend to Dad. She resented him getting the attention. She considered herself to be the recovering patient.

Suzanne and I continued our visits to France, though we no longer went over the Christmas period now that Mum and

Dad were that much older (and the grandchildren, now young adults, had other Christmas plans). It was important to spend a little time with them and, indeed, in later years they came to stay with Suzanne and me in London.

On one occasion during one their stays, Dad came down late to breakfast. This wasn't unusual, but he was wearing a homemade cardboard sign, hung round his neck with string. Suzanne and I looked on in disbelief. Mum was in the sitting-room. On the sign, in Dad's spidery writing, was the message, "I must not speak unless spoken to". We were horrified. I told him to stop being stupid and asked him to take it off. He was clearly looking for sympathy and attention but after our immediate reaction and my demanding he take it off, no further mention was made of it.

We tended to go to France for one week at Easter and another week in October and tried to spend every July there. The year Mum was still recovering from her broken femur, I was worried about her ongoing level of pain and mental stability, so phoned her GP from France. He was happy to engage at some length with me (reading between his lines was slightly revealing, but only in hindsight) though due to patient confidentiality there was not too much he could really say. What he did say has stayed with me: "It's in your mother's personality." And: "You're obviously a daughter who cares a lot."

August 2014, two weeks after our return from France, and it's about to be the Leppard Family Event of the Century (we have never had an extended family gathering before, largely because neither my brother nor I have "married").

But my father's ninetieth birthday, my mother's eighty-fifth, and their sixtieth wedding anniversary are all occurring in the space of two weeks in August.

I want to organise a family celebration to commemorate this triple whammy and run it past a very tentative Mum and Dad; my brother is a little more enthusiastic. Mum's niece Gillian and her husband own a small three-star family-run hotel in Burnham Beeches, Buckinghamshire, with my cousin Simon front of house and doubling as the hotel's extremely proficient cook; with the help of their daughter Vicki, the family manage the hotel, and they generously offer to put us all up for two nights and host a sit-down silver-service dinner.

For our family—not the biggest, not the happiest—this is a major deal. My uncle (my father's slightly younger brother, at eighty-eight) and aunt are invited, along with Natalie and Melanie and their respective current boyfriends. My brother, with his partner Kate, plus our hosts, will make up a party of fourteen.

Mum and Dad are nervous as the day approaches, insisting they don't want a fuss. I keep reassuring them it'll be a relaxed, informal, and jolly affair; the hotel will be closed to other guests and the staff have been given the weekend off. We arrive armed with champagne, wine, birthday cake, presents; I remind my brother and nieces that we need to pull our weight and help at all stages with food preparation, table waiting, clearing, and washing-up.

It's a huge success! Everyone rises to the occasion. No one displays ill-temper (although I must admit to getting a little hot under the collar with not as much kitchen support as I'd hoped). Champagne flows, as does the wine, with a superb dinner followed by a speech from Dad. He loves making speeches and is incredibly good at it. He's extremely funny and touching, talking for at least twenty minutes without notes, going round the table, finding compliments for each of us in turn, down to Natalie and Melanie's boyfriends—he compliments them on their good looks and their even better taste in girls!

(This is, thank goodness, a far cry from my father's after-dinner officers' mess speeches: "My wife and I always hold hands; if I let go, she goes shopping"; "The last fight we had was my fault—my wife asked me "What's on the TV?" … I said dust." Even more cringe-worthy: "She has an electric blender, electric toaster, and electric bread maker. Then she says, 'There are too many gadgets and no place to sit down', so I bought her an electric chair.")

Now aged ninety, and able to have responded a bit to the changed times, my father is very much more able "to go with the flow", adapting to his unconventional family. My mother is asked to say a few words. She laughs and declares she's useless at speaking—the best she can offer is "My husband and I …" and then she just giggles.

She does, however, thank my father for the diamond broach he's given her. She's clearly genuinely surprised and delighted with it. She declares that she thoroughly deserves it as a "medal" in recognition of having put up with him for so many years.

Without the generosity of my cousins and my mother's niece, we couldn't possibly have had such a very special event. They are suitably thanked and saluted by us all.

A few weeks later, Dad writes me a very touching thank-you letter; I'm slightly choked by the realisation of how far we've come together in our troubled relationship. He adds, towards the end: "It is a long time since I saw Mum so pleased and delighted with the way the party went. You must also take the credit for its favourable effect on her obvious improvement to normal health", though he amended that to read "*towards* normal health", signing off, "Fondest love and sincere thanks, Dad."

It becomes obvious that Dad can't cope with trawling Tesco's aisles. I offer to do the shopping for them online. They both put up a fight when I first suggest it—Mum saying, "He doesn't do anything else so for God's sake make him do the bloody shopping"; Dad being too proud to accept my offer and fearing he's going to lose his only chance of getting out and going into town.

Eventually he sees sense and agrees to supermarket deliveries, while I order the things that Tesco can't supply, such as Imperial Leather talc and antique furniture polish—via the love-to-hate Amazon. Mum still plays bridge once a week, occasionally twice, but complains she isn't comfortable sitting at the bridge table for such long periods of time and, it seems, her card-playing friends are not the enjoyable company they used to be.

Like my parents, their friends are gradually deteriorating physically and mentally, if not on the way out altogether, or dead. Similarly with my father's golf—he still loves playing, but eighteen holes become nine and his golf-buddies are diminishing, both in their abilities to play and in their numbers.

For my sixtieth birthday, again not wanting a party, I book the local Indian restaurant for a Sunday lunch party for twenty-eight friends. Four days later, after a visit to Mum and Dad, Suzanne and I fly off for a three-week stay with friends in Australia, with a stop-off en route to an island in Malaysia for a chilled week and, on the return leg, two nights in a five-star Singapore hotel. With the wonders of Wi-Fi and technology I continue to place my parent's online Tesco order from the other side of the world.

Singapore revisited again, and wow, has it changed. The only exception is the smell and the humidity, exactly as I remember. Although I'd been back before, I hadn't ventured out of the city, but this time Suzanne and I go by MRT (mass rapid transport), which certainly didn't exist when we lived there in the '70s), disembarking at Sembawang station, now full of high-rise apartment blocks, the street-market stalls having long gone.

We pick up a taxi, with a very grumpy driver, who finally manages to find 124 King's Avenue: still well and truly standing, in its grand colonial style. I take several pictures and stand for a while, allowing myself to be transported back in time.

A few days after our return, we go to visit Mum and Dad who were keen to hear all about our holiday, especially our time in Malaysia and Singapore. Telling them our stories and experiences rekindles theirs of fifty years ago, possibly fanning some of the embers that still lie between them.

Dad's Last Days

My father's more serious decline really only became apparent a year before his death. He lost the sight in one eye due to a fall in the garden (the cause of a mini stroke, possibly, the doctor thought) and was then prescribed steroids, which didn't agree with him. He got frailer, thinner, and more and more tired, frequently falling asleep in his chair or the sofa.

He started to get pretty fed up; he'd been used to a relatively healthy and physically active life. He couldn't read *The Telegraph* anymore and having to relinquish his driving licence hit him hard. On top of that, my mother was convinced he was "losing it", insisting he have a memory test; he agreed under duress, and, in turn, he tried to insist my mother had one at the same time.

He passed his test with flying colours but when it came to my mother's turn, she refused to take part. The visiting community matron suggested gently that it was perhaps my mother who needed some medication (due to her "nerves being on edge"), not my father for his memory.

En route back to London after visiting a friend on the south coast, Suzanne and I dropped in to see my parents for tea. Dad was just returning from his last-ever lunch at the golf club, having resigned his membership of twenty-five years. One of his golfing friends of a mere ninety-six had driven them both to and from the golf course in a very old, very dented, red Ford Fiesta.

Dad could hardly get out of the car but declined any

help, staggering into the house without thanking or saying goodbye to his old friend, another retired naval captain who, watching my horrified expression, assured me my father had not had more than one glass of wine. He agreed that my father, normally the perfect gentleman, was not himself. By the time I got into the sitting-room, Dad was sparked-out in his TV chair, with Mum muttering "typical". It was far from typical.

He developed serious "shakes", which meant he couldn't shave (an absolute must for him) and with his general overall frailty it became extremely difficult for him to wash and dress himself. It was out of the question that any help in this department would be forthcoming from my mother, so I proposed paying for a carer to come in for an hour every day, first thing.

Whilst Dad was a proud man, he was also quite vain and it was important for him to look and feel "spruced-up" after washing and dressing, so *he* thought this was a good, a valid, idea. My mother did not … "Of course he doesn't need any help, he's laying it on with a trowel … He's lazy and likes any excuse to stay upstairs half the morning."

There were further arguments, but it was one of the first and only times I supported my father against my mother: a carer, for an hour a day, was organised. But the rows about the visiting carer didn't stop as it became apparent, once again, that Mum didn't like Dad getting attention.

That summer, of 2016, whilst Suzanne and I were in France, my niece Natalie graduated from a three-year degree course at dance school, funded by her grandparents. Proud grandparents, indeed; there was nothing that was going to keep them away from the graduation ceremony. Dad was too frail by this time to even use his sticks, so my brother hired a wheelchair for the occasion; Dad having caught a bad cold really felt an invalid, so gave up his resistance to using a wheelchair, and attended the graduation ceremony.

Shortly after this, my father got a chest infection and couldn't get out of bed. It took my mother a while to realise he wasn't right as she had insisted Dad sleep in the guest bedroom—she didn't want him disturbing her when he came to bed, usually late, after watching sport on TV.

A doctor was called, who promptly made a home visit, and though he recognised Dad was far from well left him with antibiotics and paracetamol, and instructions to drink plenty of fluids. None of us knew this at the time, but the duty doctor had made it plain to my father that he urgently required hospitalisation. My father had declined and said he wanted to stay put.

A month later, at my mother's request, I will phone the practice and ask to speak to the practice manager, to find out why the duty doctor hadn't insisted an ambulance be called and my father taken to hospital. My mother is convinced that the duty doctor, on that fateful day, was ultimately responsible for Dad's death. Perhaps in her grief she is searching for someone to blame.

I make the call but don't articulate my mother's thoughts; but the doctor talks to me and explains. He tells me that at that time my father had been desperately ill but was of "sound mind" and aware of the likely outcome of him staying at home, but insistent; it was the doctor's duty of care to respect my father's wishes.

From as far back as when Dad was in his late seventies (he invariably joked about not making it to his next birthday) he had always been clear about wanting to die in his home, not in hospital. My mother on the other hand, really hadn't wanted him to die at home—"I have to go on living here, afterwards," she said, and, as usual, on one level, she had a point.

Later that afternoon, the community matron had just happened to be passing and popped in to find my father hardly breathing and called an ambulance. The medics arrived and he had stopped breathing but was resuscitated and rushed to the Royal Surrey County Hospital.

I was in France, where my brother called me with regular updates during the first two days. At first, the reports were encouraging, and the general message was not to rush back. An even more definite directive from my mother: "He'll be absolutely fine, there is no need for you to come back whatsoever."

Yet after receiving the news about my father's hospitalisation, our holiday time in France became rather less enjoyable and, given his age of ninety-one, it seemed prudent to pack up and get back to Blighty ASAP.

Dad died a week later of "the old man's friend", pneumonia, but, sadly, after a week of terrible suffering—not that he wasn't looked after exceptionally well in hospital; he couldn't eat or drink and wafted in and out of consciousness whilst doctors prodded and poked tubes down his throat in an effort to remove excess fluid from his lungs.

The only positive that I could take from his week-long misery in hospital, where he clearly did not want to be, was that it gave us just enough time to drive back from France to say our goodbyes, as indeed it did for the rest of the family to visit and spend some time with him.

My brother had the call from the hospital during the middle of the night and had tried to reach me (I was staying overnight with Mum, but I didn't hear the phone ringing) and when I did speak to him early the next morning, he was angry and simply said, "It's over, Dad's gone" and hung up.

Having waited twenty minutes to collect myself, I went into Mum's bedroom to tell her the news. She looked at me like a rabbit caught in headlights and said absolutely nothing, pulling her bed clothes up and tucking them under her chin. I sat on her bed for what seemed like forever, neither of us saying anything. I offered to make her a cup of tea (well, that's what you do, I believe—another reason I hate tea) and she didn't answer. I just sat there, silent, in tears. I suggested to Mum, for the very first time in my life, that we should have a hug. She declined.

I can't remember the exact order of all the death duties, but I know there were loads. This experience was a first for me. Shock and grief put you on some sort of autopilot and you work through a checklist: notifying immediate family, friends, the bank, obtaining cause of death documentation from the hospital, visiting the registry office for the death certificate.

And all that before commencing the funeral arrangements while looking after the well-being of my mother whose rabbit-caught-in-the-headlights-look lasted the best part of a year (though that's not to say she still wasn't able to demand exactly what she did and didn't want at any given time).

A few days before the funeral, *The Telegraph* published a half-page obituary with photos: "Naval pilot who invented the 'Twinkle Roll' and helped Rod Stewart to chart success with *Sailing*" and the online version was headed "Daredevil Pilot" (which, for some reason, Mum was not happy about). On reading the lengthy piece, I discovered many of my father's achievements for the first time. It made me feel guilty and sad, as well as incredibly proud.

Since the age of eight I had been indoctrinated into believing that my father was a bad man; it wasn't until my older, slightly wiser years—say my mid-fifties—that I came to my own, and different, conclusion. My father had indeed "fucked up" in a major way, but five decades later he was still paying a ridiculously high and unfair price.

For all sorts of reasons, death brings to the fore all the best characteristics of the deceased—and so it should—but, perhaps born out of guilt on hearing repeatedly what a nice person he was, I felt I should have been kinder and questioned longer and harder about where the balance of truth lay.

He'd been unfaithful to his wife, which in turn caused a lifetime of family unhappiness. His job always came first. He was lazy at home (no doubt partly due to the traditional husband–wife roles of the time). He was ill-tempered much of the time (probably mainly due to being relentlessly hen-pecked), saving his "perfect gentleman" manners for anyone outside the family unit.

But he'd tried to make amends and show overall concern and care for his children's welfare and mental well-being, more so than his wife who was *still*, fifty years on, emotionally overwrought about his betrayal. He was my father.

In September 1959, Leppard stunned the crowds at Farnborough Air Show with a spectacular display of aerial formation aerobatics.

I'd had no idea—nor that in the same year, and on the day of my third birthday, he'd had a near brush with death when his Scimitar suffered an engine failure.

He invented an original manoeuvre in which four aircraft passed overhead in a box formation while each in sequence made a rapid individual roll. He called the manoeuvre the "Twinkle Roll" and it is now familiar at most air displays.

Perhaps not so difficult to see why some of these exercises earned him the title "Daredevil Pilot". The obituary revealed he was "court-martialled for performing dangerous low-level aerobatics" but got off lightly with an official reprimand as the president of the court was a pilot himself and sympathetic.

In 1944 Dad took part in operations off Norway against German targets including a U-boat base, which involved flying for miles at a mere fifty feet in complete radio silence before climbing to 9,000 feet to take the enemy by surprise;

no doubt his specialist fighter pilot training in "dogfights and divebombs" stood him in good stead. He survived many sorties, whilst several of his friends and colleagues did not.

My father shared his twenty-first birthday celebrations with those of VJ Day in Singapore, August 1945. After the war he was deployed to an aircraft carrier which remained in the Indian Ocean and the Far East for several more years; he clearly had a ball on the ocean waves and declared, "Life was good, sport, visits, parties and flying which was what we all loved."

My mother was thrilled with *The Telegraph* obituary and even more so that she was mentioned:

In 1954, while at Culdrose (Naval air base in Cornwall), Leppard wooed and won his wife, Betty 'Rachel' Smith, who was then aged 22, the youngest Chief Petty Officer WRNS. When his squadron moved to Scotland, he would borrow an aircraft to fly down to meet her, and twice she returned to Lossiemouth with him in a twin-seat Vampire jet.

The funeral was a fitting send-off and the village church was full to the rafters: naval and brewing colleagues, family and friends, including many locals who offered their condolences as they filed out of the church. "He was a true gentleman." Dad's oldest friend, a retired admiral in his ninety-fifth year and his wife had travelled up from the West Country to deliver a long, detailed, and well-deserved eulogy.

A white ensign shrouded the coffin, topped with Dad's sword and hat, the flag having been sent by the Fleet Air Arm Officers' Association. They'd also suggested sending a bugler, but we politely declined, deciding it would be unnecessarily ostentatious. I like to feel that Dad would have been more than pleased with his send-off. I hope we got the balance about right.

Andrew and the twins and Mum and I sat in the front pew. My brother delivered a touching speech, citing what incredible support he'd received for his children and what a wonderful father he had been to himself and his sister, and a loving husband to his wife.

Mum still had the same startled look on her face and had shown no outward emotion and, even now, still no tears. With her bad knees, she struggled to stand for the hymns (kneeling for prayer was not an option) so I tried to help her get to her feet by holding her arm to steady her, but she just glared at me and shook me off. It felt so very cold, and I was hurt.

Sandwiches, beer, and wine were served at the local pub after the service and an hour later the immediate family reluctantly departed to accompany Dad in the hearse for his final journey, to Chichester crematorium. Thank God I'd managed to knock back several glasses of wine.

Life for my mother was about to change significantly. It was going to change for me too. Little had I bargained for what was coming.

Captain Keith André Leppard CBE

29th July 1924 – 28th July 2016

8

Falls ... and Decline

During the sixty years of their marriage my parents had each played the very traditional roles of their generation. My father had been in charge of the money, both income and outgoings, and my mother received a monthly "housekeeping" allowance for food shopping. My father had left my mother surprisingly financially "comfortable", with two pensions in addition to her entitlement of a state widow's pension—surprising as Mum always complained how useless Dad was with money. He even left a small life assurance policy to cover his funeral expenses.

However, what he thought he'd set up—but in fact hadn't—was a joint bank account, something they'd never had before but was to commence immediately on his death to make household finances easier for mother. Despite the new and untouched NatWest cheque book in the desk drawer bearing both their names, Dad hadn't completed the official paperwork with joint signatures.

My first task was to phone all the utility and insurance companies, the local council, and various suppliers and cancel Dad's accounts and set up standing orders or direct debits in Mum's name. That was quite challenging given I had to provide proof of my father's death and details of my mother's existence. Then I had to explain to my mother how it all worked, which was easier said than done: she claimed she had a "better way", without having a clue as to what was involved. At the same time, of course, she was still coping with the shock and reality of losing her husband.

Whatever the five or the seven stages of grief might be, my mother displayed her shock and denial with the continued, wide-eyed, rabbit-caught-in-the-headlights-look and showed no external emotional grief whatsoever. She was so very cold. That was when she wasn't very angry. Was this stage two of the grieving process? Or was it her usual anger and trademark bad temper now intensified by the fact that my father was no longer available to absorb the weight of her blows? Either way, several stages of her grief seemed to be coming in my direction, all at once, well-stirred into a potent cocktail with my name on it, swizzle-stick and all.

To support my mother in those early stages, I visited weekly, sometimes staying over. I phoned daily, offering to take care of anything she didn't feel up to, such as shopping, bills, house admin, Dad's death duties. We visited the family solicitor to get advice and on hearing the firm's bill would be in the region of £3,000 to £5,000 to carry out probate, my mother was adamant she was not going to pay "that sort of ridiculous money". So she asked me to do it.

There was no question that my brother might be asked as it wasn't a "suitable role for an artist". I wasn't keen and felt daunted at the prospect of the research and the form-filling involved, with much of my time already being taken up with my mother's new administrative needs on top of my own, and, indeed, my freelance work. I felt my mother didn't value my time, or perhaps it was she had little or no understanding of what was involved. I was slightly irritated (no, *very* irritated) at having to do it, but, of course, I didn't say so—I was still trying to play out that elusive role of "dutiful daughter". And so, on I ploughed, and Suzanne helped me where she could.

My mother showed few outward signs of grief, other than framing my father's *Telegraph* obituary and then, shortly afterwards, creating "The Shrine", as I liked to call it. My parents' house had a rather lovely double-aspect L-shaped sitting-room with the dining-room housed in the vertical bit of the "L", boasting a rather fine, highly polished, antique dark-oak dinner table. Four Edwardian chairs upholstered in two-toned striped gold velvet were positioned around the table with two more parked on the side, all towered over by yet another of my mother's purchases from the auction rooms, a baby grand chandelier.

The messages and cards of condolence were displayed on the table along with the flowers, until they died and were replenished with fresh ones from the garden. The condolences, after six months, were replaced with photographs of my father, both A4 and A5 in size and anything in between, all framed in silver—though, admittedly, silver plate. At first, I understood, or thought I did.

But as time went by, The Shrine grew and grew. As my

The Shrine

mother had never said anything positive about my father when he was alive, I was now somewhat dumbfounded.

One evening, during a stayover, only a couple of months after Dad's death, Mum and I, having eaten supper, were chatting about nothing in particular, with the television on in the background. She turned to me and asked if I'd like to read a letter to her from Dad written a few years previously. I said I wasn't overkeen—presumably it was written as a private letter. Mum insisted I read it, grabbing it from the bookshelf by the side of her chair where she'd secreted it, shoving it in my face.

Dated 31st July 2012, almost four years before the exact date of my father's death and the day of their 62nd wedding anniversary, he wrote:

Rachel,
As each year passes, the enormity of the devastating and unending pain to your life which I caused, becomes deeper and more hurtful.

My greatest wish as time slips away, is that I could turn back the clock to our happy Cornwall courtship and early years together.

Looking back, I cannot understand how I behaved as I did, and am more ashamed than you can possibly believe.

I am truly, truly sorry.
Keith

Welling up on reading it, I ask Mum why she's shown it to me. She replies that she wants me to know that he was still guilty. I ask her why, even after fifty years, she couldn't forgive him. "I don't know why but I just couldn't," and, unprompted, adds "and I don't feel any guilt for not forgiving him." Emotionally choked and unable to continue the conversation, tear ducts struggling to contain the flow, I leave the room and start on the washing up, in the knowledge that my father, the constant "washer-upper" had never stopped looking for forgiveness. He'd never found it.

Life continued, settling into some semblance of a new normal. Mum came to stay with us in London for her first Christmas without Dad and her grandchildren popped in for Boxing Day lunch. Mum's knees continued to deteriorate; various Royal Surrey Hospital visits were made to see the specialist for pain-relief injections in her knees and I would accompany her for most appointments. Mum began to get her head round house admin but couldn't cope when anything went wrong. Her anger would kick straight in.

The first thing was the house alarm. When the service company came out to fix it, she accused the engineer of deliberately manipulating the control panel so he could then "charge even more" to repair it. Then the stairlift broke down, the battery having failed (due to being in the incorrect "park" position, hence draining the battery); Mum wasn't going to pay the call-out charge, insisting they had paid thousands only two years previously and it was totally "unacceptable".

She was extremely angry and rude to the companies concerned. Each time, I tried to calm her down and make her see reason, pointing out there was a less antagonistic way to go about complaining; that annoyed her even more. "Don't you dare tell me what to do in my own house Katharine, and who I should pay and who I should not."

Then the central heating packed up and she called me on a Friday evening asking me what to do, saying she was cold … and frightened as the alarm system didn't work … and how was she expected to get up to bed with a broken stairlift, "On my hands and knees?"

Although it takes the best part of a year, Andrew and I collaborate regarding Dad's headstone for the garden of remembrance, with Mum casting the final vote. Black granite with gold engraving and a simple "In loving memory" message—the headstone will finally be laid where Dad's ashes have already been buried. Andrew has a friend in Dorset who can do the engraving at "a fraction of the price" quoted by the stone masons of Surrey or West Sussex.

Andrew and I seldom visit Mum at the same time, given our cool relationship; it also seems better to spread out our trips rather than doubling up. Initially, we visit Dad once a month, always taking flowers from the garden. "Your father would prefer that; he wouldn't want them bought from a shop." Standing in front of Dad's headstone, I hide my tears behind my darkened lenses. Mum has no tears to hide.

My brother recounts what could be described as a near-death experience for Mum on one occasion when he takes her to visit Dad's grave. It starts off sounding quite serious, but then turns into quite an amusing tale. On the day of the visit, Mum's knees are particularly bad, and Andrew has to support and steady her down the lengthy path to Dad's site at the far end of the church graveyard.

Having put the flowers in the vase by the headstone, they're chatting away. Natalie and Melanie are there too, and Mum wanders off, looking, she says, for friends buried there. There's a sudden scream and Andrew turns to see Mum tottering forward down a slight slope, trying, in tiny steps, to stop herself lurching forward, but failing and gathering pace. At least twenty or thirty feet away, Andrew watches in horror, aware that he's too far away to stop the imminent fall.

She stumbles and slows her downward trajectory by grabbing a large upright gravestone with both hands, which prevents her hitting her head and takes her, in reasonably sedate fashion, to her knees on a patch of unmown grass beside a newly covered grave. On catching her breath and loosening her tight grip on the tombstone, she lets out a squeal of delight: "Oh, it's my friend Muriel's! I can't believe it. Muriel, you've saved my life!"

Despite her complaints about being too tired, initially my mother continues to play bridge once a week (although no longer with Muriel!) which means that as well as helping keep her brain reasonably tuned, she also has the company of three friends, all of whom are now widows and live on their own, though one of them does have a live-in carer.

They take it in turns to host the afternoon rubbers, served with cakes and sandwiches and a pot of tea. Life experiences are shared, as well as gossip and tips about life as a widow, not to mention sharing details of their latest medication for various age-related ailments. Of which my mother has several, and plenty of meds: high blood pressure pills, pain relief for her knees, stomach pills for her hiatus hernia, thyroxine for her under-active thyroid, sleeping pills for an overactive brain.

What are never discussed, of course, are the anti-depressants, or the Bell's whisky, or her Silk Cut—she would certainly never smoke in front of her friends. Nor does she admit to the fact that she self-administers the quantities and times of her prescribed drugs, depending on her mood and what she's gleaned from around the card table. My father had been telling me about this for years: "Your mother always thinks she knows best especially if her bridge friends agree—and, with her, they always do. She'll do what she wants."

Her same friends also tipped her off to watch the daytime TV programme, *Rip Off Britain*, hosted by the all-woman team of TV presenters and ex-newsreaders, Gloria, Julia, and Angela.

So, one day, out of the blue one day, Mum phones to tell me she's cancelled all the direct debits I'd set up for her household bills, saying she'd watched *Rip Off Britain*, and they advised that direct debits payments needed to be kept an eye on. In her eyes, that translated into all direct debits being complete "rip offs", obviously!

My heart sinks. I know what this will mean ... My mother, understanding very little in these matters (she'd never had to do any of it before), wanted to be in control. She would decide who, when, and how much she would pay for services. No amount of explaining cuts through her dogmatic, angry, ill-informed reasoning. My mother will be in charge … and the more she gets a taste for her new-found power, the more she exercises it, mercilessly.

My attempts to be helpful are met with increasing hostility. It takes a while for the truth to dawn on me—I have slipped into the position of the punchbag, the role my father has so recently vacated.

My mother then decides to fire the gardener, who has been working for them for some twelve years, three hours every week. Mid-sixties and recently retired, he lives in the village and is loyal, reliable, and hard-working, often helping Dad with DIY around the house and now, more recently, doing a few household chores for Mum in addition to running errands.

However, she's never liked the fact that he isn't a "proper" gardener, complaining that he doesn't follow instructions. So, she tells me over the phone one evening, having paid him for his most recent three hours' labour, she has simply told him not to come back. I exclaim in frustration that she should have given him a few weeks' notice after his long service or at least some money in lieu. "Absolutely not," is the response. "I see no reason to give him anything."

The following evening, the now ex-gardener phones me, extremely upset; he doesn't understand why he's been treated in this way. I apologise profusely and agree that my father would be "turning in his grave". I insist on sending him a cheque, a small token of recompense, as my father would have wanted—but this is strictly on the basis that my mother must never know.

So begins the list "KL's outlay on behalf of Mum". As it grows longer, I agree with my brother that I should keep all the receipts so that one day I can claim my outlay back from Mum's estate.

When her central heating boiler breaks down again and she calls her "very nice up until now" boiler man and he won't show up, she calls me, furious and freezing cold. When I call him to plead that he go, I find the problem is that my mother has withheld part payment of his last invoice and only given him a cheque for £100. That, apparently, was the amount she deemed "appropriate to pay", leaving him chasing a shortfall of £120, which she chose to completely ignore. I immediately instigate a bank transfer to him from my account and, again, ask that it's not mentioned to my mother.

My mother's controlling personality now notches itself up a gear. I want to help, I feel obliged to help, but the more I do, the more I get kicked back. The house alarm company will no longer deal with her; she's been rude and withheld money. Mum investigates other alarm companies and asks me to help. After three different onsite visits, she chooses a company with a very personable manager—male, of course—who just knows how to turn on the charm and who draws up extensive plans for a new system and presents a quote. Well, the decision-making process goes on quite a long time.

"What do you think, Katharine?"

"I've told you Mum several times, go with the guy you liked; his quote seems fair, and the online reviews are good and they're a local company."

"Oh, I don't know. Perhaps I'll try and knock him down on the price."

Eventually, she accepts the quote but refuses to pay the 30 per cent deposit. "I've never ever parted with any money for goods before I have them delivered and fitted." Again, no amount of reasoning about how her alarm system is being "custom-made", nor how deposits work "these days", will change my mother's mind. Worn down, the new alarm company agrees to go ahead without a deposit.

On the prearranged day, when they turn up to fit it, she has simply changed her mind—"Perhaps I don't need an alarm"—and sends them away. Bills are sent by the company to claim for their wasted parts, time, and labour but their efforts, over a whole year, are met with no response. My mother will not pay them a penny.

Technology had left both my mother and my father well behind. In the years before my father's death, I had introduced them to the world of mobile phones and, over a period of several years, had given them three. They just couldn't master how to use them. It was hopeless. After extensive onsite demos, I'd leave and call them do a test at an agreed time; the phone was always switched off. They would have pressed the red button so hard to end the previous test call that, unwittingly, they'd turned the phone completely "off".

And if it wasn't off, it wasn't charged, so when they thought about trying to use it, such as when calling on the way to see us to say they were held up in traffic, it didn't work. They had given up at a time when quite a few of their friends had persevered, learning to use iPads and how to have Skype conversations with their children and grandchildren. Not Mum and Dad. "Can't be doing with all that." The lack of patience has always been a strong family trait (to be honest, I must include myself!).

After my mother's femur breakage and the installation of the stairlift, even though my father was still alive at the time, it was suggested that a "fall alarm" (or panic button) be fitted, in case Mum fell in the night whilst going to the loo or during the day when Dad was in the garden or in a deep sleep with a crumpled-up *Telegraph* on his knees in front of the TV. This turned out to be a very good move in the long run as it was used increasingly after my father's demise.

Quite often the landline would be solidly engaged or "out of service" and I would be unable to get through to my mother. Over the years, I spent many an excruciating hour or so on the phone to TalkTalk via India demanding to speak to a manager but getting nowhere. "She has no immediate neighbours, she's elderly and on her own, she has no mobile", and so on.

On one occasion, whilst I was out having an early evening drink with some friends in Vauxhall, she phoned from her landline, complaining her phone had been working only intermittently. She was furious and yelling at me (little did she know she was on speakerphone): she'd phoned Care Line (the company who looked after her fall alarm) and had told them to get her landline fixed "IMMEDIATELY". They, in turn, explained that her landline was nothing to do with them (I'd explained this too ... many times) but my mother wasn't having it and said she would withhold her monthly payments to them.

Five minutes later, I had Care Line on the phone; my mother had hung up on them and they didn't know if the landline was working properly or not, but I should be aware that when it didn't work, neither did the "fall alarm". I elevated my complaint to TalkTalk and had to plead with them to send an engineer (it took six hours on the phone via India, over a two-day period). To get my mother's fall alarm service reinstated, I quietly paid the missed payments, adding that cost to the list "KL's outlay on behalf of Mum".

Day-to-day life admin with all its niggly problems is tedious at the best of times, but managing it for my mother, under these circumstances, was making me feel like I was going round the bend. Maybe I was. Maybe *she* was. But on and on and on she carried …

2018—two years since Dad died. My head feels like an empty slot machine into which the pennies are beginning to drop with a vibrating clatter … *how on earth had Dad coped?*

The summer is approaching, the weather is improving, armchair Wimbledon is round the corner; her dizzy spells have abated, and all seems calmer—on the surface anyway; not that *I* am particularly calm or happy—in fact, I'm becoming increasingly fed up with the demands Mum is putting on me and the arguments that ensue.

Then begin multiple cases of "I'm not paying that bill". Since she's cancelled her direct debits, quarterly bills are coming in thick and fast and cheques need to be written, or not. "Why do I have to pay for water, I don't shower, and my dog drinks bottled water?" "I'm not paying that ridiculous amount of money for my gas when there's only me in the house."

The more I try to reason with her, the more she digs in. She refuses to pay if she doesn't agree on the amount. Even when "red" bills arrive, she scoffs: "Let them try and take me to court, a poor widowed pensioner." At first, I'm worried, then progressively more wound-up, frustrated, and resentful at giving up my time to help, only to be continually knocked down.

I'm finding it sickening that, although not very well-off, she isn't short of a monthly income but is claiming to be "a poor naval widowed pensioner", despite having two private pensions plus her state pension and an Attendance Allowance (which I'd secured two years previously, after her femur fracture, and she'd been quietly squirreling away).

I start to pull back and to largely ignore the pile of admin and the stack of unpaid bills. Mum wants me to go through them and give her my advice, but when I do, she ignores it. Quietly raging inside, I gradually realise it has become a game for her, a way of provoking me. I stop arguing with her (almost). I am tired of standing in for Dad.

A new gardener had been found, but has now been fired, so I offer to write an ad on a postcard to put in the local newsagent's window; she'd liked the previous gardener, who was a retired policeman no less, but he'd cut out the dead wood of her cherry tree and "stolen the wood, no doubt to cut into logs and sell". Something similar happened with her long-serving cleaner of fifteen years whom she fired because she kept "going on holiday expecting to be paid for not turning up". The dog-walker, however, didn't get fired; after years of walking little Leo, she was half an hour late one day, so my mother locked the back door (Colleen was used to letting herself in) and refused to answer the doorbell. Coleen never returned.

In the run-up to my mother's eighty-ninth birthday, I plan for her to come and stay in London, thinking things might be easier with her being a guest in our home. We can pull out the stops and spoil her, possibly even have a laugh.

I am going to be proved *so* wrong.

Major Mother Meltdown No. 1

The food has been bought, menus worked out, and presents wrapped. When "on form", my mother can be extremely funny, kind, generous. Very much a live wire—though always a little too dogmatic—she is full of amusing stories and seldom boring, so we're looking forward to some fun time on our home turf, though we know there's going to be a degree of waiting on her hand and foot thrown in.

It's all planned: I'll drive down Friday morning to pick her up and bring her back to Battersea in the afternoon. Friday night, we'll take her for a meal to our favourite local Indian restaurant, the long-standing proprietor Nassir having met my mother and father on previous visits. Saturday, she can have a lie-in, breakfast in bed with her beloved dog Leo, while I prepare a lunch party for the following day, her birthday, with her niece, and her niece's son and daughter (the cousins who'd hosted Mum and Dad's special triple celebration, three years earlier). I've already prepared a meal for the three of us for that night, Saturday.

We'd got off to an edgy start when, just after collecting her and during the drive back to London, she started making racist remarks about "Pakis" as (unusually) she relived some of her time in Bradford. I ask her to stop, but she didn't like it. "I'm a racist, I don't care," she'd declared, as if it was a badge of honour. But when, on arrival, she cracks a joke about our new marble-veined kitchen work tops— "Oh look, you've already had an accident and cracked it"— all three of us laugh. The meal out is a great success; Nassir flatters her to the hilt and tells her she looks younger than her daughter—she just loves that. Suzanne and I have a bit more wine when we return home, and Mum has a Bailey's with a brandy top-up.

She takes her breakfast in bed and some hours later the next morning I go into her room to tell her lunch will be in half an hour. She says she isn't getting dressed and is it okay to come down in her dressing-gown? I reply that, of course, it'd be fine but ask if she's feeling unwell; no, she says, she just doesn't feel like getting dressed.

Due to her chronically crumbling and painful knees, I help her down the stairs for lunch—as one of us always does with every step involving stairs; sadly, we don't have a downstairs loo and certainly no stairlift! We have cheese, wine, and salad. Mum has a coffee and a couple of cigarettes and then says she'll have a rest, and can she have a cup of tea later? When she's ready to come down, she calls from the landing at the top of the staircase; she's standing in her nightie, dressing-gown, and slippers. I ask if she's going to get dressed. She simply replies, "I can't be bothered".

It's now drinks time—normally 6.00pm in our household but 5.30pm in my mother's—so I pour her a Bells. We've been chatting for a short time and Mum, sitting with her whisky and a cigarette in her dressing-gown on the sofa, asks to watch the news. My mother is even more addicted to the news than she is to her whisky, and, left to her own devices, she'd watch rolling news all day.

Aretha Franklin had just died. Loads of archive "in-concert" footage was being shown on TV. Suzanne and I are huge fans and had been suitably shocked by her death. Mum suddenly pipes up, "Oh change channels and get that fat black thing off the screen." Suzanne and I just look at each other in disbelief. We change channels and, unfortunately for my mother (and for us, as things turned out), Aretha is on every channel.

Again, Mum says the same thing: "Turn over and get that fat ugly black woman off the screen." I calmly ask her not to talk like that, saying that *she* might feel that way, but it's unacceptable to talk like that in our house or anywhere else. There's a moment's silence while she lights another cigarette; I pour her another small whisky and three or four minutes elapse before I leave Suzanne and her to talk while I go to finish preparing supper.

It can't be more than five minutes later that Suzanne comes into the kitchen, looking furious but ashen. "I can't cope with your mother. You need to go in the other room and sort her out."

Long story short: Suzanne had suggested to my mother that she just had time to dress for dinner; my mother replied that she didn't want to. Suzanne told her I'd gone to a lot of trouble so it would be a thoughtful thing to do for her daughter. She said her daughter had not gone to any trouble; a meal out last night and only bread and cheese for lunch and how "DARE" Suzanne tell her to get dressed. This was the point at which Suzanne came to get me.

Things then escalated. My mother, with eyes popping, face bright red, spittle flying, rages at us and starts making spiteful accusations and assumptions about Suzanne's mother, who died in tragic circumstances thirty years previously. My mother had never met her, knew next to nothing about her, and was simply foul.

I am shaking with silent fury by now. My mother announces she wants tomorrow's lunch party cancelled and orders me to call a taxi for her to return home first thing in the morning, "never ever to return here again". With my voice trembling, I tell her, in no uncertain terms, to go and pack immediately. I am taking her home, there and then. I don't help her up the stairs, or down.

In the car we are silent; for an hour and a quarter, not a word is spoken. I feel shaky, acutely stressed, and shocked to the core. It's dark when we got to Little Holt. I stay long enough to take her overnight bag up to her bedroom and put some lights on in the sitting room. She sits in her chair, with that same wide-eyed cold stare, her jacket still on, cigarette lit, and asks me to leave, saying it would be a good idea before she says anything more.

But she does say more ... very coldly and calmly: "I don't want to see Suzanne ever again and I certainly don't want her coming to my funeral." I tell her this is a horrid, cruel thing to say, and I leave in tears.

I sit in the car in a terrible state, having pulled into a dark lay-by a mile from Mum's house. I decide to phone my brother to tell him what has happened, seeking his advice and support. I recognise Mum has been acting weirdly and it just flashes through my mind that she might "do something stupid". My brother thinks it's a good idea for me to go back and just check she's okay but says he doesn't think she *would* "do anything stupid", that it would be best to let her cool off overnight. He promises he'll call her first thing in the morning and report back as soon as he's spoken to her.

I do go back. She is still in her jacket, she hasn't moved from her chair, although she has a whisky on her side-table, her dachshund at her feet. Quite choked, I tell her why I've gone back and that I am worried about her and can't believe this terrible blow-up has occurred. She just stares at me and calmly repeats that she doesn't want to see Suzanne again nor is she to attend her funeral. Still feeling shocked and unbearably upset, the second helping of her cruel words make it easier this time to turn my back and walk out the door. I drive back to London in a zombie-like state.

When I get back home, Suzanne is still up and dressed but stressed. We sit and talk, both of us full of angst. Before going to bed and for only the second time since I started wearing it forty-five years ago after my car accident, I tug at the tight-fitting gold bangle and ease it down my right wrist. Squeezing it painfully over my knuckles, I remove it—along with any prospect of a future mother–daughter bond.

After a terrible night of worry, tossing and turning, I waited for Andrew's "first thing in the morning" call: 10:00 came and went; 11:00; midday. Nothing! I phoned his mobile, he didn't pick up. I phoned his partner, "Oh yes, he spoke to your Mum several hours ago, she's fine." When Andrew finally called me, I was amazed and horrified by his stance: "How dare you and Suzanne tell my ninety-year-old mother that she's not allowed to wear her dressing-gown, and she's got to get dressed when she doesn't want to."

So the family divisions deepen ... but without the captain to adjudicate.

For three weeks after that I didn't speak to my mother, nor my brother. I felt incredibly low. Shortly after the mother meltdown episode, I phoned the community matron again and relayed recent events, asking her to keep an eye on Mum. She was supportive and adamant that I put my relationship with Suzanne first and look after my mental health. She also suggested that my mother could have a UTI (urinary tract infection), highly treatable with antibiotics, but along with the physical side-effects there was a tendency in older women to present agitated behaviour, in some cases an acute state of confusion.

The matron also hinted that Mum's behaviour might— she did emphasis "might"—be caused by the start of a form of dementia—a particular type known as FTD (frontotemporal dementia), symptoms of which are also changes in behaviour like my mother's. However, as it was a mental disfunction, rather than a physical one, it was a little more complex to treat, with no known easy remedy or cure.

Mum had a urine test, and, to my relief, it proved she had a UTI, and she was prescribed a course of antibiotics, the first course of many for what became a frequently reoccurring ailment.

Shortly after the birthday incident, Suzanne, knowing how upset I was, offered to be the "bigger person" and, in an attempt to end the wall of silence (my fear was my mother would die before amends had been made), write a card to my mother, apologising for the "misunderstanding", saying of course she shouldn't have to get dressed if she didn't feel like it.

Having offered the olive branch, we waited ... and waited for the response. None came. It transpired my mother, on recognising Suzanne's writing, thought it was a birthday card and made a point of not opening it, until I finally called her and asked if she'd received it. Having digested Suzanne's apologetic words over a period of days, limited verbal amends were made by my mother. She said she'd removed it from her brain and didn't want to talk about it.

But that wasn't really enough to effect a true repair; family relations were not the same. In addition, my mental health was wavering, and I started to feel physically quite unwell.

During that November I started to see an experienced psychotherapist. Yes, I had been gently persuaded! I'd always railed against seeing anyone about any mental health issues because I'd been blessed with friends who were excellent sounding boards. (And to be honest, I've never been someone who's been accused of not being able to talk about my feelings.)

But now I'd started to feel emotionally out of my depth and was worried I was beginning to bore my chums with never-ending sagas about my mother—not that I wasn't getting good mileage out of making them laugh at the almost unbelievable but true dramas—oh yes, I was still capable of seeing the funny side when in a social setting after a glass or two. "You should write a book," said a couple of good chums, as did my new psychotherapist: "express the need to get it out, to reflect to yourself the truth of the situation and to hold that truth in the written form."

The beauty of this psychotherapist was that she was local and flexible—she didn't insist on weekly appointments and, in the first instance, when I explained what I thought I needed, she was happy to take me on an ad hoc basis, provided I could slot in around her busy schedule.

I told her that I didn't want to analyse my family's dysfunctional history, as I believed I understood why it had all happened and its consequences; now that I was in my sixties, I was getting bored with it all. What I needed help with was how to deal with my increasing rage and resentment and the relatively recent feeling of sheer hatred towards my mother.

Cynical at the start, I was thankful for being pushed into the therapy sessions. Only five over a six-month period, but they helped enormously. Two new tools I found extremely helpful: "Manage the situation, calmly". And "When the going gets tough, leave the family playing field so the game can't continue."

Digging deep into my newly equipped toolbox, I was doing my best to pull back from resentment, though I carried on performing ongoing admin tasks for my mother, but only those specifically designated by her; I helped with her doctor and hospital appointments; her Tesco online shopping. And, of course, repairing any damage caused by my mother's unnecessary rudeness and hostility to neighbours or suppliers.

She successfully managed to get a Tesco delivery guy fired! Coming back late from the hairdressers, my mother found the large Tesco van parked near the top of her drive and the delivery man unloading it there. She couldn't drive up to her door and wanted him to reverse back, so put her hand on the horn … and left it there.

Unsurprisingly, he wasn't too happy and asked her to stop being so aggressive and let him finish unloading before reversing. But she wasn't having it. Tempers flared. By the end of the day, the branch manager had returned her call of complaint and "by way of compensation" offered my mother £200-worth of delivered shopping, free of charge, and confirmed that the driver concerned had been dismissed. She was thrilled with herself. "You see Katharine, it pays to complain and always make sure you demand compensation."

During this time, the "fall button" had been activated several times and I became increasingly uncomfortable about the fact that a neighbour was repeatedly having to drop everything and go round to check on my mother's welfare—although I was, of course, grovelingly grateful to her. Often, having established an ambulance wasn't required, she nevertheless had to call a second neighbour to help lift my mother up off the floor.

One evening that spring, Mum again "had a fall" and an ambulance *was* required, the paramedics recommending that, to be on the safe side, she go to the hospital in Chichester to be checked over. She spent the night there and I drove down and picked her up the following day; no harm had been done this time, though she moaned all the way back in the car about the terrible nursing she'd received. Apparently, they hadn't even given her a glass of water …

To harmonise family tensions, I suggested to my brother that he and I visit Mum on the same day in mid-February, to coincide with both our birthdays, which were only two days apart. It went sort of okay; there were still tensions but the day passed without any outbursts. It wasn't until a couple of months later, while having an Easter break in France, that I received an email from my brother Andrew.

In it he tried, in my view, anyway, to worm his way even further off the hook of responsibility regarding the dreadful situation we found ourselves in. His assertion that my version of events was "distorted" particularly wound me up. I was incensed by the fact that he was claiming to be "contributing". As far as I could see, all that amounted to was him phoning in on a Sunday evening.

Despite my strong feelings, I nevertheless managed to send a reply that I thought was calm and considered. On the plus side, I felt a bold sense of validation; he'd unwittingly given me the opportunity to really let him know how I felt, and I reckoned I'd managed it in a non-confrontational way

In his email Andrew had suggested we "have a chat soon, on whatever level you choose!" We did have a brief chat just before he and the girls went off to Bali (Granny generously funded the trip by giving the twins £5,000 each for their birthdays, enabling them to visit their place of birth), but only in as much as he acknowledged that my email was "a well thought through response with some valid points", that it would be better to discuss the finer details on his return. Of course, we never did have that particular talk.

Summer 2019 was fraught. First, Mum had another fall, possibly brought on by a recurring UTI. She broke two ribs and seriously bruised herself and there ensued a ten-stay in Guildford Hospital. Like a yoyo, I was up and down the A3 almost every day, but in between times I was having my own tests at St George's Hospital in South London, to investigate ongoing stomach problems.

At the same time, our beloved dog Purdey became seriously lame, which resulted in her having a major £5,500 operation at a specialist animal clinic, making the NHS seem even better value! By the end of one particular day, I'd visited three different hospitals, leaving me extremely stressed and physically and mentally exhausted!

We were due to go to France for the month of July but as Purdey had a metal frame on her rear leg, a fixator fitted with various nuts and bolts, we decided it unwise to go, particularly as our vet advised she would be prone to infection. Not only that, but our poor dog struggled to walk (not a dissimilar situation to that of my mother!).

The problem with cancelling our drive down to the French Pyrenees was that I'd invited a long-standing dear friend and business partner to come and stay for a few days with her two teenage children; her husband, an equally good friend of mine, had tragically had a sudden fatal heart attack six months prior at the age of sixty.

Judith and the girls had booked their flights months before and she mentioned that she didn't feel confident behind a wheel when abroad ("Tony always did the driving"); given the shocking circumstances, I felt I couldn't let her down by not being there to host and ferry them round.

I flew out and rented a car for ten days. I washed, shopped, cleaned, cooked, and taxied—and that was all fine, it's what I'd chosen to do. But this, in turn, put an additional strain on my relationship with Suzanne; she'd had to stay at home (save for a whistle-stop four-day visit), none too happy, nursing a sick dog, only for me to then return completely drained and even more stressed than before I went, and then throw myself straight back into my annual music industry contract.

Having only partly recovered from her spring fall, my mother's ninetieth birthday in August was low-key; that's what she wanted—no fuss. Andrew, Natalie, and Melanie stayed overnight, and I went for the day taking a couple of presents, bubbles, and an Ottolenghi seafood salad.

Suzanne didn't come—my brother suggested it was better that way and that he wouldn't be bringing his partner Kate. The family rift was far from healed.

Three weeks later, my mother ("I can cope perfectly fine on my own") had yet another fall ("I just don't know what happened"). This time she spent a week in Guildford Hospital, where she was a complete nightmare.

She reduced one nurse to tears by asking her why she was so fat. She complained about the food, the staff, the cleaners. She insisted on having her own room, saying she couldn't sleep in a ward with women moaning and groaning all night and went on demanding until the ward sister finally gave in.

She would rudely dismiss the cleaner if they ventured into her private NHS-funded room to mop the floor whilst she was eating. "This doesn't suit me, can't you see I'm eating." Perhaps she would have had a point had she been a private patient.

The doctors were mainly Asian and every morning she'd ask the on-duty consultant where he or she was from.

Despite numerous different types of pain-killing drugs, pain management was a problem, and she continued to complain. Nothing they gave her worked, even though they'd gone to the maximum of safe doses. She was assessed by occupational therapists, and mental health nurses. The latter asked her to do a memory test, but she refused.

Up and down the A3 again, I was racking up outrageously expensive hospital parking charges, but, on the other hand, quite good value in exchange for The Royal Surrey looking after my mother.

After a week's hospitality at the Royal Surrey's expense, she was taken by taxi, or rather ambulance, for two weeks care and rehabilitation at Haslemere Community Hospital. Lady Leppard was back! Treatment proceeded very much the same as before; for cracked ribs, bruised and sprained arm, and bruising on and around her recently repaired femur. The nursing staff and physiotherapists had to cope, once again, with her interminable non-compliance. "I shouldn't be here," she told me. "I should be in a private hospital".

"No Mum, you and Dad gave up Bupa years ago even though I pleaded with you at the time not to do so."

There was one ray of sunshine, however: a male nurse named George, I think he was Greek. She was absolutely smitten with him, and he just knew how to deal with her. "If you do your exercises Betty, I'll take you out for a drink, as long as you pay!" and he'd roar with laughter as he gently escorted her down the ward on her three-wheeler walker.

Mum loved flirting with men and George was in the right place at the right time and was a helpful distraction and a restorative remedy. She nearly always got on better with men in her new but increasingly shrinking day-to-day life: Fabio the dentist, Alex her doctor, Tibor the care manager, Jon a neighbour (and the *chairman* of her private road residents' association).

She flirted and joked, they smiled and responded in an amused but knowing way; any choppy waters were calmed. Professional and caring women like nurses, carers, and her daughter (a chip off the old block) were "far too bossy" and she would ignore their advice. Betty always had to be the absolute "boss", endlessly harking back to her days of being the youngest Chief Petty Officer in the WRNS.

A visit to her young "good-looking" GP was a highlight for Mum. Being asked to "get up on the bed" for her knee injection, she replied "Oh, I'll *jump* up." Or, when she was being difficult about taking her medication: "I don't want to take these as it says on the leaflet a possible side effect is that I could get mouth ulcers"—to which her doctor replied: "I can assure you that you'll get more mouth ulcers from smoking your cigarettes and drinking your whisky than you will from taking these antibiotics."

Even visits to the dentist were relished: the handsome Italian Fabio would work his charm, flattering her and making her laugh—that is, until the day he fitted her with a bridge that was "like having a double-decker bus put in my mouth."

Yet another time when she refused to pay.

9

How Many Carers Does It Take?

On a visit to Mum's, I stop off in Haslemere to pick up a few bits from Waitrose. In the car park I meet one of her few remaining and oldest best friends, a very spritely eighty-five-year-old who has recently lost her husband to cancer. After we've exchanged pleasantries, she says that for the last couple of years, right up until they'd stopped meeting for regular bridge, they'd witnessed Mum's physical deterioration and had been trying to persuade her to get a full-time carer.

I roll my eyes and smile: "I've been trying hard", and I disclose that though she can afford a carer she's being plain stubborn, that I'm incredibly worn down, tired of "picking up the pieces" after my mother. Her friend replies: "We all love your mother but she's a very difficult woman who's becoming increasingly difficult."

Suzanne and I attempt to gently bring up the matter of "live-in care". In the spring of 2018 she has a fall, after "a dizzy spell". My mother thinks her knees had given way and she'd hit her head on the coffee table, but she couldn't quite remember. Coming round, she'd been able to press her fall alarm, the ambulance had arrived and, fortunately, nothing was broken. But the shock of this fall was enough to change her mind about getting full-time care.

The saga of my mother's home care is long and fraught (not without humorous incident but with some excruciatingly frustrating ones, too). It could fill another thick volume, but I'll try to hold back. A chapter will have to suffice.

I prepare the spare room for the first carer's arrival and suggest we need to buy a cheap television so that both Mum and the carer can have some "space" of an evening. I also mention Wi-Fi for the carer, pointing out that "these days it's essential".

"Essential for whom? Not me, she's coming to look after me, I'm not looking after her."

It was only because the monthly phone package was cheaper with a modem than without, and better value than the old-style contract she and Dad had been on for years, that she allowed me to get the basic Wi-Fi bundle. But forgotten it wasn't, as every time she wheeled her walker through the hall to the kitchen, the green and red lights on the modem blinked and irritated her, reminding her she was paying for something she didn't want.

"Get rid of that box-thing, I don't want it, I don't need it and I'm not paying for it." Frequently she'd simply rip the wires out of the wall sockets.

Over time, carers are hired ... and fired; it becomes apparent my mother is finding it increasingly difficult to accept anyone in her house. Her logic is that they are benefitting from "free board and lodging", at her expense; that they are either "completely useless and lazy" or "fat and greedy" or "too controlling". All that before she claims items of food and some of her trinkets have started to "disappear".

Having someone come to live in your home to care for you cannot be easy, especially if you are paying them to be there and you resent it. The question on all our minds is: how long does it take to find the right carer, one that you can get on with and accept their presence? The answer, in my mother's case ...

Danuta, No. 1 and Tenzi, No. 2

The first carer, Danuta, and the second, Tenzi, both Polish, who, in retrospect, managed quite well, last approximately ten weeks each. We had found a Polish care agency which charged £630 per week, almost half the rates of the locally recommended Surrey- and Sussex-based home care agents.

Fiercely independent and used to doing things *her* way, my mother was always going to find it excruciatingly difficult having someone in her house and watching them doing things *their* way. I encourage her to allow some time to "train them up", agreeing with her wholeheartedly that she is "the boss" but suggest that perhaps she should tone down her manner: for instance, "Would you be very good and get this for me", rather than, "Get this for me NOW!"

Danuta's downfall was she was "too controlling and ate

secretly" and the problem with Tenzi was that she was "fat and ate too much".

"It goes back to the war when the Polish didn't get enough to eat and if they think they can make up for it now at my expense, well they can think again."

Two carers down, it was at this point my mother decided she could cope on her own. And promptly ended up in the Royal Surrey and the Haslemere Community hospitals, recovering from yet another fall, as I've already recounted.

While mother had been in hospital, my brother had driven up from Dorset on an agreed day so we could meet over a beer and sandwich and come up with a plan that we could jointly present to Mum at visiting time and suffer her wrath by taking equal flak.

We couldn't find a decent open pub anywhere in the locality so ended up sitting on a brick wall with a can of lager and packets of peanuts; we agreed that there was no time to waste in finding more full-time care for our mother.

Partly because of the email exchange we'd had in the spring, Andrew and I were making some headway on improved sharing of mother-caring duties. With a two-pronged pincer movement, we put it to her that she couldn't be on her own in the house any longer but placated her by agreeing that this time she didn't have to have a Polish carer if she didn't want one. We did point out the cost would be considerably more.

Andrew and I got on the case and found a recommended home care agency serving Surrey and Sussex, at double the cost of the Polish agency. I filled out the corporate-style forms and an appointment was made for a care manager to visit Mum while she was still in hospital, to make "an assessment" of the type and level of care she needed.

Anne, No. 3

Anne from South Africa got off to a flying start. I picked her up from the station and immediately saw the advantage of using a more up-market agency. Neat-looking, middle-aged, a woman in pearls. And blow me down, she had a dachshund back home! My brother and I were so excited, we thought we'd cracked it. We luxuriated for a while in the relative peace and quiet at Little Holt.

It all seemed to be going swimmingly. Several weeks went by, then Mum received the first invoice, and she was reminded of the cost. The invoice remained on the top of her desk for two weeks until the area manager made an appointment to visit and assess how Anne and my mother were getting on. She clearly hoped to pick up a cheque at the same time.

The meeting didn't go well. The manager had a "tick box exercise" of questions for my mother, which in turn she put to Anne. It was part of the company's "duty of care" policy to attend to the welfare of their carers as well as their clients receiving care. The question of smoking came up. The manager made a point of saying to my mother that she hadn't mentioned being a smoker before, explaining she had to designate carers accordingly and respect those who had requested to work in non-smoking households. Anne had.

My mother didn't like this at all. "I AM PAYING YOU for a carer, they are here in MY house, how DARE you tell me when and if I can smoke." Mum did usually have half a point. Following this visit, she simmered for a few days and then one night kicked off big time. Fraught calls went between myself and my brother and Mum, who hung up on both of us. She wanted Anne out, and "OUT NOW".

It was ten o'clock at night, my mother's house is in the country with little to no public transport, and poor Anne had taken to her room to escape my mother's escalating rage. I was on the phone trying to advise Anne, but I could hear my mother the other side of her door banging and screaming, armed with whisky, cigarette in mouth (reportedly), and pushing her walker, "I WANT YOU OUT NOW, GET OUT, GET OUT!"

There was no lock on Anne's bedroom door (my old bedroom) and my mother rammed the door open with her metal walking frame and burst in. Then, in a final peak of rage, she threw the frame at Anne. My brother took over speaking to Anne and advised her, for the sake of her own safety, to pack as quickly as she could and get out. She was picked up by a friend who drove down from London to collect her at 11.30pm.

My mother dug in and refused to pay the agency until legal threats started; only then did she decide to send them half the total. She continued to ignore the repeated claims for full settlement and Anne's travel expenses.

I felt incredibly upset and even more angry that Mum was causing me yet more sleepless nights worrying about her being alone in the house. She was affecting my life to an unreasonable degree. My brother thought it best to leave her to get on with it until she was calmer and came to the realisation she couldn't cope. Or had another fall. We waited ...

Maggie, No. 4

Some weeks later, when my mother was showing signs of her vulnerability, we were able to convince her to try Maggie. I can't remember exactly how we found her—part recommendation, part internet, I think—but it was a direct booking (no agency fees, thus pleasing Mum) and she had references. And she was English! She lasted two weeks because according to my mother, she was "fat, lazy, and uncaring".

Maggie called me one morning, frantic, saying she was concerned about Mum, that her speech was slurred, her breathing was strange, and she couldn't wake her up properly. I phoned her doctor's surgery and requested an urgent home visit, then got in my car and drove down to Little Holt.

My mother was on the highest dose of the controlled pain killer Pregabalin and had ignored the dosage instructions on the box. She'd been taking them "like smarties" whenever she felt in pain. No matter the instructions, or the person trying to administer the meds reminding her it was time to take her next dose, my mother *always* self-administered what and when she wanted.

She always had her secret stockpile (leftovers from previous prescriptions) which she squirreled away in her bottom drawer, enough to open a pharmacy. My mother thought she knew best, of course, exactly as my father had been saying for years and years. I was present when the duty doctor arrived and, on learning of the considerable amount my mother had taken over many days (and phoning a colleague for back-up info on Pregabalin and its side-effects), insisted Mum go to hospital without delay.

Maggie was not to blame, but Maggie got it in the neck, and whilst waiting for an ambulance to take my mother to the Royal Surrey, Mum suddenly found the energy and words to be rude to Maggie and told her to leave immediately. Maggie by this stage had clearly had enough and was unable to contain herself any longer so she answered back, rudely, and Mum went crazy with rage, despite, or perhaps because of, her overdose. It was only because Mum was in the process of being carted off to hospital, and therefore unable to physically throw her out, that Maggie was able to wait until the next day before leaving.

And that was that. Carer No. 4 didn't get full payment.

The Royal Surrey Hospital stay this time was different. Take my mother's previous visits and multiply her obstreperous behaviour by ten! Once having checked and stabilised her vitals and established she wasn't going to die, the consultant wanted her to stay in for two or three days "to be on the safe side" and to get her meds back on track, particularly the Pregabalin.

Easier said than done. She started to display serious side effects of the controlled drug overdose: aggressive and angry behaviour, anxiety, irritability and mania, and panic attacks—she started "to see things" on the ward and became demented. The problem with this drug, despite there being too much of it in her system, was that they had to continue giving it to her in small but controlled amounts to avoid severe withdrawal symptoms.

But no, my mother was not going to take it. Sitting with her in the visiting corridor bay area (she was causing too much commotion on the ward), I, along with the ward sister, the consultant, and two nurses, tried to explain what needed to happen and why.

"I'm in here because I've been half poisoned by the pills my doctor gave me and now you're wanting me to take more of them." Again, my mother seemed to have a point—in her eyes!

The following day, my niece visited. My mother was adamant she wanted to discharge herself and made my niece complicit, in other words bullied her, into wheeling Mum into the lift and down to the ground floor. Melanie, having left her grandmother parked in the wheelchair by the main hospital exit, went to get the car and called me in tears not knowing what to do, saying "Granny is far from alright."

Fortunately, I knew the sister's name and the phone number of the reception desk on Mum's ward. They immediately dispatched a young doctor down to the main doors and as luck would have it, this doctor was "terribly good looking and really quite charming" and he worked his magic, retrieving the wheelchair and its passenger back to the ward on the third floor.

Two days later, Mum was discharged and to avoid her being at home alone, Melanie, who was between jobs and still trying to find somewhere to live in London, offered to stay at Little Holt for a few weeks. This was a win–win situation and Mum was happy and offered to give her granddaughter some money in return for looking after her.

Irena, No. 5, and then in quick succession, Beata, No. 6

More research, more form-filling, more assessments. Carer No. 5 was found from another Polish agency, because it was by far the cheapest and this was the maximum my mother was going to pay. She is "too full-on and touchy and has stolen my expensive Royal Worcester ashtrays." Her other big error on Day One was to arrive on the back of a motorbike and ask if it was okay for her boyfriend to stay the night as he'd brought her all the way from Poland and was tired. That got the relationship off to a bad start. Irena lasted two weeks!

Beata, the next lamb to the slaughter, arrived in mid-January 2019. I picked her up at the station and the drive home gave me seven minutes to give her the low-down based on the previous carers' stumbling blocks: let my mother feel she's in control, agree with everything she says, just do what she asks, when she asks—within reason.

Over the course of the next three weeks, my mother started complaining about her.

"She's a typical Pole, she eats too much and steals my food to send food parcels back to Poland … and she's a liar."

I knew from doing Mum's Tesco shopping online that she wasn't ordering enough food for the carer. My mother ate very little and instructed Beata that she could only eat what she ate, and at the same times. She was not allowed to help herself to anything at any other time, "under any circumstances".

Mum continued to rant when I called. I struggled to keep my cool. "Mum, please stop it, you've unfairly got it in for the Polish who are amongst the most hard-working, honest and reliable people I know, so please stop saying such unpleasant things", whilst pointing out she'd end up on her own again, that this Polish agency, like the last one, was half the price of any others, and that was why she'd agreed to have them.

I started to dread it when the phone went. I could see Mum's number displayed but my conscience wouldn't allow me to ignore it, just in case it was an emergency. Around this time, I took up a new anti-social habit, that of screaming at the top of my lungs every time I put the phone down. God knows what our neighbours thought.

On a sunny Friday in late January, Suzanne and I decided as a treat to make an outing and walk Purdey in Dulwich

Park, with a pub lunch afterwards. As we were parking up, the mobile rang. It was Beata saying my mother had locked herself in the car which was parked in the garage. She was out of control, screaming her head off behind the steering wheel, but obviously with the car going nowhere.

Beata took her mobile into the garage so I could hear Mum carrying on. "For Christ's sake, get me out, what's wrong with you, you stupid woman?" Beata's English wasn't great—it didn't have to be to understand my mother's predicament—but as the car was firmly sealed, she couldn't pass her mobile phone to Mum so I couldn't speak to her to calm her down. The shouting and abuse coming from inside the now streamed-up car was truly shocking and I was completely helpless to do anything about it.

In my mother's usual impatient fashion, she had, whilst trying to get the car started, pressed every button on the dashboard, somehow jamming the central locking system. I immediately called the AA who, as it was an emergency, said they'd be there within an hour. Meanwhile, the postman arrived to witness the carry-on in the garage—worthy of a scene from a comedy drama; somehow, he managed to get the car unlocked and release my mother, who was furious that she'd missed her appointment at the hairdresser's.

Whilst the disruption had lasted less than a couple of hours, our day out had been spoilt; my nerves were completely ragged and Suzanne was, quite rightly, pretty fed up with yet another drama with my mother in the leading role.

There were other emergencies … of course. Such as when her television "blew up" resulting in no injury or damage but certainly no TV to watch. Despite it being only ten years old, I suggested she buy a new one, explaining it would cost more to repair than replace, unlike in "the old days". To my amazement she agreed and told me to order one "on the line or whatever you do".

Within twenty-four hours it arrived, but unbeknown to my mother or Beata, the delivery guy had not rung the bell and had left it sitting in the secluded front-door porch where, fortunately, it couldn't be seen. My mother complained it hadn't been delivered, I asked Beata to check outside, where, indeed, she found the big cardboard box. Mum went completely mad: "How DARE they just leave it outside … I will not stand for this … who is going to tune it up? … I want you, Katharine, to send it back NOW".

I agreed that "not ringing the bell" was bad form, and tried explaining how delivery companies worked, and how "a man" didn't come to "tune it up"—technology had moved on and it was no longer necessary. But she wasn't listening: "I will not deal with companies like this Katharine, GET IT SENT BACK NOW!" And she slammed the phone down.

Beata sent me a sweet text telling me not to worry, that she would deal with it when Mum was calmer. And Beata did earn herself a gold star when, the following day, my mother calmer, Beata offered to unpack it and set it up, which she did and then … she plugged it in and, hey presto, it worked! Mum couldn't believe it. "It's a miracle," she declared on the phone.

Amazingly, and almost a first, she apologised "profusely" for her outburst. Come to think of it, it *was* a first.

I began to let Andrew know as and when things were revving up at Little Holt and asked him to take over with the care problems, as my nerves were becoming frayed. We agreed that he had more patience and a better way of defusing things and calming Mum, perhaps because up until now he had remained relatively removed from the dramas and was therefore relatively unscathed.

The new plan worked … to a point.

Mother's Molten Lava Flowing

I'm on my way down to visit Mum, on my own. I haven't even got my jacket off before my mother starts up; Beata has just asked me if she can take her two-hour break early, seeing as I'm there, and can she take an extra hour because it'll take her that long just to walk to town?

I'd said I thought it'd be fine, but I'd just go and ask "The Boss" … "The Boss" goes crazy! "How DARE she ask for extra time off … She's lazy … She's a stealer … a liar" … and with that she wheels herself and her walker down the hall to hurl more abuse at Beata. I intervene and ask Mum to stop being so rude and please go back to the sitting-room and calm down. But no luck. "I want her out NOW", to which I explain it isn't possible, she has nowhere to stay and would have to book a flight back to Poland first. No, my mother isn't having it. "She can get out now and she can sleep in the gutter where she belongs … And you can get out too, NOW!"

Beata is on the phone to her manager, in tears; as am

I, in the garden, relaying events to Suzanne. An hour later, Beata is packed and waiting in my car. I go to say goodbye to Mum.

She's sitting in her chair with that familiar cold look and simply says: "Get out and don't come back and just so you know, today will have been the most expensive day of your life as I'm removing you from my Will."

In the three weeks of non-communication with my mother—including my birthday, which she completely ignored—I go through every emotion under the sun. I raid my precious stash of diazepam (normally used for long-haul flights), which indeed do help me sleep. My brother advises me to do nothing, as does Suzanne; it isn't difficult because I feel devastated, at times completely numb.

I don't want to contact my mother. I do, however, call her GP to inform him that my mother is living on her own again, describing how in a fit of rage she's sacked Carer No. 6, and how she's also expelled me permanently. I ask if it's possible, given my mother's extreme behaviour, for the community matron to visit to take a urine sample to check for a UTI. The doctor agrees to organise a home visit.

When my mother finally calls me three weeks later at Bell's o'clock, she simply declares: "I'm missing my daughter, and this thing shouldn't go on." But she makes it clear she doesn't want to talk about what's occurred. I'm reminded of her repeated mantra: "Anything bad that has happened, I don't want to remember, so I don't." She does say she hasn't been well and is on a course of antibiotics for a urine infection. I say nothing, reluctant to come clean—earlier in the year she'd asked me not to "interfere" by calling her GP "at any time, under any circumstances".

Though now back on telephone-talking terms, relations remained nevertheless lacklustre. I certainly didn't rush to visit and, as the Covid crisis was just beginning, it seemed I had a pretty good reason to stay away for a while.

My mother continued trying to be fiercely independent and "manage perfectly well" on her own (I guess it depends on what one understands by the word "manage"). She thought it was very amusing when she set off to a dental appointment but ended up at the vet, not understanding why the veterinary practice hadn't got an appointment for her darling Leo.

On another occasion she decided to take the car out—it was being used less and less now—to fill it up with petrol. When she got to the garage, she found that she couldn't get out of the car because she'd forgotten her walking frame, so asked "a kind young man" if he'd fill up her tank. When he'd done so she asked that he "kindly help her out of the car" and escort her to the payment counter inside the shop on the garage forecourt but, standing in front of the till, she realised she didn't have any means of payment. Fortunately, the garage, obviously accustomed to an increasing "seniors" population, merely took her car registration and details and later that day the garage duty manager received delivery of cash via my mother's current gardener.

Up until now, these had been relatively harmless

incidents—apart from the one or two prangs getting in and out of the garage—so I laughed along, but with the nagging awareness that Mum was on borrowed time driving-wise and her days behind the wheel were definitely numbered.

I knew from my father's experience what a soul-destroying final wrench it is to have to give up driving … and independence. If it had been hugely difficult for my father's pride to deal with, in my mother's case it was going to be an almighty blow-up: she wasn't going to be told by anyone that she should no longer drive. I decided that it was best for me to steer (forgive the pun!) well clear, for the moment, at least.

Things changed quite soon: my mother thought it better to "tune-up" the car in the garage rather than take it for a spin. The AA had been called out half a dozen times to charge the battery and had told her that she'd have to pay the next time. So, one late afternoon, Bell's o'clock, she went to the garage and started the car to leave it running for half an hour behind the closed garage door … and forgot about it!

The next morning, on coming down to let Leo out and make her breakfast, she was hit by fumes as she entered the kitchen. Then, going out via the utility area and into the adjoining garage, she found herself engulfed in clouds of thick black smoke; intense heat was radiating out from under the bonnet of the car, oil was spilling out over the garage floor, and the engine was still running. She tried to turn off the ignition, but the key was, unsurprisingly, too hot to touch. The engine had been running for fourteen hours; it was a miracle there hadn't been an explosion or a fire during the night.

That incident—combined with the death of a local ninety-two-year-old widow who drove her car into a tree en route to Haslemere—left me in no doubt that it was time to broach the subject of abandoning the car. I decided to get advice again from the community matron who knew my mother only too well.

A whole series of communications took place over several months. My mother's female doctor (who looked after her gynae problems—too embarrassing to discuss with her handsome young male GP!)—tactfully suggested to her it was time to give up driving, only to get extremely short shrift—she slammed the phone down.

The community matron, paving the way for social services to enquire if they could offer practical support when she gave up her car, got the response, "I'm not interested." But the community liaison practitioner for psychiatric services managed to get permission to visit my mother, who finally and incredibly agreed to a memory test, along with a general assessment.

Meanwhile, the Covid crisis was worsening and the first lockdown, though still not announced but just around the corner, was making everyone on edge. What had been, until then, quite straightforward home visits became extremely challenging for all concerned. But still, the most pressing matter was to solve my mother's home care as she was clearly not able to cope in the house on her own—despite her protestations to the contrary.

Eileen, No. 7

As luck would have it, in early March, one of my mother's neighbours gave us a glowing recommendation of an independent freelance live-in carer, meaning no agency commission. A woman in her early seventies from Deptford, small but spritely, with bags of care experience, including some nursing, was willing and able to give it a "trial": so she did a couple of days and my mother agreed for Eileen to start straight away.

The only slight fly in the ointment was Eileen's payment—she understandably didn't want a cheque (there were no longer any banks locally for her to pay it in), so, as is the modern way, she requested a BACs transfer every two weeks. Mum obviously could not do online banking, but that was not the point. My mother demanded she should be the one to decide how Eileen was paid, not Eileen, and insisted she would pay her by cheque.

Having decided the subject was best dropped for a while, I casually mentioned it again a week later and offered "to make life easy" and set up the electronic transfer, explaining how it worked and assuring my mother she could tell me to stop payment at any time.

This was the only time I made bank transfers on her behalf and, boy oh boy, I never heard the end of it. Every time she checked her paper bank statement she complained: first, about Eileen's £700 per week ("It's far too much seeing she gets free board and lodging"); second, she resented not being in control of that payment, she wanted to write a cheque as and when she felt like it.

Eileen did quite well to last as long as she did. On for a couple of weeks, then off for a two-day break, she got through March and April until there was a big fall-out and Mum wanted her gone. Eileen started indicating she was finding my mother increasingly challenging, her main objection being the way my mother spoke to her.

As they were sitting down to lunch, my mother would tell Eileen, "Go and scrub that dirty mark off the carpet." Eileen would reply, calmly, that she would do so after lunch (not mentioning it was not strictly her role, particularly as Mum had a cleaner) but Mum wanted it done "NOW!".

"If I am paying you, you do exactly what I tell you to do when I tell you."

Eileen in her timid but experienced way, tried to reason: "Rachel, I'll do it after my lunch, please don't speak to me like that, I'm not a domestic servant." Things went from bad to worse and Eileen was asked to leave … fortunately not in the middle of the night.

Eileen (again), No. 7 (b)

My mother had another spate of "I can cope on my own" but after a few weeks, when she clearly couldn't, my brother and I pleaded with Mum to give Eileen another try (it had, after all, worked well for many weeks); we equally implored Eileen to have another go, telling her we'd had careful words with our mother about how she should be less acerbic and more appreciative. Eileen agreed, but perhaps unsurprisingly, requested a rise of £100 per week, which after talking to my brother, we agreed as a separate confidential payment, out of the budget otherwise known as "KL's outlay on behalf of Mum".

In April 2020, out of the blue, I get a call from the community liaison mental health practitioner, a woman I'd spoken to months previously. She's subsequently visited my mother to carry out an assessment and a memory test (after four years of failed attempts) and has prepared a detailed report. She's sending a copy to Mum's GP and asks if I'd like a copy (I've by now established Power of Attorney); under the circumstances, she continues, it wouldn't be appropriate or helpful for my mother to see the report for the time being. She's made recommendations to Mum regarding medication to slow down her memory loss but has been met with formidable hostility.

"The bottom line is, I'm afraid to say, your mother is suffering from dementia and my official diagnosis in the report is specifically that of Alzheimer's dementia."

I suppose, deep down, I'd suspected something like this was coming. Nevertheless, I stand there with the phone in my hand, feeling numb with shock, reeling backwards in my mind over all the episodes of inappropriate behaviour; the aggression and the stubbornness; the irrational, impulsive decisions; the thin-skinned responses; the short temper …

What I've just been told raises all sorts of questions: how long has she been suffering from this? When did the erratic agitated behaviour of a UTI turn into dementia? At what stage had my mother's behaviour stopped being the "real" her—a year or three years ago, or four years ago when my father died, or twenty years ago, or fifty or sixty years ago? How much of what she displays is her "character" and how much is dementia?

I'm being buffeted in a storm of feelings: stupid, and guilty, for not having suspected this before; relieved that there's now a reason why my mother has turned into a complete monster; extremely angry that I'm now going to have to make even more fucking allowances.

I read the info pack from the Alzheimer's Association; I research online; I speak to the GP and the community psychiatric services. One of the key things that strikes me about dementia is that (similarly to what happens, as my mother always said, when people are drunk) the usual mental filters stop working sufficiently well and, out of your mouth, to varying degrees of inappropriateness, tumble the words that you're thinking but which, under normal circumstances, you wouldn't dare utter. In other words, it exaggerates your existing character, while ripping away the veil of social inhibition.

My mother was visited by the community mental health nurse a week later and refused to accept the diagnosis; likewise, any medication to help slow down the loss of her memory. Mum called me in the evening to tell me of "this visit" and categorically denied that there was anything wrong with her memory. "I haven't got whatever this thing is that they say I've got." I said very little. I certainly didn't risk arguing or letting her know I already knew.

Mum's female GP also talked to my mother over the phone, only to realise she was still in total denial. Despite this, the doctor *had* to persevere with the subject of driving: she gently suggested it was now time to give up her car, but Mum was adamant: she wasn't ready to do that, she could drive perfectly well.

The doctor called me to tell me that I had to tell my mother it was now illegal for her to drive due to her recent diagnosis and that she or I had to write to the DVLA and relinquish her licence. Fortunately, the doctor kindly offered to write that letter; I had no hesitation in accepting, as I knew Mum would go berserk if I were to do it.

During one of Eileen's weekend breaks, I had a lengthy conversation with her. We talked about Mum's diagnosis, me hoping it would make Mum's "rudeness" easier and more acceptable for Eileen to bear. Eileen assured me she had had lots of experience in looking after elderly clients in their homes and in nursing homes with and without dementia, but she said that she'd never come across someone with such a controlling character who treated her like a servant. She agreed she'd use her best endeavours to maintain the status quo and carry out my mother's instructions. Eileen clearly needed the income.

That took us to May, when a combination of "She's lazy and a liar, she's too controlling, she's stolen my ashtrays and she won't follow my orders", brought Carer No. 7's stint to an abrupt halt. Eileen had to leave within hours; a friend from Deptford was called and drove her home— due to the Covid crisis there were extremely limited safe transport options. On the, slightly, brighter side—it wasn't the middle of the night, and she didn't have to get herself on a flight to Poland!

Natalia, No. 8

I felt extremely low at this point, and with very muddled emotions. My mother continued to dominate my everyday life with her problems, wanting support only to argue and have things done *her way*. Carer No. 7 being fired meant me taking up the slack. More sleepless nights, wondering if she'd fallen, or set fire to the house by leaving a pan on the cooker (this had become a regular occurrence).

I had to dig deep, try and turn off and distance myself from "the playing field" by having less contact. I cut down my phone calls to a couple of times a week. Andrew and I agreed to stand firm: she'd have to find the next carer herself.

Unbelievably she did! Unbelievable, too, was that the new lamb to the slaughter, Natalia, a nineteen-year-old Polish girl, arrived via a Polish care agency (a different one to the one *we'd* used). Even more unbelievably, she and Mum got on well. They seemed to like each other! We just couldn't believe it, but the relief was enormous. I could breathe. I was beginning to feel like a normal person again. And we could take off, guilt-free, for four weeks in France.

Perhaps it was because Natalia was so young that my mother treated her a bit like a grandchild (she taught her to make a cheese sauce!), or perhaps because she just did exactly what my mother asked straight away and never questioned anything she said. Or, perhaps, it was because my mother had got this care company off her own back, and she wanted to prove she was both capable and completely in control. And work it did, through June, July, and up until the first week of August when Natalia took a few weeks off to go back to Poland.

Katie, No. 9, but not for very long

Carer No. 9, Katie, from the same Polish agency, lasted twelve days. Mum accused her of stealing and eating too much. My mother told her to "get out now" but Katie explained that under the terms of her contract she wasn't allowed to do that. And so, my smouldering mother called the police.

In the six days it took to organise the next carer, my mother managed to require the aid of the other two emergency services. First, the fire brigade, when she couldn't turn off her coal-effect gas fire because she'd tampered with the "coals" (to clean them, she said) but had put them back incorrectly, which caused a flame to burn through a control wire. She called me, late one evening, to say flames were "licking up the chimney" and she couldn't turn the fire off with the remote so, thinking the remote was faulty, she thought it best to take the batteries out!

Having failed to get her to put the batteries back in and with the fire still on full blast—with Mum insisting she'd leave it overnight and call the gas-fire company tomorrow, and me having my very own melt-down—I decided to call the fire brigade for advice; without hesitation they said it was "a serious fire hazard" and they'd attend without delay, which they did.

Then, a few days later, my mother stumbled and fell

but was able to push her fall button. I was called by the care line. The usual neighbour was out, so I called another neighbour who kindly dropped everything and went straight round to find her lying on the kitchen floor in a pint of spilt milk. The paramedics arrived and checked her over, with, fortunately, no damage done.

Agnes, No. 10

The next carer arrived, again from the same agency. Mum started complaining on day one because Agnes wanted a boiled egg for her lunch as she couldn't eat cheese (my mother's everyday lunch), but Mum wouldn't allow her to have an egg. That started an argument, and it went from there … downhill!

Mum accused the Polish of being "greedy" and, yet again, said she didn't want another Polish carer. I had to point out, again, that it was she who'd gone to the *Polish* agency, which had provided Natalia, who she liked, and that they only provided Polish carers. And I reminded her that she'd chosen them for their exceptionally good weekly rate. She denied having chosen the agency, said it was Andrew, and thought the £700 per week was a "complete rip-off".

The dementia diagnosis in spring had taken its time to fully filter into my conscience, partly due to my mother's vehement refusal to accept it herself, which meant that the subject was never brought up in conversation. I kept having to kick myself into remembering that there was no longer any point in arguing. This now had truly become a "manage-the-situation" scenario. I didn't need to expend my emotional energy trying to make my mother see reason or sense—those things were long behind us.

Due to several more bouts of UTI, I had more conversations with Mum's GP (there were two—her "good-looking young male doctor", and a "very nice female doctor" who dealt with her gynae problems but was now pushed by my mother almost out of the picture, as it had been her who had written to the DVLA). It was now easier and entirely permitted for me to talk to Mum's GP, being in the best interests of her physical and mental well-being, following the diagnosis of Alzheimer's.

Diminishing memory loss was one thing, but increasingly agitated out-of-control behaviour was another and I felt that I was clutching at straws in hoping the decline was mainly due to UTIs and could be monitored by urine tests and controlled with antibiotics. Mum's GP had been incredibly supportive to her physical and mental needs over many years (he was totally in the loop with my mother and father's history of an unhappy marriage), and he showed great understanding of her character, especially when I asked him for advice in "managing" the situation.

"She still has cognitive ability but with variable capacity that makes the problem more complex as she's still able to make decisions, albeit the wrong ones, but there's nothing you can do about that."

He also added that he'd never come across anyone quite like my mother and that she had a deeply "destructive" side to her personality.

Despite my mother's adoration of him—"No one can help me like my doctor"—he, too, had experienced my mother's venom. Two years previously he'd phoned and asked Mum to apologise to his receptionist at his surgery after she'd been abusive. Mum was so affronted she wouldn't speak to him for at least a year (this was partly why she started seeing a female GP), but when she did see him again (on my request for a home visit) she was all "butter-wouldn't melt-in-the-mouth" smiles. She even asked him to remove his face mask so she could see his "good-looking" face. After he had gone, she looked very pleased with herself and said to me, "You see, I've still got him in my clutches."

Natalia, No. 11 (previously No. 8)

A huge sigh of relief when we heard Natalia was coming back (now in slot No. 11). On visiting Mum one Sunday, I went for a brief dog walk with Natalia, an opportunity to check all was okay. She said she had no problems with my mother; all was fine, except, except, except ... she could only stay four weeks—she needed to get on with her life in Poland, being a carer wasn't suitable for her long-term because she was too isolated and needed to be with people her age. My heart sank, but I totally got it.

The Covid pandemic was ramping up and Christmas was approaching. It was back to the worry board for the umpteenth time. My mother had repeatedly said she would *not*, under any circumstances, *ever* go into a care home, and, of course, this was the very time *not* to do just that!

The Polish care company somehow hung on in there. Fortunately, the male area manager, Tibor, had a way with Mum and was able to cajole her into writing cheques for outstanding payment (quite an achievement!) when he visited and, as she was so smitten with him, she allowed him to provide her with yet another Polish carer.

Aleksandra, No. 12

For the four weeks until the end of November, my mother had the next carer, Aleksandra. There was still the food problem, but another issue raised its head—the Watergate affair! Mum, still arguing about paying her water rates and withholding payment, decided that Aleksandra was using too much water and told her she couldn't use the washing machine.

In addition, the handheld shower head and tap fitting (only fifty years old!) used by the carers in the spare bathroom, had broken, and, at a mere £30 for the part and, allowing for a worst-case scenario of £150 for a plumber to fit it, along with new taps, Mum refused point-blank to get it fixed. From this point on, no one, including Mum's grandchildren, could rinse their hair or have a shower in the spare bathroom. "I'm not paying this ridiculous amount for water."

And I decided to do and say absolutely nothing, I'd had it!

Izabella, No. 13

Exit Aleksandra, enter Izabella. She was fired three weeks later. It wasn't about food this time. "She was only interested in herself", apparently.

We were heading for fucking Christmas and the home-care dramas were on repeat, and everything was being made worse by a global pandemic. But, hey, my mother had it in her to take things to another level.

Roughly once a month, her care bill would arrive and each time there would be a drama. She'd stuff the bill in her desk and say she wasn't going to pay it, which meant the outstanding amounts went up and up. "What sort of Christmas present is this bill? I'm being put through absolute torture with these carers … it's a rip off and to think I could spend the money on a skiing holiday instead of living with this torture."

My mother was serious; in the car on the way back to London, Suzanne and I were in fits of laughter at the thought of my ninety-one-year-old mother, with bad knees, careering down a mountain, probably with her arse plumped down on the back of the skis.

Patricia, No. 14

Patricia was never going to last! She'd arrived, just in time, we thought, before total Covid lockdown, and Christmas. Phew, we sighed. But no sooner had she arrived than my mother wanted her "GONE" for the three days over Christmas when her son and grandchildren were coming to stay (Suzanne and I were to visit for a day). The agency explained it didn't work like that ... Patricia had nowhere to go for Christmas and couldn't fly back to Poland for three days and, anyway, with Covid travel regulations it would be impossible.

My brother talked Mum down and Patricia joined the extremely truncated Leppard Christmas, which, due to Boris's Almost Completely Cancelled Christmas, turned out to be just Andrew and Mum ... and Patricia.

I'd kept in touch with Natalia via WhatsApp, just in case her plans changed, and she should consider coming back to look after Mum, via the agency or not. I offered to pay her more, but she was contractually tied to the agency (and penalties were too great to take any risks) but Mum was keen to have her back—and so was I, as the thought of preparing for another new carer, taking it to fifteen, was weighing on me.

So, clutching at straws, I remained in touch and tried to make her feel wanted, being careful not to put too much pressure on the nineteen-year-old. Around Christmas time, she texted me saying her plans had changed, and she'd like to come back in early January as long as the agency could work their way round the ever-changing quarantine rules and could organise for her to have a Covid test before arriving at my mother's.

Natalia, No. 15 (previously No. 8 and No. 11)

Natalia recommenced on 14 January 2021—her third visit!

Six weeks in, my mother phoned mid-afternoon. This was normally her rest time, so I knew there was trouble. My mother was in a revved-up state, having just seen her latest bank statement. She wanted to cancel her care immediately. She couldn't bear to see that two cheques for £2,800 each had been cashed (this was payment for two months' care).

"I'm not paying this amount of money. I'm just not wearing it. I'm a poor widow living on a naval pension, and I'll manage without care … and my Tesco bills are just too much, and the food keeps disappearing."

I felt my body go tense and prickly, my stomach churned, but I paused and allowed her to go on … and on … and on. Holding the phone at arm's length, I practiced my yogic breathing. Calmly, I went through all her objections, one by one.

"You wrote two cheques Mum because you said to the handsome very nice manager, Tibor, that you couldn't psychologically cope with writing one cheque for £5,600 so you asked to write two for £2,800 … You are not a poor widow just living on a naval pension, so please stop saying that. You have three pensions and an attendance allowance, you have more than enough money coming in to pay for your home care … your income is there for your living expenses—that's what it's for. If you go into a care home, it'll be at least double, but you want to stay in your own home."

Keeping calm, on I went, gradually knocking back all her arguments and reminding her how good Natalia had been and how much she had approved of her. Poor Natalia, I thought; we exchanged texts (and I found out later that my mother had reduced her to tears and asked her to pack her bags).

This was one of the few times my mother listened to me without shouting or hanging up and I couldn't believe it when, finally, she agreed to take my advice and calm down. Was it my yogic breathing or was I learning better how to cope, even if I was having to make even *more* allowances due to her recent dementia diagnosis?! Or, perhaps, was it simply that she was deteriorating and losing the energy to be angry, let alone the ability to argue cogently?

Nevertheless, later the same day, the gardener, having just completed his weekly three hours at Little Holt, phoned to say he was finding his job challenging. She'd now banned him from having bonfires and accused him of almost setting the house on fire, despite the damp smouldering heap in the corner of the garden being at least a hundred feet from the house. And that was before she went ballistic over his "butchery" of the overhanging branches on the driveway. A week later, Gardener No. 4 was fired.

Oh Dad, how did you cope for so many years?

Natalia managed to hang on without a break for another three months before returning to Poland.

Aleksandra, No. 16 and Agnes, No. 17

Between May and July 2021 two more Polish carers, Aleksandra and Agnes, came and went, after both being told by my mother that they were less than useless—not to mention accusing them of stealing her Crown Derby ashtrays, using the washing machine, and eating too much.

Andrea, No. 18

Meanwhile the pandemic rolled on and the Polish agency, mainly due to the Covid boarder control restrictions, ran out of available carers (and, I suspect, patience). So, for the very first time, they employed an English carer from Birmingham. Andrea, believe it or not, *was* totally and utterly useless. *And* she stole (although only cigarettes). She was the only carer who *had* stolen anything but still, it gave my mother the ammunition she needed to claim another big fat point! And eject Andrea.

My mother then suffered a very serious UTI and was very unwell. Both my brother and I were away in France at the time—on *separate* holidays, I hasten to add.

It felt as if the wheels were finally coming off … and I didn't have a spare. Heroically, my nieces, so worried about their Granny's state, stepped in to resolve the immediate care crisis, and suitable remuneration was put in place to appease all.

10

She's Lost Control

There's a thin line between love and hate; there's a chasm between love and murder.

Since the death of my father, I've been reflecting on everything that's happened; slowly, but steadily, a complicated set of feelings has been brewing. I'm now feeling *duped* by my mother; but at the same time, I love her and feel sorry for her as she suffers physical and mental deterioration. I'm left feeling completely torn.

Much as I long for reconciliation and happy endings, the feelings of anger and resentment carry on bubbling away. I can't keep a lid on them any longer. My mother has been making me extremely unhappy all my life, but now, it's more than that—she's making me both physically and mentally ill. And I hate her for it.

The diagnosis of dementia isn't straightforward: according to her doctor, "your mother still has limited intermittent and varying cognitive ability". Up until now, I've always dreaded the idea of seeing my mother in a care home—but really, if only she could be less foul to the people around her trying to help her have a decent quality of life whilst enabling her to continue living in the familiar surroundings of her own home. After eighteen carers and now, to top it all, her grandchildren, having looked after their Granny for six months, announce they mentally need a complete break, and want to move out and get on with their own lives.

This constant raging against everyone's caring endeavours is exhausting, and very sad, and options have run out. Residential care is now firmly on the cards.

Mum agrees to give a care home a week's trial, after being persuaded by all members of her family and her "handsome" GP, but we certainly don't mention the fee of £1,500 per week! My brother and I jointly register and settle her into her private room in the highly recommended home, just outside the local town centre and five minutes from her doctor's surgery. All is calm. Then, after a tricky first two days of strong vocal objections and denial that she'd ever agreed to the residential care (the care home assuring me this was completely normal and to be expected), on day three I receive a call from the manager, asking me to collect my mother that afternoon as she is threatening to call the police, saying she is being held there against her will. The care home matron relinquishes the telephone receiver, or rather my mother snatches it from her, unable to contain her rage. "Come and get me NOW Katharine! You put me in here, so you bloody well come and get me out NOW!" And then, she accuses me of trying to "lock her up".

There's only so much abuse, over so much time, that any one person can take and that includes the daughter of the person who is doling out the abuse; after decades of having lived with it, she's decided she's had enough.

It's a Friday in the summer of 2021, with the Covid crisis still going on, when I drive down to see the Monster Mère in Haslemere. I'm only too aware that this is going to be my last visit to the family home, that is, with my mother in it.

I've spent months, and years, going through this in my mind. Up until now, it's been no more than a fantasy to help lessen the anger and frustration; it's always eased the pressure, made me feel better. But now my thoughts are focused on how, once I've done the deed and people question how I could have been so cruel to my mother at this stage in her life, I'm confident I can count on enough friends to testify that I've spent years being subjected to mental abuse by her …

Forty-six years on from leaving the family home in my Wolsey Hornet with its walnut dashboard and gleaming chrome, accompanied by a police escort, I make my final crawl, slowly, surely, up the worn gravelled drive, now in a dark green Range Rover Evoque. I park in the top corner of the garden, by the house, leaving the car hidden in the dense and overgrown rhododendrons.

In the back door I stomp, down the hall, straight through to the sitting-room. My mother is in her reclining chair, half asleep. The carer is, as I planned it, on her two-hour break. After more than fifty years of holding back, it's my turn to erupt.

"Oh, darling, what are you doing here?" she stutters,

blinking to make sure her eyes are registering my presence correctly.

I barely take a breath before I unleash my tirade. There's no way she's going to be allowed to say a single word more.

I want to talk to you, so don't even start … You can just shut the fuck up. I've spent most of my lifetime listening to you, being bullied and manipulated, and now you're going to listen to me. I hope it hurts you, hugely, but the good thing for you is, it'll be relatively short, not like the near-sixty years I've had listening to your shit.

All this time, you've played the *blame* game. Oh, poor you. In 1964 your husband made a big bad error and fucked the "Whore in Singapore". You chose to forget that other naval couples went through similar marital messes. You couldn't forget, you couldn't forgive, you couldn't move on. Oh no, you chose to stay put and punish Dad and in doing so you punished all of us and made our lives a misery. And, into the bargain, you gradually unravelled, and you destroyed yourself.

The problem was, no one recognised your increasingly "out of control" behaviour as being as out of control as it really was. We got used to it. It became the norm. *You* were the norm, *Dad* was the evil one. Not to be trusted, not to be loved—"Remember, Katharine, he fucked a whore in Singapore on your eighth birthday." Poor you, Mum. Dad had let you down and you were going to make him suffer and suffer, slowly but surely. You were going to take control, total control.

I've loved you all my life. I've looked up to you, I've respected you, and I knew—sorry, thought—you were always right. "Mummy is always right, darling", and in later years you never stopped saying "I once thought I'd made a mistake, but I was wrong." What I realise now is you were *often* wrong, but I was terrified of you. We were *all* terrified of you.

There's no question I've much to be thankful for—yes, as you said to me once, "poor little rich girl"—my middle-class upbringing showing me the values of right and wrong. How to save and not squander—not to buy anything you couldn't afford and never borrow money. "Never put off 'till tomorrow what can be done today"; "If a job's worth doing it's worth doing well"; and on and on and on. Oh, and before I forget, "Never ever trust men."

My boarding school education toughened me up and taught me how to survive, thank God, even if it contributed fuck all to my intellectual education—you took your eye off the ball there, Mum. Too busy wrapped up in your own ongoing drama that lasted for a total of fifty-two fucking years, until Dad died, and over all those years, Dad pleaded for your forgiveness but NO, NO, NO, you weren't going to give it to him.

I feel hoodwinked by you—you're not the mother I thought I had. You're a fraud, a deeply manipulative, destructive, controlling fraud.

At every step of my life you've tried to take

control: not allowing me aged seventeen to have a say in my own career path; putting a stop to my first proper in-love relationship aged twenty-two; and yet again, aged thirty, you did your best to end the most significant relationship of my life, which, thirty three years later, I'm still in—absolutely no thanks to you.

That really irks you, doesn't it? You've tried on the surface to accept me as a lesbian but you really, really hate it! Your traditional values have been compromised by my choices in life but, you know what, I think, deep down, you envy the comparative freedom I've had. I might not have delivered you grandchildren but if I had done, you wouldn't have benefitted from the amount of my time I've given you and the loyalty I've shown you, because my family nest would have been my priority and not my ageing parents. You don't stop to think of that do you, as you continue dealing me more of your shit, double-helpings now Dad has gone?

Have you once stopped to think how your behaviour, and the havoc it's caused, has affected your daughter's mental and physical health? No, of course you bloody haven't, just as you didn't bother to think about the damage you were doing to your young children fifty years ago, because "it was all Dad's fault". So why should you suddenly reflect and care now he's gone?

You had the nerve to say to me on several occasions in my adulthood, "This is not what I want for my daughter." And when you were in danger of losing control of me, the threats would start: "I never want to speak to you again if you continue down this road."

Then I'd step back, so hurt and frightened by your threats of punishment—twice, at least, we've gone six months or more without any contact, all because I had the nerve to stand up to you, and now, looking back, how very pleased I am that I challenged you.

My big mistake over the years was to repeatedly come back to you, because I wanted your approval and encouragement in my life choices but, in trying to achieve that, I overcompensated in my efforts to please you, trying to make up for letting you down by being gay.

It's little wonder that for a whole decade, between twenty and thirty, trying to come to terms with my sexuality was a complete and utter unhappy living nightmare made ten times worse by you. Rather than concentrate on healing the wounds in *your* life and marriage, you found the time and energy to attempt to control *my* life.

And you did your best to make sure I didn't have a good relationship with my father. Or my brother. After all this time, finally it all makes sense. Divide-and-rule, Mum. You divided, and you ruled, to give yourself more power. You're a bully and a bitch.

Poor you—how unhappy Dad made you, how "lazy" and "untrustworthy" he was! How you resented cooking for him, how you resented being his wife—he didn't deserve you—your traditional values suddenly vanished and bitterness and resentment stealthily and increasingly crept in. Year after year, you'd want to unload onto me, while I was trying to get on with *my* life, to tell me what a liar Dad was and all about your endless fights.

But—and this is where it sticks in my craw—I always took your side, didn't I? I always supported you. I believed all the shit you told me … "Oh your father's having an affair with his secretary"—he wasn't but your deep jealousy and suspicion drove you to getting the poor woman dismissed from her job.

So Mum, not poor you. It was poor, poor Dad. Only I didn't see that until it was too late, and I feel so sad that unwittingly I ganged up with you against Dad and I never had a chance at a proper father–daughter relationship.

Let's look at who you *really* are. You're a bigot of the first order. Your deeply held racist, sexist, snobbish opinions are still there, just bubbling under the surface, but now, with old age, your "filter" has broken, and you can't help but expose your real self, just like when you used to say, "When a man's drunk, he exposes his real personality."

I've tried so many times to make allowances for your unlucky start in life and the generation you were born into, but it still leaves me far short of understanding your behaviour. You were clearly damaged as a child by your father getting himself killed while out drunk and being unfaithful to your "good-time girl" mother, leaving you as good as parentless. The Wrens must have been a huge escape for you but ten years after having married the "right man", you were let down by him too. Of course, I do understand what hurt, shock, and anger this would have caused you. But was this the double damage that rocked your mental stability?

Did you give Dad a double whammy of revenge to help make up for your father's unfaithfulness. Unable, or unwilling, to recover, you swung your wrecking ball and destroyed our family. It's only in hindsight that I've come to realise you were a damaged woman *before* you married Dad—more than he, or any of us, thought possible. Perhaps Dad, over the course of your first ten years of marriage, before he had his affair or possibly even at the start of it, had begun to realise he had bitten off more than he could chew with you … otherwise, why would you have replied to his letter in April 1964 "I do wish you could understand that I'm not different from other women" [her letter in the Prologue on page xi].

Or perhaps it's just a personality disorder that's been allowed to flourish whilst everyone around you has been too scared to question it, so busy making allowances for your unhappiness. That's a regret I have; in being so loyal to you, I never asked Dad what sort of person you were before he had his affair; but then again, if I had, it would have meant going behind your back, which I never would have considered.

You never unpacked and sorted through your baggage at any point in your life. Your shadow has just got longer and longer and the bag you drag behind you it now is too heavy to pull. Bursting at the seams, it's all unravelling.

You tried to hide your former family, leaving only the faintest trace. I never met your three brothers, my uncles. How weird is that? Your father died "in the war", so you say and your mother, Nana Smith, she embarrassed you, Mum, didn't she?

"Betty, I've heard of chicken and Bisto but never chicken and almonds," she'd pipe up as you cringed, serving up supper from your prized hostess trolley during one of her once-every-decade-stayovers. "Oh Betty, if I blacked-up my face I'd get far more money down Social Security." She was actually very funny because she knew how to wind you up—not that I appreciated that at the time. She wanted to publicly remind you, in the presence of your new middle-class family, where you'd come from and about your working-class Bradford roots.

No, Mum, there's nothing wrong with bettering yourself ... pulling yourself up by the bootstraps, striving for a better life for yourself and your children. Of course, there's nothing wrong and it should be applauded ... *but* ... in your newfound position in life you became so completely intolerant of anything that wasn't the "norm". And your "norm" definitely excludes so much, and so many—working-class, black, gay, foreign, fat, or any sort of minority group.

How people look, how they talk, their political views—"Oh, they're not our sort of people, not out of the top drawer"—okay, to be fair, this was also one of Dad's expressions.

I've only recently found out from the couple of remaining "Smith" family members that your mother, my Nana Smith, was in in fact, "a bit of a slapper and a good time girl". Of course, this was during the war, where people took what they could get for fear of dying before getting anything. Nana, I'm told, had a child before she married your father, the grandfather we never met. So that would make a reason perhaps for one of your brothers, Jack your half-brother, to get swept under the carpet.

And your mother, having lost her husband "in the war" as you say, took to booze and bingo and left you home alone to fend for yourself, whilst your other two brothers, Eric and Eddie, were out and about town, presumably too young to be conscripted. Your older sister Jessie, or rather Jessica, who, rather like you, renamed herself, did look after you. "The one with the brains, but no common sense" left home to study and eventually went on to become a professor and top educational tutor after emigrating to Canada and working her way through several husbands and live-in affairs—obviously her way of blotting out her unhappy childhood.

Your equivalent, Mum, was to first join the Wrens, oh, and become "the youngest ever Chief Petty Officer in the Navy", as you never stopped reminding your family, and every new carer who comes into the house. Then you planned to marry the "right" man, the next stage on your escape route out of the working-class unhappy hell of Bradford. Oh, and let's not forget, you could have married at least two other men who you go on and on about, especially the one who was a millionaire but, you hung out bait for Dad and played hard to get.

So Mum, all that is allowed. It's fine. You've achieved and you should be applauded but, and this is the bottom line: at what cost? How much does your fucking unpacked baggage weigh now?

Funny how, all things considered, I "achieved" in my work and my life, but, of course, not in the way you wanted. My further education wasn't important. I was a girl, only to get married and have babies. Your son needed to have a career and was sent to university and at his wish he studied Fine Art for three, or was it four, years? Funny how I've always been the one to be fully independent and have *never* asked you for money. But, yes of course, I didn't deliver you grandchildren, and it's transpired that the plans you had for your son and daughter have turned out to be exactly the opposite of what you wanted!

You couldn't and didn't and wouldn't applaud me—the wrong job, the wrong partner, the wrong fucking shoes, and, even during my forties and fifties, the wrong-coloured garment—"That colour really doesn't suit you, darling." What a fucking nerve you've always had. Oh, and how about "Why don't you wear a wig Katharine, you'd look so much better in one."

Yes, Mum, we never really talked about the cause

of my alopecia, did we? Now, let me see, could it have been a result of my unhappy and damaged childhood or perhaps alopecia ran in the Smith side of the family, and it was genetic—perhaps a bit of both but, one of your brothers had it and so too his son, but you decided not to mention it! Why was that Mum? I only learned this from Dad, who told me not to let on that I knew. You couldn't bear for anyone to find out any of the shortcomings of your family background—you were so deeply ashamed of the lot of them, Christ, even if they had no hair through no fault of their own.

Yes, you became a snob. It wouldn't have been so bad if you hadn't spent your life slagging off Dad's side of the family, like how his mother, my Nana Leppard, was "mean and dirty" and her husband, my grandfather, was "lazy, unsocial and bad tempered". He, too, died young, but of lung cancer. At least he wasn't drunk coming out of a pub with his mistress. God, you make me sick.

You went on and on about how useless Dad was with money and yet look at you now; sitting pretty with three pensions and an Attendance Allowance which you've stashed away for years, refusing to spend it on care because you claim to be a "poor widow on a humble naval pension". It's crap, but you keep saying it. To think Dad took care of all the household bills for over sixty years; all you had to manage was the housekeeping budget for your food.

But, somehow, after Dad died you thought you understood direct debits and utility bills and how to be decent to the gardener and dog walker and anyone who came to the house to provide a service. You didn't like paying and you couldn't be civil. Were you by any chance trying to re-live Chief Petty Officer Smith, very much in charge after the captain's departure to the officers' mess in the sky? The way you punished Dad became an *obsession*, and since he's been gone, you've punished everyone around you.

Sure, Dad's unfaithfulness made you lose all trust but, you think the worst of all people and suspect they have ulterior motives, so you dig and you dig and you dig and cause so much trouble and upset. Your small family is all you've got left but in case you haven't realised, even that is hanging by a thread.

So here you are sitting in your lovely house surrounded by a beautiful garden. You have your beloved dog, you have your treasured possessions, and perfectly adequate income to stay here and maintain a good standard for the rest of your life with live-in care. You have grandchildren, a son and a daughter who love you and have both tried so hard to be supportive, but without doubt, it's me who's gone the extra mile with you, that is, up until now. You've made what could have been a relaxed and relatively content part of your life into a living hell for all concerned, including yourself but particularly me. I've had it with you.

I'm going to leave you now and I'm not coming back. You can digest what I've said, or not. I don't care. Because it's too late for you to do anything about it. It's not too late for me though. Today is the first day of the *rest* of my life and now I've unburdened myself with this I can, at last, move forward.

And what have I learnt from all this, apart from there's strength in human nature as well as fragility? Well, let's keep it simple: I'm not going to remain bitter or hold on to any resentment—all that's dumped today. You spent your life blaming Dad, and I don't want to play a parallel blame game by holding you any longer responsible for the unhappiness and the stress in my life.

And my biggest challenge now is this: *to make sure I don't turn out like you*—granted, it's probably nearly every daughter's wish not to turn out like their mother, but, luckily for them, they never had a mother anything remotely like mine! *I've* clearly got my work well and truly cut out.

I'll try and remember some good times when you were at your best, Mum. I know you loved me and wanted the best for me, but it was always on *your* terms. You just couldn't help yourself or your "out of control" behaviour.

For what it's worth, I *have* loved you all my life, even in between the hate. I *still* love you. Why? Because you are *my mother*. Someone, a little while ago, said—sadly I can't remember who—oh god, I hope that's not a bad omen—that people who display the meanest and most damaged behaviour are probably the people who deserve the most compassion.

Whatever, Mum, the time has come for me to

walk away from you and get my life back on track …
before you cause me any more mental, and physical,
anguish.

Goodbye Mum.

I walk out and leave her with mouth wide open and with
that all-too-familiar, shocked, cold stare.

Epilogue

Well, Dear Reader, there are no prizes for guessing! In the end I didn't have the courage to say any of this to my mother, never mind murder her with that gorgeous Georgian candelabra (the one that you perhaps eyed in the Shrine photo and noted as a suitable, and entirely appropriate, weapon!).

Of course I didn't—though I've played it out, countless times, in my head. *That's* been my crime (but I'm hoping it's one that you can now pardon, having stayed with me this far).

After reading my story, I hope *you* don't feel duped too—but, if you do, just consider this: it'll only have been for the time it's taken you to read this book, not for the lifetime it's taken me to cotton on.

Now that I *have* cottoned on, I'm able to look back and tell the whole story. Sure, my mother will always be somewhere inside me, wrapped up in a perverse parcel of anger and resentment, physical fear and emotional confusion, love and admiration … still demanding attention, still needing vindication, still causing chaos.

Unavoidably, guilt is being stirred up in writing this. *But—and this is key—I no longer live in fear of her.* The terror that had always bound me to my mother's iron will has faded away.

In being honest and giving a fair and balanced account of my parents' trials and emotional struggles and where and how they impinged and impacted on my life, I believe I've released much that enables me now to emotionally put all this to bed.

In a way, I guess *I have* now murdered my mother. Writing this story has felt like dissecting her, cutting her up into little pieces—and holding each piece up to the light and seeing her for who she *really* was. And that includes the positive qualities I was in awe of during the early decades: energy, determination, generosity, and humour—that is, of course, when she was on form … on a good day.

Another positive is that, in this process, I've been able, to some extent, to bring my father to life and to get to know him a little better. During the Little Holt house clearance, my brother and I found a shoebox full of Mum's letters to Dad (she had destroyed his letters to her), some written during their courting days in Cornwall and the other batch from 1963–4, when my father was away at sea, before it all went so wrong. Gut-wrenching, but equally heart-warming, to read just how much in love they once were. I wondered why my mother hadn't thrown these letters away and it occurred to me that, perhaps, she'd wanted me to read them after she was gone.

As for me … well, it feels as if I've been doing the same thing to myself—cutting myself into pieces. But as I finally dig myself out from under the wreckage of my mother's influence, I can put the pieces back together and find a different, a better, shape.

So, this slow, *necessary* murder of my mother has been more about repair than revenge. And the remembering has made it possible for me to begin to well and truly put behind me *nearly* everything that's happened.

There's sadness, yes ... but there's also a huge sense of relief. I can now get on with the rest of my life.

My mother and her family

My mother died in the early hours of her ninety-third birthday in August 2022, at home with her daughter, son, grandchildren, and dachshund gathered around her. We were lucky enough to have found another live-in carer (by this time Mum was too frail mentally and physically to complain) plus a palliative care team who visited twice a day "to make her comfortable", but the end was rather longer and rather more protracted than I thought "comfortable".

We all cried … and we cried together … for the first and, probably, the last time ever.

Acknowledgements

A huge thank you to Nick Downing, who totally got it! I couldn't have done this without your editing and proofing skills.

Maureen Chadwick and Katherine Gotts for their never-ending encouragement. You gave me the confidence to continue when I had so many bouts of wavering.

To my longest-standing boyfriend, Philip Durell, thank you for being such a good listener and aiding me with your photographic tech skills.

My friends and family, both mentioned in this memoir and not, for putting up with my angst throughout the years and supporting me through many an ordeal. Thank you.

Finally, to my partner Suzanne, thank you for enduring the twelve-year "Book Project" period, for your pearls of great wisdom and understanding and for helping keep me sane. Even more significantly, enormous heartfelt gratitude for coping with my mother for almost four decades.